“ALRIGHT S

FLYING BY THE SEAT OF MY PANTS. FROM THE STREET TO THE FOOTPLATE AND THE BOARDROOM.

A TRAIN DRIVER’S MEMOIR

BY

DAVID TYSON

ESSEX TRANSPORT PUBLISHING
40 Broadway, Silver End, Essex, CM8 3RA
Publishing History
First published 2024
ISBN 978 0956683212
British Library Cataloguing in Publication Data
A catalogue record for this book is available from the British Library
© David Tyson 2024
Cover design concept by David Tyson
Cover design artwork by Cherie Chapman
Typeset and designed by Essex Transport Publishing
Printed by Crescent Card Company, Tiptree, Colchester, Essex

All rights reserved. No part of this publication may be reproduced, stored in a retrieval system, or transmitted, in any form or by any means, electronic, mechanical, photocopying, recording or otherwise, without the prior permission of the author. The images may be viewed for personal use only. They may not be used for any commercial purpose, nor may they be displayed on any web site.

DISCLAIMER

This book is a memoir. It reflects my present recollections of experiences over the last sixty years. Some names and characters have been changed, some events have been compressed and some dialogue recreated.
Where possible I have made reference to real events that took place and information has been provided in the 'references' section. Such material has been taken from publicly available resources, research libraries, my own files and my memory.
The author is responsible for any faults in his memory as many of these events happened a long time ago in a world that was very different.

To Peter Tyson, who is seen crouching in this photograph

Foreword

The best writers and the best books take you to the places and characters in your mind's eye as if you are there, there is a saying on the railways that you can go into a messroom anywhere in the world close your eyes and listen and know you are at home.

What is rare in the many of the autobiographical railway books I have read is to be transported immediately to that world of characters living history and honesty, that you do not have had to have been a career railwayman to enjoy or engage Alright Spider does that.

There is a forthrightness and natural story telling ability that reflects the author in a true mirror of his personality: a construction not of a narrative but this is a living world experience whose simple truth cannot be denied.

What shines through is an abiding love for a role and a way of life articulated without rose tinted glasses the fun times the good times the difficult times and rationale honestly expressed behind without spin.

The managing of train driving with a trade union career through some of the biggest industrial changes and internal difficulties the trade union faced candidly opined, but a tribute to the man himself that did not walk away and was the President of ASLEF.

Anyone who knows Dave would expect a self deprecating recounting of a life representing others and then going off to protect and serve looking after peoples deferred wage as a trustee of the railway pension scheme whilst still driving trains, it is and was for him always about a greater good.

In this book Dave Tyson brings the human aspect of our unique sector to the fore in a way that anyone can identify with and understand, I may be biased as his friend but can attest that this is his life and how he lived it, openly honestly with great humour and true railway man and great trade unionist.

Mick Whelan
General Secretary ASLEF

Introduction

"ALRIGHT SPIDER!" VIC called to me as I climbed down from the locomotive cab or footplate as it has been known ever since the very first locomotive trundled along. I had made a monumental balls up which resulted in a delayed arrival at Dereham, a town situated in deepest Norfolk. Vic would continue to greet me this way whenever we crossed paths. Why?..... I have absolutely no idea!

Over the years, numerous books have been written about the rail industry charting the time the first locomotives puffed into life right up to the modern era that led to locomotive or 'footplate-men' being the envy of many a young lad. I take a completely different look at the modern rail industry through the eyes of a railman of 41 years service who was destined to follow in his fathers' footsteps and become a locomotive driver.

As a youngster I was heavily influenced by my father and later encountered the formidable Aunt Ida and her puritanical views (she marched a Jackie Collins novel back to the local library and demanded they remove "such filth" from the shelves). In my teens I potentially ended the career of an England world cup winning soccer legend as you will find out later.

"Alright Spider" charts my career from my first day in June 1980, when I set foot in the mess-room as an enthusiastic young man and was paired with my regular driver, Felix—who reminded me of the caveman like character Stig of the Dump created by children's writer Clive King— right through to my retirement in 2021. I recall tales of all manner of characters I encountered over the years such as the driver who would bring a shotgun to the footplate and bag a few pheasants, then accidentally blew a hole in the cab roof of a locomotive. I will also introduce you to serial prankster Gary Strange.

I learned that drivers were the Kings of the railway after being told by my driver to advise a manager to "kiss my arse" after being "ordered" to alter our work schedule for the day! Many of these men had lived through a world war and dedicated a lifetime to the industry, however, as I was to find out, many were as strong as oxen and nimble too. I was taught a lesson after giving one such driver a load of lip, then chased, caught by the testicles, and given a love bite as punishment, not on my testicles I might add!

Many of us were young men and we would often fool around and I soon received a telling off from my boss for riding my 750cc Honda motorcycle around the mess-room lockers!

I recall my extensive training, driving incidents, accidents and hazards that came with the job. Not forgetting near misses and fatalities, none more striking than poor driver Albert Brown who was involved in two fatalities on consecutive days at the same station.

As a local union representative I progressed to be president of the train driver's union, The Associated Society of Locomotive Engineers and Firemen (ASLEF), and I speak of the situations I found myself in, members I had to bail out, and representatives who were, at times, harder on their colleagues than the management. My part in settling the 1995 national rail dispute, my resignation from, and reinstatement to the unions executive, and later sacking the then President and General Secretary for entering into a drunken brawl in the garden of the union's offices, then dealing with the acrimonious fallout.

I would like to put a tale to rest as a romantic picture has been painted of the driver and fireman enjoying a hearty breakfast after cooking it on the shovel, but due to a lack of toilet facilities, footplate men would also defecate on the shovel and throw the contents into the firebox.

My father and I attended a reunion at his old depot in King's Lynn where he reminisced with an ex colleague. They spoke of baking an onion on the shovel and soon the conversation took a more sinister twist. My father's ex colleague spoke of the time he put the contents of a sack his driver had brought to work into the inferno of the firebox: it turned out one of his greyhounds had died the night before. My father knew the driver well and had been with him many times. However I was shocked when he revealed that he had to put a litter of dead puppies in. I think it's fair to say the firebox was often the best way of disposing of many unwanted secrets.

The book contains many stories about the high jinks we got up to over the years and finally, in 2021 I retired completely from the industry after completing 38 years on the footplate and 20 years as a director of the railways pension scheme.

In a career spanning 41 years I have encountered many, many people. The vast majority were, and still are, passionate about the industry, they conduct themselves with the utmost professionalism and keep the industry running safely day in day out.

This book may well leave the reader wondering if we actually got any work done at all!

Chapter 1: Early Days

I WAS BEGINNING to fight for breath. The clods of wet earth from the newly ploughed field were clinging to my Wellingtons which were weighing my feet down and I was starting to tire. As I struggled along each step became difficult. My left boot got stuck, my foot slipped out and I fell face down into the cold wet mud, not for the first time that afternoon. I picked myself up and after some considerable effort the mud relinquished my boot with a shluup.... at that moment I concluded my attempt to catch up with the 'big boys' was futile and decided to make my way home.

The older lads, who were about eleven years old, were much bigger and stronger than me and made their way to a small bridge that spanned a drainage ditch that split two fields where they planned to have a crafty fag.

I began my early years in Clenchwarton, just across the River Great Ouse from King's Lynn in North Norfolk, on the southern edges of the Fens, where I used to mess around in the streets and surrounding fields with the children from the village. I was four years old and covered from head to toe in mud. As I made my way back to the lane that ran alongside the field, I jumped out of my skin. "Oi....get yourself back here!" I looked up to see a rather angry farmer, cloth-capped with a leather gilet and a shotgun by his side standing at the exit from the field. I was terrified as my eyes focused on the shotgun. With some trepidation, and after falling over again, I finally returned to the lane. "Best you get yourself off home young man," he said and uttered the chilling words, "Your Mum's gonna be pleased to see you!" The sight of the farmer terrified me, but the prospect of facing my mother in such a state, my new anorak with its pointy hood (my head wasn't pointy) covered in mud, petrified me. My worries were confirmed when I arrived home and announced that I had "fallen in a heaped up puddle" which failed to convince her that my state was a result of some freak accident.

There's a photo of me being pulled on a sledge through the snow (below). One of the lads hauling me along was actually wearing his wellies and short trousers. We

were tough in those days. During spring and summer I tried to spot the skylarks: I would listen to their distinctive shrill tune as they rose high above the fields behind our home. Whenever I hear them I am taken back to those early days.

When I was about three years old my uncle, aunt and their three daughters Rosemary, Louise and Alexandra came to visit. My father had created a fishpond in the back garden with a rockery around it. It had a fountain and I would marvel at the colours the sunlight made. If you caught it at the right angle you could see all the colours of the rainbow.

My cousins and I were playing in the back garden, the girls using a rope and taking it in turns to skip. As the youngest, as well as being the only boy, I clearly did not figure in their plan to let me have a go despite me repeatedly asking. Alexandra was jumping in time to the rope and ignoring my pleas, but despite my repeated requests and protestations I did not get the opportunity I thought I deserved. So I decided to administer swift justice by pushing Alexandra into the fishpond.

According to my cousins my first attempt failed, so I walked away, turned around, took a run up and was successful on my second attempt. There was a scream and a rather large splash! I got a monumental telling off and was made to apologise to my cousin. It was only many years later that my two older cousins, now in their sixties, admitted to egging me on!

Around the time I was born Dad worked on the footplate as a 'passed fireman' at King's Lynn depot. He would fire steam locomotives, shovelling the coal into the firebox to power the engine but when required he could perform duties as a driver.

Progress through the grades was based on seniority and many men spent most, or in a few cases, all of their career as passed men only to make the grade as driver in their sixties. Much depended on the demographic of the depot. At places such as Stratford in East London the churn of drivers was high and promotion happened quickly. I often heard tales of Stratford drivers in their twenties speaking to who they believed to be the driver of a Norwich crew he was relieving who would be in his sixties, only to be told, "Hang on mate, I'll go get the driver!"

Many men were eager to progress through the grades and keen to take advantage of better benefits such as higher wages and a pension that a driver's rate of pay provided. They would move to depots in the London area or the Southern Region to get their check as it was known, then immediately apply for a driving job back at their old depot. The poor promotion prospects at Lynn prompted Father to seek a driving job elsewhere. Not long after my fourth birthday he was a successful applicant for a driving job at Norwich.

The appointment happened very quickly and within a month Dad was taking up his new position. There was no time for our home to be sold so he lodged with my Mum's 'Aunt' Ida, a lady very much in the mould of puritanical campaigner Mary Whitehouse. (For those who can't remember her she campaigned against social liberalism and accused the media of encouraging a permissive society - she complained about Tom and Jerry cartoons as those were too violent).

Ida was no blood relation to us but had been friendly with my grandmother when they were both wives of captains in the British Army and had remained friends over the years. Sadly she was widowed at quite a young age and never re-married, but re-mained friendly with my parents for many years after the death of my grandmother. In fact they treated her as if she was a member of the family.

My mother and I visited Ida only to find out that she had borrowed a Jackie Collins book from the local library. After reading the first few chapters she marched back and harassed the librarian into removing such "Utter filth" from the shelves. I remember sitting in Aunt Ida's immaculate lounge with my legs dangling off the sofa, while she kept repeating, “Marjorie, it was filth, utter filth!” Being rather young and naive, I thought she was talking about a gardening book or the like. Filth to me was muck, grease etc. not the rampant sex portrayed in Ms Collins’ novels.

Dad would spend his time at work route learning and traction training while lodging with Aunt Ida in Sprowston, a suburb of Norwich. I looked forward to seeing him on his return on a Friday evening when generally he would bring me a present. One time it was an Airfix model of a steam locomotive which he duly ‘helped’ me assemble. I had just started school in the September of 1969 and by the December we moved into a new build bungalow in Sprowston.

Within days of moving my mother’s father George, or as I later called him, The Captain, passed away after succumbing to motor neurone disease. I can only imagine that this was an extremely stressful time for my parents, what with the move to a new area with no friends, a new job and the death of my grandfather. Not the greatest start to a new chapter in our life as a small family.

Being young, my new start was probably easier for me than my parents. My mother knew hardly anyone, but dad was part of a fraternity that was generally open minded and curious of any new member, and having daily contact with locomen made life much easier. Dad always said to me that he knew he had begun to be accepted by his new colleagues once they started poking fun at him. Mum soon made friends with our neighbours and through friendships I made at school.

I was befriended by Stuart Church at school. One day I complained of a loose tooth. “You need to see Mrs Mattin,” he told me, so off we went in search of dinner lady Mrs Mattin. On locating her he shouted, “Mrs Mattin, Mrs Mattin, David’s got a loose tooth.” She was a tall slim lady, and wore a red coat with a head scarf. “Oh dear, come here David and let me take a look at it.” Naively I opened my mouth, pointed to the offending tooth by giving it a wiggle. The next moment she had inserted her fingers and hoiked it out. I didn’t know what the hell had hit me. With stunned bewilderment I let her stuff a tissue into my mouth to stop the bleeding. I spent the rest of the day in some kind of trance not actually appreciating what had taken place. Years later I was talking to fellow Driver Nick Mattin and I made the connection. The infamous Mrs Mattin was married to Bernie who was a Norwich train driver and Nick was their son.

The influence of my father and my experiences with him, along those I witnessed as a child, sowed the seed to embark on a career on the railway. Dad was based at the ‘loco’ as it was referred to, or depot, which was close to the engine sheds. Each Thursday he would collect his wages and if I was at home I would go along for the ride. I was fascinated by the size of some of his colleagues and the smell of the loco messroom which was a mix of tobacco smoke and stale diesel fumes. I loved to see the locomotives stabled in the sheds, the wagons in the goods yard, their various shapes and sizes and varying names of companies painted on their sides. In contrast was the uniformity of the passenger stock in the station.

The pay office was in the loco and wages were paid out in cash from noon until 8pm. This was well before the time of credit transfers and electronic banking. Wages were paid out in clear packets, with the pay slip wrapped around the cash in such a manner that the employee could check their wages along with the hours and bonuses from the previous week without opening it. I would come to know those characters who would check their wages down to the last penny. One driver caused a fuss because he had been underpaid by one minute.

I was maybe eight or nine when my parents took me to London for the day by train. They even managed to get me off school as the trip was considered to be educational. We visited the Science Museum in Kensington where my overriding memory is of staring up at the prototype Deltic locomotive that was on display. It seemed so big as it towered above me and I was very impressed by its size and sheer presence, all in pale blue with white stripes at the front. Little did I know at the time, but I would eventually get to drive one of its successors, a BR Class 55.

Dad was always as smart as paint when he left home for work and looked hardly any different on his return. I sometimes wondered if he actually did any work at all, although I rarely saw him go to work and return the same day due to the uncompromising shifts. These were of any hour of the day and generally on a three shift system, mornings followed by afternoons and then nights. There were odd times when he would leave for work and within a couple of hours be home. “Blimey Dad that was a short day,” I would exclaim. Alternatively there were occasions when he would not appear when expected. Mum would often say, “Your Gran always used to say ‘God bless the railway’”. This was well before the advent of the mobile phone. It wasn’t until the mid 1970s that we had a telephone installed, so before that it was a case of just wait and see when he would turn up.

In exceptional circumstances Mum would make a trip to the phone box down the road to call the loco just to check all was ok. This pales into insignificance compared to the experiences of my grandparents who were apart for years during the First World War. Both of my grandfathers served in the British army in Northern France. Later my Dad’s father served as a Rolls Royce armoured car driver in North Africa.

On occasion Dad received telegrams to advise him of his duty time the following day after having a day off work. Most of the time a driver would be aware of his work for the week, however if he was ‘spare’ (to cover short notice sickness or special workings) then he would have a datum time and could be moved two hours each side of this to cover holidays, leave, training or sickness. Although a weekly list was produced and a man could be moved to cover a week's vacant work, there was also a daily supplementary list that would be posted at noon showing the following day’s work allocation. If the driver did not have a home phone a Royal Mail telegram boy would be dispatched to deliver an advice note.

I was proud of the fact that my Dad was a train driver. Anyone I met for the first time, I would let them know of his profession.

The years at school dragged. I did well in subjects such as history and geography but on reflection I did not work as hard as maybe I could have at high school. To my regret I would not speak up when I did not understand something. I remember the frustration I felt after opting for CSE chemistry, opening the text book for the first time and not understanding the various equations. Rather than speak up I tried to knuckle down but soon gave up.

In chemistry lessons I sat with two lads and the usual schoolboy capers ensued in lesson. I remember the teacher shouting at us while in stitches of laughter after “Tufty’ had just set light to one of his farts with a spill. I’m not kidding when I say a blue flame shot out of his backside by at least a foot.

As I approached my CSE’s it was time to focus on some form of employment. It was 1979, Mrs. Thatcher had gained power, and we had experienced the winter of discontent with rubbish piling up on the streets and there were regular power cuts. I had a great interest in photography and wanted a single lens reflex camera as I was keen to pursue a career in photography. After a busy summer of Saturdays cleaning hire cruisers at a boatyard in Wroxham, as well as helping out at the local newsagents doing paper rounds when the regular lads were on holiday, I had saved enough money for one.

I enjoyed doing the occasional paper round which was generally evening work. One summer’s day I had the potential to be the scourge of every Norwich

(Above) Deltic D9000 at Yarmouth on 31 August 1998, the prototype of which the young David Tyson saw at the Science Museum. (Steven Goodrum)
(Below) David Tyson's grandfather, Harry Lamb Tyson, is seen second from the left whilst on Army service in North Africa.

City, Tottenham Hotspur and England football supporter. The paper shop where I helped out was called 'Griggs Newsagents' and was situated in a parade of shops on the Wroxham Road in Sprowston. Generally I covered my mate Steve's evening round when he was on holiday and soon I gained the trust of the proprietor, Mr Graber, who asked me to cover other rounds which were generally in the evening.

Some of the paperboys would use their own bikes rather than use the shop owned ones, as they got paid a bit extra, but if the round was larger we could use one of the shop's trade bikes. These were the old sit up and beg style bikes with a big leather seat and a huge metal basket on the front to hold newspapers. Worryingly, the brakes were less than effective! I had been out on an unfamiliar round and had a spot of bother locating a particular street. This put me back a bit and I was eager to get back to the shop before it closed at 6pm when Mr Graber locked up.

I belted back as fast as I could on the heavy, squeaky old bike. I shot across the car park and aimed for the alley between the paper shop and the petrol station. I was no further than thirty feet from the alley and travelling at full tilt when the newsagent's door opened and a chap came out with a copy of the local evening paper, the Eastern Evening News. I immediately slammed the brakes on and continued to hurtle towards the alley at the same speed which was now blocked by England World Cup winning legend Martin Peters!!! "LOOKOUT!" I shouted. He glanced up and cool as you like stepped back to let me pass. I was still travelling at warp factor six into the alley. With a crash and a bang I landed in a heap at the end. 'My God,' I thought, 'What if I had taken him out?' I sheepishly went back to apologise but he had disappeared. I would only see him again from the terraces of Carrow Road, Norwich City's home ground.

Can you imagine seeing the headlines? 'Reckless paperboy ends England hero's career'. Not long ago I read an article in the Eastern Evening News about a rumour that Martin Peters was 'thinking' about buying the Blue Boar pub not a stone's throw from my paper round related incident. What an absolute non-story. Maybe I should relate my tale as I'm sure I could make the letter's page, or given their clear desperation for news, maybe even make the headlines.

After saving up enough money from the boat cleaning and paper rounds I was able to afford the camera and later a telephoto lens which would help me carry out my other passion, watching and photographing wildlife. Although I was keen to become a photographer and my parents certainly encouraged me to go down this path, deep down I knew that this would be beyond me. My academic achievements would be well below what was required and I still had an overriding desire to join the footplate.

Around May 1980 the school arranged for us to attend a job's fair at the cathedral in central Norwich which was a very impressive venue. After wandering around aimlessly I came across a British Rail trade stand and began talking to the gentleman who was representing BR. He gave me some leaflets and I recall seeing a photo of a group of lads standing in overalls around what seemed to be a boiler which puzzled me as steam locomotives were long gone.

I knew there and then that this was to be the path I wanted to tread. My father was not so supportive but did not discourage me from joining the railway, far from it. However, he was of the view that I should seek to find a trade within the industry such as an electrician or fitter. These were wise words. With a trade I could go anywhere, a footplateman only had one place to work. It was sound advice which I immediately ignored.

I made other inquiries and soon brochures arrived through the post from the British Army. Could I follow in the footsteps of my grandfather 'The Captain', or should I go to sea? My Uncle Eric was a commander in the Royal Naval Reserve. There was a brochure from the police force and I even considered being a traffic warden. In those days of high unemployment it was important to keep my options open.

Soon I thought, 'David, it's time to start writing some letters'. I sat down and wrote to British Rail in Norwich. A short time passed and soon a letter popped through the door addressed to me. I only used to get one letter a week and that was from my grandmother who lived in King's Lynn. When I was younger she would send me my weekly TV Comic with Tom and Jerry and Mighty Moth. As I got older I progressed to Shoot, a football magazine...not a porn mag. A formal letter was somewhat daunting. I could not believe it when I read that I was to attend an interview at Grosvenor House, the administration offices for BR in Norwich.

I had to fill in an application form which was pretty much the first form I had ever filled in. There was a section where I had to nominate a referee. 'What the hell is that all about?' I thought. My parents soon put me right, so I had to rack my brains as to whom I could ask as it could not be a relative. Without any consultation I nominated Stuart's Dad, John Church. John was a man I always looked up to as he was well disciplined, with a good sense of humour and extremely clever.

Soon after returning the application form I received a phone call from John. I had forgotten about the referee part of the application and generally when he called it was to speak to my Dad. I was somewhat perplexed as to why he wanted to speak to me and he said he also wanted to see me. I popped around immediately but was worried that I had done something wrong, but for the life of me I could not think what it could be.

John had been written to by BR. They had asked him to write a reference. I must admit, I was somewhat embarrassed as I had not sought his permission for which I apologised. He assured me it was not a problem and in fact he was flattered that I had named him as my referee. He then went on to tell me he said he was about to do which was the opposite of what BR had asked of him, which was to share with me what he had written. I was bowled over by the reference and felt ten feet tall on my way home. I am eternally grateful to the late John Church for his words of wisdom and support. I sincerely hope I paid him back in the manner in which I conducted myself over the next 41 years.

I attend the interview at Grosvenor House some weeks later. However in the meantime I found out that two school friends had also been called in for interviews so there was some competition. As the country was in recession, many of my friends were struggling to get interviews, let alone employment. I was duly whisked off into the city by my mother where she bought me a brown pinstripe suit, shirt and shoes. I felt I looked the part as my father drove me into the city for the interview but I was extremely nervous.

I sat in a side room with some other lads waiting to be called in by a kindly gentleman who I later came to know as Ray Wardale from the Personnel Department. I was given a reading test and some basic maths and English questions. I was then shown to a room where two middle aged gentlemen were sitting. As a lad just short of sixteen, they looked ancient! The two gentlemen were Eric Wilkinson who was a Traction Inspector and his boss Norman Duggan, the Area Manager.

I was asked a series of questions one of which was about going into the engine room when the locomotive was under full power. I distinctly remember stating that I may be a bit nervous at first but I was sure I'd get used to it. In truth the thought of it made the hairs on the back of my neck stand up. They also wanted to know if I knew anybody who worked on the railway, I explained that my Dad was a driver however I'm pretty sure they already knew. My father always denied that having a parent on the footplate was the reason I got the job. Personally I think that given his reputation it would have been a no brainer for Messrs Wilkinson and Duggan. There are many cases of the railway being a family affair with several members of one family all being employed in various aspects of the industry. I was thanked for my attendance and was told they would be in touch.

It was time for me to focus on my CSEs which in all truth I was not looking forward to. Chemistry was a dead loss and, a couple of years earlier, I had been placed in a maths class with a really nice teacher who had no control over the kids at all—it was a complete riot. I was no angel and contributed to the mayhem which I was to regret when I sat my maths exam. I became even more indifferent when I received a letter not long before they were about to start. It stated that I had been successful in gaining a position as a Traction Trainee and was to start work on 16th June 1980. I was elated and really pleased that my two friends from school had received the same letter.

The final few weeks of school passed by until I took my final exam in late May 1980. The last lesson I attended was art, and I recall the teacher wishing us well. I thought, 'Up yours mate..I'm free'. But it felt a bit of an anticlimax walking out of the school gates for the last time. I was safe in the knowledge that in a couple of weeks I would begin a new chapter of my life.

Chapter 2: Traction Trainees, The First Six Weeks

ON MONDAY 16th June 1980 at the ripe old age of 15 years and ten months I mounted my bike and cycled around to Steve 'Mac' McLean's house which was a stone's throw from where I lived. The two of us, along with fellow school mate Andy Taylor, set off for the ride to the railway station on Riverside where we were to begin our railway career. I recall the day vividly. We chained our bikes to the railings of the railway station and made our way up Prince of Wales Road to the Personnel Department that was located in Grosvenor House.

We were shown to a side room, very similar to the one I had fretted in prior to my interview several weeks before where three other individuals were also waiting. We all sat nervously not saying a word and weighing each other up. I'd known Mac for eleven years, pretty much as soon as I moved to Norwich and we went through infant, junior and high school together. Andy and I had been acquainted since the first year at high school. The other three lads were unknown to me. One was a slim handsome chap in a denim jacket with AD/DC painted on the back. There was a blond lad who carried a bit of weight and clearly had never seen a razor. The other guy was older than the rest of us and was lounging back in his chair, fag between his fingers giving an impression of coolness and being totally unfazed by the situation.

After a short wait we were introduced to Ray Wardale who proceeded to conduct our induction. Our first act was to read and sign our contract of employment. I just signed it as I could not see the BR changing things I did not agree with. He then dished out our publications; five of us received rule books and a pile of other publications that meant absolutely nothing to me! The confident smoker received a small handbook rather than a compendium of publications. This intrigued me— did he know it all already, or was he there for some other reason? He was joining the maintenance department as a fitter. I later got to know him well and called upon him on many occasions when trying to deal with faults and failures.

Eventually it was time to meet our instructor, so like a bunch of school kids we followed Ray over to the station, down the platform slope, and across the wooden walk ways.

These prevented us from stepping on the rails and the old cinder or 'clinker' which had laid on the ground for years and were the remains of coal from steam engine fireboxes which was used for many years as ballast. Even today if you get the chance to walk along any disused railway you can generally see nuggets of clinker laying around. (I did get confused some years later when the driver I was with commented that he had a "Bloody great clinker up his nose." 'How did you that get up there?' I thought, only to realise he was referring to a large bogie up his nose.) Through the passenger yard and around the back of the signal box we walked, and then over to the loco.

All five of a us were wearing our high visibility jackets which were a pain in the backside to put on. At the time very few locomen actually wore them. I remember a track worker saying to me sometime later, "You can always tell when a locoman is on the track, he never wears his high visibility vest." We then walked over to the loco sheds where I noticed a distinct lack of locomotives. Obviously this was because they were all out on the mainline.

We followed a line of buildings that were typical of the turn of century railway architecture, single story red brick with slate roofs which had been weathered over the years. We passed a small office with several people in. I was later to learn it was one of the most important offices at the depot– it was the pay office and general loco administration. This was where we would pick up our privilege travel tickets: we were entitled to so many per year depending on our length of service.

We rounded the end of the terrace and passed a huge water tower which years later one of my secondman colleagues would climb up and wee off just as a senior driver was passing by. This particular driver was also an accomplished boxer as well as a first aid expert. To add to this he also had a very short fuse. He would use his boxing skills to administer instant justice to any person that gave him any lip, then administer first aid on his unconscious victim! The wee caper passed without incident apart from a comment from the victim about not expecting any rain that evening!

We passed the sludge pit which had raised sides and emitted a quite unique smell which I could never quite put my finger on. Lord only knows what was in it. It had a kind of grey crust and would stink to high heaven during the summer. We rounded the bike sheds, crossed a footpath and entered two sets of double doors into the stone floored messroom.

To the right was the pay wicket where the wages were handed out on Thursdays, then the entrance to the toilets. Beyond a fruit and video game machine was a large hall rather than a room. Down the middle of the messroom was a line of lockers. Long tables with benches were set either side. To the left of the lockers were the fitters' tables where no locoman would trespass, and to the right a mirror image where my new colleagues and I would sit. At the far end were yet more lockers, and to the right a fire exit which was often locked.

There was an entrance to another area known as the old canteen which comprised a couple of sinks, a work top, a hot water geyser and a waste bin containing stewed tea, tea bags and tea leaves. There were also two offices on the right, one where the ASLEF Union reps known as the Local Departmental Committee (LDC) hung out and next to them was the Timesheet Clerk's office.

To the right of the far end of the main messroom and its lockers was the entrance to the notices area where rosters were hung along with letters from management as well as Union notices. To the left of this room was the foreman's office which was attached to the time keeper's office that led to the roster clerk's 'lair', where 'Jakie' the roster clerk conjured up his evil: he wasn't biased......he hated everybody! At the far end of the notices room was another set of double doors where there was a drying room for hanging wet overalls, and then the outside main gates which were opposite the Clarence Harbour pub. There was no harbour and as far I as know no-one called Clarence.

I was to spend many long hours in this spartan place (the messroom rather than the pub) although the pub was used by locomen over many years. One evening the time keeper Billy Sadler asked me to go over to the Harbour and get the foreman out as there was an important phone call for him. After passing the message on I thought, 'Oh well, while I'm here I might as well have just the one!'

Ray introduced us to our temporary instructor. The chap who was supposed to take the course was on annual leave, so a substitute had been drafted in. He was a driver but had qualified to act as an instructor when the need arose. He carried what looked like a briefcase which had been constructed out of wood—furthermore it also had his name painted on it. Clearly it was a case that he had constructed himself which contained his tea making utensils along with his lunch and not much else. He had a Scottish accent and on our introduction he advised us that he was from Cambridge depot and "we would not be hanging around too long" as he wanted to get away.

With most of the paperwork done it was time to have a spot of lunch with my new colleagues. There was myself, Mac, Andy and now we had got to know Steve and Gary. Steve would be with us at Norwich and Gary was to be based at Great Yarmouth. While I had a packed lunch I did not have a mug or any tea making equipment so it was down to Jock our instructor to provide us with what we needed for the day. "Make sure you have the right things tomorrow," he said sternly.

My father and I had one of those man to man chats before my first day at work. "Now then David, you'll find that there is a lot of bad language on the railway." I recall thinking to myself, 'Can't be any worse than school." Most of the kids I hung around with could swear and if the truth be known I was no angel.

We were having lunch when all of a sudden the sound of raised voices broke the silence, not in anger or anything like that, more in a jovial sort of way. "Hey Sword, how the fuckin' hell are you getting on?" There followed a conversation that was peppered with the f-word in just about every second or third word. 'Christ on a bike,' I thought, 'This puts the kids at my school to shame in the bad language stakes.' I thought Mac was going to choke on his cheese sandwich! There was no doubt my father had been right to warn me considering my first working encounter with locomen. If swearing was an Olympic sport these guys would certainly be in the England team! Later I encountered colleagues who could actually insert swear words in the middle of a word. "Fuck me I'm fuckin' knackered I've been con-fuckin-creting all fuckin' day".

After lunch we were taken to our classroom, if you could actually call it that. It was situated at the end of the terrace of railway buildings we had passed earlier on our way to the messroom. It was cold, dark and there was a desk in the middle of the room which was akin to a bank manager's desk with chairs around the outside. Books were stacked up along with cups, paper and large boards with various diagrams and explanatory notes on signalling and other things that were of no meaning to me whatsoever. This was to be home for the next six weeks.

Our first day had come to a close somewhat earlier than I had expected. So the three of us made our way home loaded down with books, new equipment and for me a sense of euphoria as I was embarking on a new chapter in my life. I had got my first day out of the way and soon we would get into a regular routine of arriving at work at around 08:00 and working through lunch so that our instructor could get home to Cambridge which would mean we would leave around 15:00

Each day was planned out for us and would consist of a morning in the classroom drinking tea and learning about the various rules and regulations that would apply to our job. Much of our training would take place on the job as secondmen, or as we were soon to be known, drivers' assistants. You could throw as much theory as you liked at a group of lads but there was no substitute for being out on the rails with a driver with years of experience. Nevertheless we would take in as much as we could about signalling and track safety with the overriding message being safety first!

One driver's assistant duty involved being stopped at a signal and having to walk to the signal box to ascertain what the problem was. Many signals did not have telephones and once in the signal box we would then be obliged to sign the book. This was not a visitor's book like you get in a hotel or guest house, this was the signalman's train register. We had the mantra drummed into us 'train-line-name-time'. This would be the train identification or head code, for example '1K65'. We would have to state which line the train was on, either the up or down main, followed by my name, and the time displayed by the signal box clock.

I only ever signed the register once and made a balls of it by putting the time first rather than the head code and subsequently crossed it out. I made a right mess of the train register and received a scowl from the signalman. I apologised and scuttled back to the locomotive leaving him to mutter dark thoughts!

After lunch our instructor would pay a visit to the loco foreman to see which locomotives were available for us to play with. We had certain duties to perform as driver assistants, one of which was to attach and detach locomotives to and from the train, or to couple locomotives together when they were booked to work in tandem or multiple. Typically two Class 31 or 37 locomotives (see opposite) could be driven from a single driving cab thus increasing the horsepower to haul heavier and longer loads. Once we had located a couple of suitable locomotives we would take it in turns to tie up and untie during the course of the afternoon. I must admit that this was an area of the job that I had not bargained for. I had some rose-tinted view that I would be riding around on a train with the driver looking important and not doing too much until I became a driver.

We would have to climb in between the two locomotives that had been squeezed together then put the coupling on so that the driver could ease away to take up the slack. It was also a way of confirming you had not forgotten to put the coupling on. Couplings were very heavy and there was a method to putting them on the hook of the adjoining locomotive or coach. Generally you would crouch down and haul up the link of the coupling with your left hand, then take up the weight of the rest of it with your right, then push it up while guiding it with your left hand onto the hook. Easier said than done for a skinny fifteen year old.

Not only were the couplings heavy but the various air and vacuum brake pipes that had to be attached to each other along with the steam heat pipes could be difficult to manipulate. I did not have the strength in my wrists to bend the pipes to attach them to each other. Later a shunter watched me make a complete dog's breakfast of the process and commented, "Looks like you've pullin' yer puddin' too much mate!" It took me a while to work out what he was talking about. Some years later as I removed the coupling too quickly it swung down and it crashed into the side of my knee. I thought I was going to pass out at first but miraculously I sustained no damage.

Each week we would have a trip out on a service train to observe the drivers and secondmen in action, and to take in the various characteristics of the lines we were going to be working over. These were like family days out with the five of us trailing behind our instructor. Two of us would jump on the footplate with the crew while the rest would get into the train and drink tea, chat or play cards. We would take it in

Two of the loco types that David experienced during his training.

(Above) 31318 at Ipswich in 1975, showing the steam heating working well.
(Alistair Barham)

(Below) A pair of Class 37s at Thorpe Junction, Norwich — D6722 (later renumbered 37022) leading.(John Longman, East Anglian Railway Museum)

turns to swap around onto the front at pre-arranged points along the journey. I always enjoyed these days the best. They were the practical side of the job and were far more exciting than sitting in a classroom or crawling through dirt and grease in between a couple of locomotives.

Mac was friendly with one of the more senior secondmen, a chap called Barry Ketteridge. He actually lodged at Mac's home and they were good friends. Barry was a larger than life character who always wore the full uniform, even the daft cap, and was railway mad.

We were going to London on the footplate for the first time with our new instructor Allan Waites, who would later rise to greater things in the railway industry. Our driver on the journey was one Geoff Begley who was one of the more senior mainline drivers. He was in his mid fifties, single and was renowned for being a stickler for the rules. He was a man who said little, liked a pint and deep down I think he suffered form an element of nervousness which was underlined by the amount of fags he would smoke during a journey. The saying went that fag ends would fly out of the window of a locomotive like machine gun tracer bullets and that he could smoke a Capstan full strength in one drag! Geoff was also known for his meticulous time keeping and for maintaining his train in its path. It was also rumoured he had contempt for the youngsters who knew nothing. Judging by my limited experience at the time, this seemed to be a general view held by quite a few of the older drivers, some of whom still hankered after the good old steam days.

Mac had been tipped off by Barry about Geoff's quirks and how to touch a nerve. As the journey went on Mac and I were standing there watching the driver's actions and the secondman sitting there with his cup of tea. At the time, the driver of each London train was issued with a running time sheet. It contained information such as stops for the journey, arrival and departure times at each station, along with what were known as passing times. Passing times were certain points on the journey where the train was expected to be at a given time. Additionally, the odd minute or two was added which was known as recovery time. These were allocated to account for any temporary speed restrictions as a result of engineering work or repairs.

As the train left Diss Mac looked at his watch and said nothing. The next stop was Stowmarket with a passing time at Haughley Junction which we were to pass prior to stopping. The journey progressed and as we were approaching Haughley Mac again looked at his watch and then looked at the running sheet and announced, "Blimey we're a minute down." Geoff said nothing. His mate sat bolt upright and I noticed Geoff had gone a dark shade of red. Out came the Capstan full strength which was duly lit. He took a long draw then exhaled as a cloud of blue smoke filled the cab. We arrived at Stowmarket on time where Mac and I bailed out. Mac was chuckling to himself and let me in on his little wind up.

When we arrived at Liverpool Street our instructor came back and asked Mac, "What the hell did you say that for?" Mac played the innocent. Apparently Geoff was none too happy having some kid questioning his skills. Whether he had to buy another packet of fags at Liverpool Street I do not know.

There were a few occasions when we would come into work later in the day to experience the railway in the dark. The network was a very different world compared to sunny days when visibility was good. It turned out to be pretty much a waste of time because it was late June and it was daylight up to almost ten o'clock at night!

I left home with my rucksack on my back and my lunch which had been kindly packed by my mother. "I've put a nice drink in there for you love," she told me. 'Great,' I thought, 'that will make a change from tea on a hot summer's evening'. We were to travel on a Norwich to Birmingham service with the stop of an hour at March in Cambridgeshire. The journey passed without incident and we made our way over to the messroom on the island platform at the station. This was a place I was to become very familiar with over the years with its only real charm being a massive kettle that sat on the stove and always seemed to be simmering. It weighed a flippin' ton due to the fact that it was half filled with a massive build up of limescale. Pouring the hot water was a skill in itself and any unsuspecting secondman could be caught out by its weight.

We were all sitting in the messroom with a driver from another depot who was engrossed in his newspaper and tea. I declined the offer of tea and produced a can of lager which I promptly opened and swigged down. Allan stared in amazement at me, his jaw dropped and his eyes were on stalks. "Dave....what the hell do you think you're doing, you can't drink that!!!" I felt my cheeks turn red and then realised that we were not allowed to drink on duty. I was embarrassed and felt a complete fool. I was going to say it was my Mum's fault for packing it but that would have sounded really stupid, or should I say, even more stupid.

The driver who had been reading his paper looked at us agog. Allan just looked at him, smiled and said, "He's a lad isn't he?" After about five weeks on the railway I could have been sacked if it were not for Allan giving me a telling off and letting that be the end of the matter. I was later to understand that the rules on drinking on duty were ignored by many drivers.

It was a great feeling to turn up at the pay office on the second Thursday of our training to pick up my first wage packet. As trainees we earned about thirty pounds a week. Once we passed out we were to increase our rate to sixty pounds a week which was almost treble the wage some of my mates were earning at the time.

We were approaching the end of the six weeks training and were in the classroom with three other more senior secondmen, Kevin Brown, Adrian Burrage and Alan Cobbold who were training to be drivers. It was quite a squeeze in that small room but nonetheless we all managed to find a place to sit. Their instructor was a large gentleman by the name of Lou Bickers who was also the chairman of the Norwich branch of ASLEF. His primary job was as a driver but he would train colleagues as and when required. Lou was what my Dad described as a regimental chap being renowned as a stickler for the rules. He was as smart as paint with big bushy black eyebrows, black slicked back hair with grey side burns. Some of the drivers, or those who could get away with it, called him 'Blue Knickers' as opposed to his proper name. Our instructor kept calling him "Brother Lewis" on account of the position he held with the Union. It wasn't too long before Lou got fed up with this kid's cheek and told Allen to "Cut the Bro Lewis sonny", and that was the end of that!

It soon became clear that Lou seemed to want to test us new boys out but first he was curious to know which one of us was "Young Tyson". I sheepishly smiled and put my hand up. "Well you've got some big shoes to fill," he told me and then went on to question each one of us about various aspects of the job. After about half an hour he told us that if we wanted to pass our exams we would just need to fill a form. It turned out to be an ASLEF application form and we didn't hesitate to make our applications. Little did I know what sort of journey I was going to take with ASLEF in the coming years.

A few days later we took our examinations, all five of us in the same room with part-time instructor Billy Lincoln. He was a real gentleman and the couple of hours we were with him flew by after which he advised us we had all passed.

Chapter 3: Felix and Me

IT WAS TIME to begin life on the footplate proper. We were paired up with our drivers and worked our way through the links, or rosters as they were known. Promotion through the ranks was, and still is, based on seniority. The day you joined the railway along with the day you entered the grade count for just about everything on the footplate. Given that five of us all started on the same day, we were placed in link positions according to our seniority and age, the oldest being allocated the first vacancy.

We were all placed in the drivers' assistants 'B1' link which was the most junior link at the depot. Later I found out it was named after the 'B1' steam locomotives that were allocated to Norwich.

At the time it was illegal for anyone under eighteen years of age to work night shifts but due to a legal loophole we were able to do so as we were not working unsupervised, the presence of the driver or 'mate' (as they were often referred to) being the supervisory element. Fortunately I was placed in a part of the link with a late morning shift which meant two days on the Fakenham goods signing on duty at 10:40am. Later in the week there were three days of trips to London just before noon. My driver for the next four months was to be John Cabon or 'Felix' as he was known to everyone. I never did find how he came to be known as Felix.

I told my Dad that John Cabon was to be my regular mate. "Oh Felix," he said "He's a rough diamond ... but he's alright." I didn't quite know what to think of my father's comment as I had no idea what a rough diamond was. Furthermore, it didn't sound like a ringing endorsement, not like saying, 'Oh he's a really nice bloke, you'll get on with him.'

Come Monday morning I made sure I was at work in good time but was in a state of heightened apprehension. The only clue my Dad gave me about Felix's appearance was that he was a short stout chap who drove a red Robin Reliant, a small three wheel car that had been given the affectionate nick-names 'Plastic Pig' or 'Resin Rocket'.

As I entered that large messroom I was full of trepidation and there, sitting on one of the benches, was a stout gentleman in his full uniform including the daft driver's hat. (I always thought the driver's hats looked daft.) 'Ah, there's my man,' I thought. "Are you Driver Cabon?" "Nooo, I'm afraid not, I'm Frank, Felix will be in shortly, I'll tell you when he arrives." I thanked Frank with whom I was later to enjoy many happy times on the footplate. As I waited, so my anxiety built up.

"Here he comes," said Frank as a faded red Plastic Pig trundled past the messroom windows followed by a trail of blue smoke. Shortly Felix hauled himself through the fire doors. Much more of a contrast to Frank you could not imagine. He too was about 5'6" but with a very large stomach that was held in by his pale blue railway shirt, the buttons of which were straining at the pressure of his huge tummy. He wore a shabby driver's jacket, his grey hair was in need of a good cut and he had a roll up fag hanging out of the corner of his mouth. I was reminded of 'Stig of the Dump' by children's author Clive King, a book I read in my childhood about a caveman-like character who lived in a chalk pit and was discovered by a young lad. Felix was my Stig. "Are you driver Cabon?" I asked. "Aye," came a gruff reply, "I'm your secondman." He looked me up and down and said, "Oh." Felix was not the greatest conversationalist.

We were booked to get road transport to Fakenham which is in deepest Norfolk and relieve a crew that had brought the train down from Norwich earlier that morning. We walked through the depot and across the lines of the goods and passenger yards then along the platforms to the rear of the station. We were met by Peter, the van driver and then clambered into the back of a small yellow Bedford van which had no windows in the back and no seat belts. The guard joined us and sat in the front. This was our transport to Fakenham.

As we were passing through Great Witchingham the van shuddered and came to a halt. After several attempts to restart it we pushed it onto a grass verge and Peter went off to find a telephone. As we sat on the grass in the sun waiting for alternative transport to arrive I remember commenting that this was good, sitting in the sunshine doing nothing and being paid. Felix grunted which I took to be some form of approval, then produced his tobacco tin and rolled a thick 'un.

After a while the Norwich Station Manager Arthur Wiffen arrived to take us on to Fakenham. Once we finally arrived we received a somewhat frustrated reception from the morning crew. "Where the bloody hell have you been?" the driver exclaimed, which was to be expected really as it meant they would be late getting home. In those days we had been unable to warn them of our delay as there were no mobile phones to keep people posted.

This was to be the first and last time I worked a train from Fakenham. The line from Great Ryburgh to Fakenham was closed not long after. It was also at Fakenham where I first encountered Vic, the leading railman who was in charge of the line between Dereham and Fakenham. After relieving the disgruntled morning crew we made our way to Dereham where we would normally stop for some lunch and a few hands of cards. Due to our late arrival it was decided that we should push on to Wymondham as there was work to be done once we arrived. The sooner we returned to Norwich, the sooner we could get off home.

My first day on the footplate proper was over although it had not gone according to plan, but at least I had met my new 'mate' and my first day nerves were out of the way. I was indeed looking forward to later in the week when we would be on the mainline to London for the first time.

London jobs were always popular because they went with a mileage bonus payment. These were a throwback to the steam days when the work was much tougher, especially for the fireman who would have to keep the fire tended which involved shovelling a great deal of coal. For this extra work the unions negotiated various mileage payments - journeys that accumulated more than 200 miles in a shift would be graded. A journey to London and back via Ipswich meant the lowest band mileage payment. If the trip was via Cambridge in both directions then you would slip into a higher band. Depots such as King's Cross and Euston were renowned for the vast mileage payments drivers would accumulate, especially if the crew were on a King's Cross to Newcastle round trip.

The driver and his assistant would be allocated a signing on time which included adequate time to look at notices, walk over to the station and relieve the crew who had prepared the train ready for departure. This particular day, being my first week, and our first London, I really wanted to create a good impression with my new mate. I made sure I had a tea can with all the necessary tea making equipment. Once we were on the locomotive I paid particular attention to making sure the windows and cab were clean.

Very shortly before departure, Felix leaned out of the cab window looking back in anticipation of the right away signal with a roll up fag in his mouth, and his hand resting on the horn ready to acknowledge the departure signal. Soon I heard the whistle from the platform staff. Felix sounded the horn in acknowledgement then he released the brakes and opened the regulator to notch one. We were working a nine coach InterCity train hauled by a Class 47 locomotive. Soon we were under way passing the various signal boxes at a breakneck speed of 15mph!

The lines around Norwich had not been upgraded for many years and the signals were of the semaphore type (see opposite) that were operated by the signal box they were related to. This was an antiquated way of working which meant there were many signal boxes with their associated sections on a journey up to London.

Due to the condition of the track and the curvature of the line we had to keep to a lowly 15mph, especially when we passed over the River Wensum via Trowse swing bridge. During the Second World War the Luftwaffe targeted Norwich on several occasions and it came to light that an unexploded bomb was buried in the mud close to the bridge. During the electrification of the line between Norwich and Colchester in the late 1980s, construction of a replacement swing bridge was halted as attempts were made to recover the bomb. No matter how hard the engineers tried to locate or remove it, it just kept sinking down into the mud, where it remains to this day.

Once through Trowse Lower Junction, where the line splits off to the left for the main line towards Ely and to the right to Ipswich, we began our climb out of Norwich up through Lakenham passing behind the houses of the estate there. Many of the residents whose gardens backed onto the railway obviously thought they could dump any old rubbish over their fence onto the embankment behind their gardens. Old bikes, mattresses, grass clippings would all be fair game and once over the fence it would be a case of out of sight out of mind to them. I often thought it would have been quite fair of BR and later Network Rail to sling the lot back.

By now Felix had the regulator wide open, the cab was vibrating and the generators were bellowing out their high pitch distinctive scream to provide electricity to the traction motors. It was a summer's day and I was again full of the joys of my new job. This was better than school any day and I was being paid as well.

Soon we were getting up to a top speed of 95mph and the various crossings and signal boxes were flashing past. Our first stop was to be Diss. The platforms at both Diss and Stowmarket stations were not long enough to accommodate a nine coach train so we had to run through the station platform and stop at marker boards. All the coaches had slam doors that were opened by the passengers. It was not unusual, especially during the dark, for unsuspecting people to open a door and step out into thin air with a rather considerable drop. Later, during the electrification process, the platforms were extended to cater for a full ten coach set along with a locomotive.

Soon we were at Shenfield and thundering through the many suburban stations at 80mph. It was always a bit more exhilarating travelling in the London area: the signals were much closer together and they were the modern colour light electronic type. It's when passing along this stretch of line that I got a real feeling for the sheer speed we were travelling at, especially when passing stations as the buildings and the platform made everything look faster.

On the flip side of this, it was a most unusual sensation after travelling at almost 100mph to slow down for Chelmsford which had a maximum speed to pass through of 60mph. It felt like you were going that slow that you could get out and walk. I wouldn't recommend it though.

By now we were through Stratford and then on to Bow Junction where the London skyline came into view. As we arrived at Bow Junction we passed the iconic Bryant and May match factory. It has been converted into flats now but still retains its character. As we rounded a bend St. Paul's Cathedral and the Post Office Tower appeared. Due to the vast amount of development over the past forty years neither can be seen at all these days.

As this was my first trip, my mate pointed out the Kray twins' old stamping ground at Bethnal Green. We were passing right by peoples' windows and could look directly down on to those houses that were fortunate to have gardens. It was a

(Above) Old fashioned semaphore signals seen from the cab of a train in the platform at Norwich station—in the centre of the photo the signalbox that operated these signals can be seen. (Steven Dey)

(Right) A modern colour light signal at Witham: the angled section at the top would illuminate if the train was to be routed into the loop. (Dom Shaw)

snooper's paradise. We looked down on playing fields and roads with their shops where people were going about their daily business.

At Bethnal Green Junction where both the Norwich and Cambridge main lines meet, the line is elevated. In the arches below there would be all manner of businesses, some of which I imagine were a tad shady. There were numerous car workshops where no doubt the odd 'cut and shut' would be in progress. One particular tyre dealer had so many old tyres stacked on the roof of the workshop, I was amazed it hadn't collapsed. We were slowing now as we approached Liverpool Street. My mate drew my attention to how the rails were worn, the rail head being much wider and cleaner than further down the line. This was as a result of the sheer volume of trains passing over them during the course of each day.

As we approached our final signal of the journey it changed from red to yellow with a number '9' indicating we were cleared to go into platform 9. Again the engine throbbed and the generators made their high pitched whine as we crawled across the myriad of points and criss crossed lines, past the loco where a locomotive was waiting to back onto our train ready for its return working.

I began to put my dust smock on and the big cumbersome orange rubber gloves ready for the moment we would come to a stand and I was to untie the locomotive from the train. As we slowed I opened the driver's side door, turned around with my hands on the vertical grab rails and lowered myself out of the door and down to ground level. I then alighted just at a point where the gap between the train and the locomotive would come to a stand.

Felix brought the train to a halt and there was a loud 'wooossssh' as he put the brake handle into emergency to vent all the air from the brake pipes so that the train wouldn't move. This was my signal to climb in between the train and the locomotive. My first act was to place the brake pipe isolation cocks to the up position and then split the pipes that linked the air brake systems on the locomotive to the train. There were two pairs of rubber pipes to split, the brake pipe which was painted red and the main reservoir pipe which was yellow. Both pipes had different connections so they could not be connected incorrectly. Once I had got hold of the train side brake pipe I pulled the isolating cock down thus venting any air in the train pipe; it meant that any locomotive backing onto the other end of the train could not move until I had but the brake cock in to the up 'closed' position. It was my insurance against the train moving while I was in between.

It was at this point I looked under the coach and noticed a particularly evil pair of beady eyes staring straight at me from the darkness. This made me jump – it was only after I had shooed it away did I realise that it was a large rat. It would not be the last one I would encounter over the years. By the time I had got the pipes apart Felix was in the cab directly above me and ready to ease up. The most unpleasant part of getting in between was the potential of being exposed to the irresponsible actions of those passengers who chose to ignore the instruction in the toilets, 'DO NOT FLUSH IN STATIONS.' There was a very good reason for this instruction. The effluent passed straight out onto the track below and over the years I encountered all sorts of unpleasantries!

Easing up involved the brakes being released by the driver on the locomotive. Only then would he power up so that the buffers would squeeze together thus making the coupling sag. The assistant, who was in between, could then easily lift the coupling off. Generally once the assistant was ready for the driver to squeeze up, he would shout, "Coupling," and then, "Ease away," once he had removed it.

As a new boy, and this being my first proper uncoupling, I remained outside when Felix squeezed up. (Later, as I grew in confidence I would remain in between.) I then climbed back in between, removed the coupling, climbed out and shouted up, "Ease away," which Felix then did. It was at this point that I noticed the yellow main reservoir pipes were still connected and beginning to stretch. I held my breath and waited for them to ping apart or become detached from the locomotive. This all happened pretty quickly but it seemed to be in slow motion. The pipes got longer and longer as the locomotive eased further and further away from the train, and then there was another wooossssh as the pipes split at their joins. No harm was done, they had remained intact and were hanging there waiting to be hooked up onto their dummies. I breathed a huge sigh of relief. I'm not sure Felix was any the wiser as to what had just happened so I chose to keep the matter to myself.

The Liverpool Street station of the 2000s is a clean, bright and airy station with its marble concourse, coffee shops, eateries, supermarkets and retail outlets. Not forgetting the occasional bird of prey —from time to time Network Rail will employ a professional falconer to give the resident pigeons a fright.

In the 1980s Liverpool Street was quite a dismal looking place and was split into two, the low number platforms being separated by a wall from the higher numbered ones. There was a subway that led to platform 10 and upwards. The whole station was grey and caked with the soot and grime of many years of pollution from steam and diesel locomotives. As with any busy station there was always plenty of hustle and bustle, people meeting one another, rushing to catch that train home with only seconds to spare, the rumble of diesel engines and the clatter of Brutes being hauled across the platform.

Brutes were large metal cages that had wheels very similar to supermarket trollies, with the same minds too. They would be used to carry parcels, newspapers and the like around the station. They were hauled by a small electric power cart, and sometimes you would see ten or more Brutes being hauled around which needed no warning of their approach.

While training, Lou Bickers would emphasis the importance of clear communications. He gave an example of an incident where a train was stopped at a signal just outside Chelmsford. The secondman got down to use the signal post telephone and was advised by the signalman there was a "Boot" on the line, which he relayed to the driver. It was only when they hit a Brute that had fallen off the platform onto the line did the miscommunication come to light.

Soon the train we had brought in was ready to make its return journey to Norwich, and a couple of minutes before it was due to depart Felix started up our locomotive. The hustle and bustle of the station disappeared as the engine fired up and a cloud of diesel fumes puffed out of the exhaust ports on its roof. Passengers who were heading for the Norwich train would suddenly break into a fast walk or a run. I guess they were fooled into believing it was actually leaving. As the train departed we followed along the platform as far as the signal at the end which was by this time displaying a red stop light. We waited a few moments and a smaller disc signal or dod as locomen called them, flicked over to a proceed position and we made our way over the criss crossing point work into the small loco. This was where minor inspections were carried out and the locomotive would have its fuel and water topped up. It was also our chance to have another brew.

The fuel point at Liverpool Street station is long gone now. It was situated at the north end and sat between the suburban lines that led to Chingford and Cambridge to the west and the Great Eastern lines that led to Colchester, Norwich and Southend.

Most of the trains on these lines were electric so it was just the Norwich and King's Lynn services that were hauled by diesel locomotives. Additionally there were

(Above) Class 47 hauled London train departing Norwich under semaphore signals, seen from Carrow Road bridge. (John Longman, East Anglian Railway Museum)
(Below) The view from the cab on the Up Main at Ilford, with the flyover on the right and Aldersbrook Sidings to the left. On the extreme left is the Ilford training school. (David Tyson)

trains direct to Lowestoft as well as a boat train service to Harwich. The fitter and his labourer at the fuel point were not exactly over worked. While our locomotive was being fuelled and checked over I popped upstairs to the messroom to boil the kettle. It is many years since the fuel point was demolished due to the reconstruction of the station but to the best of my recollection the room was a bit of a tip! Most drivers chose to stay on their locomotive rather than go up there to have their break.

Liverpool Street was a really busy station, with the bulk of its trains being commuter services in the morning and evening peaks. Many drivers would sit on the locomotive actually watching the trains coming in and out of 'The Street.' Others would read the papers they had managed to get from the train we had brought in from Norwich or the guard would pass on a few copies of whichever dailies he could get his hands on. These days it's almost impossible to pick up any, the decline in newspaper circulation having been so dramatic as a result of the 24 hour news media circus and mobile Apps.

Some years later I was lucky enough to attend a union event in London where Dennis 'The Beast of Bolsover' Skinner was speaking. He reminisced about a time he was travelling to London by train where a man who sat close by was reading the Financial Times. Dennis noticed tears were rolling down the man's face. Once the train arrived in London, Dennis explained: "I made a beeline for the man's discarded paper as I was curious to see what the chap had been crying about. I was also lucky enough to get it before the driver came through and nicked it!" When Dennis opened the paper, a particular company share from the FTSE had been circled in ink. He exclaimed, "I could only assume his tears were ones of joy!"

Once the locomotive had been topped up with fuel and water, it was time to fire it up ready for the arrival of the inbound Norwich train which would form our return working. As the up Norwich ran in, it was preceded by the throb of the locomotive engines and clattering of the wheels over the point work along with the occasional screech of the wheels rubbing on the edges of the rail head.

Soon we were backing onto the rear of the arrival. Fortunately, I tied on without incident! Generally when the secondman tied up he would shout, "Ease away," once he had put the coupling on. This meant the driver would release the brakes on the locomotive and the coupling would raise and tighten. The brakes were solid on the train so it would not move. This gave the secondman more space to move around and it was a good way of remembering to put the coupling on first.

One secondman, Des, decided that he would put all the various pipes on and then the coupling. It was only when the driver applied power did Des' error become apparent. The locomotive drew forward a few feet and all of a sudden there was a loss of brake pipe pressure and the train then came to a stand. When the driver went back to investigate he was confronted with an array of split pipes, wires and the sound of air escaping from the locomotive. Des had forgotten to put the coupling on..... a schoolboy error, one that took him a while to live down.

Two hours later we arrived back at Norwich. My first trip on the mainline was complete but not before we had clouted a couple of large tins of grease that had been placed on the rail head in the Mile End area. By the time we hit them we were doing about 60mph. Felix made no attempt to put the brakes on and seemed entirely unconcerned by the incident. The tins were made of metal and were full of a particular type of grease that was used to lubricate the joints on point work. We guessed they had been put there by kids, clearly bored due to the long summer holidays. I must admit as soon as I saw them I sat up in the seat but Felix just looked at me after there had been a dull thud and said, "They won't need to give this loco a grease up for a while." When we arrived at Colchester we both got out to take a look to see if there was any damage but there was hardly any sign we had hit anything at all.

Although we had only been to London and back which involved me observing and sitting on my backside for the majority of the journey, it felt like I had done a full day's work. It would have been hard to imagine that some fifteen years later we would be doing two trips to London in one day without any mileage payments either. In later years I was to understand the way in which mental concentration can be tiring in a very different way to feeling physically worn out.

As the weeks passed life on the footplate was not quite what I had expected. I was enjoying my new found freedom as well as the experience of working for a living rather than having to listen to teachers. The examination pressures associated with my final year at school were thankfully well and truly in the past. My parents used to say that school days were the best days of your life. Well, I couldn't have disagreed more. I counted down the days until I would walk through those school gates for the last time. I was fifteen years of age, I had a job in the bag and a good loving home. I could want for no more.

However, there was something that was not quite right as there were times when I did not look forward to going to work. Felix would very rarely strike up a conversation and if I did find a subject that interested him then it would only last a few seconds. If we were on an early duty then a conversation before eight in the morning was just out of the question, so I found working life somewhat difficult. This was amplified when I would be booked out with other drivers as we did not always shadow our regular mate to whom we had been allocated to for the year.

Needless to say, my regular mate was a good railman and there were times when I needed his help. On a couple of occasions I would not be able to get the coupling onto the hook of a train and he would waste no time in getting in between to help. I would receive a scowl and told that he was having trouble explaining to his Missus why he was coming home filthy.

One bitterly cold morning I remember having trouble operating the train heating boiler which was situated in the engine room of the locomotive. It would not fire up. Having just been on a boiler course I should have been able to diagnose the problem but for the life of me I could not get to the bottom of the fault. "I can't get the boiler to fire up Felix!" I exclaimed in exasperation. "Have you cleaned the magic eye?" came the gruff response. I had no idea what the magic eye was so was somewhat confused. With some reluctance he made his way into the engine room squeezing his massive stomach through the narrow door and then down on all fours and onto his side. He then reached under the boiler and unscrewed the photo electric cell (the magic eye), cleaned it, replaced it, and the boiler then fired up. Another scowl and David was in his bad books for the rest of the day.

Looking back I think I was on trial. Felix's previous mate was a "bloody liar" according to him, and "No flippin good" and later left the industry. In some way I could see why, having been through the 'tests' that had been set for me, only to fail. He cited one particular incident when they were stabling a locomotive for the night. He asked his mate if he had shut the tail lights off on the locomotive to which he replied that he had, only for Felix to find that they were still on. When a locomotive was left on the depot or 'disposed of' being the official term, the crew would be expected to shut the engine down, screw down the hand brake, turn off any lights and operate the battery isolating switch so as to prevent the batteries from going flat.

One evening we were disposing of a Class 31 locomotive. Felix asked me if I had turned off the tail lights which seemed strange as he never normally asked this. I confirmed that I had ....or I thought I had. For some reason this particular locomotive had a different bank of switches in the cab. Rather than the normal two taillight switches there were four and in my confusion I had actually turned two more on!

As we were walking away from the locomotive he turned and looked and said, “You’re a bloody liar, look at them tail lights, you told me they were off!” Before I could apologise he threw his driver’s bag down and stormed back to the locomotive to turn them off. I was going to wait for him to return but I thought, ‘Sod you ...up yours,’ and I walked over to the messroom and went home questioning whether this really was the career for me? In reality I knew I would not chuck the job in. It was getting towards the end of the year so I knew I would be with a different mate who I hoped would have a completely different attitude.

Chapter 4—“Alright Spider!”

THE FAKENHAM BRANCH line was very different from almost all of the other lines we worked on. It was known as a freight only line with just one train being allowed to travel on it at any one time. Passenger trains ceased to run in 1969. It was accessed from the junction via the main line at Wymondham which is about eight miles from Norwich on the Cambridge line.

The early morning crew would bring some wagons up from Norwich and await the arrival of the Whitemoor goods which would leave March in Cambridgeshire overnight. This was where freight from all over the country would arrive and then be shunted onto the relevant trains for further distribution.

Years ago Whitemoor was the largest marshalling yard in Europe, but as rail freight traffic declined and BR moved to a policy of bulk traffic its usefulness declined and it became dormant in the 1990s. Later a high security prison was built on some of the old yard. Soon after being opened it was the subject of an inquiry after six high risk inmates breached what was believed to be impregnable security. Later it came to light that four prison officers were playing Scrabble at the time of the escape!!

The Whitemoor goods would drop off wagons at various yards along its journey to Norwich and Wymondham was the penultimate stop. The early morning crew would then attach the wagons that had been left for them and proceed to pick up the train staff, or ‘staff’ as it was generally known, from Wymondham signal box. The staff was basically a block of wood with a brass plate which had ‘Wymondham to Fakenham’ stamped on it. The possession of it, along with the clearing of the relevant signals, was the crew’s permission to proceed onto the Fakenham line. It also meant no other trains could enter. Thus it was their insurance against any collision. Attached to the staff was an emergency box which had some basic medical supplies.

The crew would then work the train through some of the best of Norfolk’s countryside. They would stop at each level crossing where the secondman would alight from the locomotive to open the gates. He would wait for any traffic to pass and then swing the huge wooden gates with their distinctive white frame and the large red disc in the centre, across the road. The gates were kept padlocked and could be rather temperamental at times as they would frequently become jammed or freeze in cold weather. We also had to be careful to secure the gates properly. If the secondman failed to do so, they could swing back onto the train as it passed which could lead to them becoming damaged.

Once clear of the crossing the train would stop and the guard would jump out, close the gates, and then give the driver or secondman a hand signal so they could proceed down the line to the next set of gates.

It was on my first trip over this line that I encountered the leading railman Vic.

A Class 37 hauled freight train at Dereham. (David Tyson)

He was a man in his mid to late fifties and a real country character, with a broad Norfolk accent and a shock of thick grey hair that was topped with a plain flat cap. These seemed to be part of the unofficial uniform of many in the farming communities. Vic was in charge of the shunting movements and would liaise with the various companies that used the railway, predominantly grain and fertiliser suppliers, and he would generally ride in the brake van to help the guard.

I learned on my first day on arriving at Dereham that the Norwich Road gates that were adjacent to Dereham station were considered to be within Vic's domain. Woe -betide anyone else who opened or closed them!

Once we drew into the station we would generally de-camp from the locomotive to have our lunch break in the station buildings. These were not the most salubrious of facilities. After years of neglect they were in a state of disrepair with damp running down the walls along with graffiti, and were always cold even in high summer. Some drivers chose to stay on the locomotive.

If the train ran on a Thursday, Vic would take an order and then walk to the chippy to get fish and chips. Most days there would also be time for a card school. It always felt a privilege to be out in the countryside, trundling along with nobody breathing down my neck checking to see if I was working or making me do things I did not want to. Many of my mates were either employed in factories or unable to find work, so I considered myself to be in a very fortunate position.

When on the late return trip, on arrival at Wymondham we would hand the staff and emergency kit over to the signalman which meant the line was no longer occupied. We would then shunt the train over into the sidings where we would wait to see if the Ketton cement wagons were ready to be released to us so that we could haul them to

Norwich. The cement wagons would have been dropped off by the Whitemoor goods train earlier that day. There was no use in getting there too early as you would just have to wait for the lorry drivers to finish pumping the powdered cement into their trucks. Some crews used this as an excuse to take an additional liquid break in the Railway Tavern which was adjacent to the station.

Long before I joined the railway I had a really good friend called Paul and we would knock about with each other at school and during the holidays. Paul became a really keen bird watcher and soon was an expert in bird behaviour and identification. Sometime towards the end of our time together at high school his family moved out into the country to a village called Hardingham. Their house looked across a small valley onto the line. My Dad would take me to visit from time to time and one particular day, Paul's Dad asked my Father about some strange bangs that would sometimes come from the direction of the train as it passed by. Occasionally it would come to a stand and then there would be a series of explosions very similar to those made by a shot gun. Surprisingly my Father confirmed that there was an individual who would bring a shot gun to work!

One afternoon I saw a driver walking across from the goods yard at Norwich with a long item wrapped up with sacking and string that looked suspiciously like a shot gun. In fact, I don't really know why he had wrapped it up as it was glaringly obvious what he was carrying.

The individual was Jack. I was to work with him later in my career and found him to be a very nice, quietly spoken man, but he always had to be somewhere else. Many drivers would supplement their incomes by cleaning windows, several worked at the Norwich Theatre Royal scenery shifting, and a few managed boilers at various establishments. Jack was one such person, so if you were on the relief staff (relieving crews as their trains arrived at Norwich and preparing them for departure), he would disappear for a while and return later once his other duties were complete. I am led to believe that one of his alternative exploits was to act as a chauffeur for a local judge.

It was absolutely true that he would take his shot gun with him on the Fakenham goods and when approaching the Hardingham area he would get the secondman to drive while he would take a few pot shots at the pheasants. If Jack successfully scored a hit the train would come to a stand, and he would scuttle off into the adjoining field to locate the unfortunate pheasant. He would proceed to pluck it in the cab on the way back to Wymondham, much to the disgust of those secondmen unfortunate enough to witness the performance.

Early one cold winter's morning I climbed up into the cab of a Class 31 locomotive only to notice what appeared to be a hole in the ceiling above the secondman's seat that had been patched up with tape and painted over. I asked my driver what had happened to cause such a hole in the roof. It transpired that Jack had been on the Fakenham goods and planning on getting up to his old tricks. The gun was loaded but unattended and resting up against the handbrake in the cab. The train jolted and the gun tipped over, there was a loud bang and debris was scattered all over the cab which resulted in a gaping hole in the roof. According to my driver it was down to pure luck that the secondman was not in his seat at the time as he would have surely received severe injuries or possibly been killed. Much as I liked Jack, I found this to be a rather risky strategy for bagging a few pheasants and the consequences could have been terrible.

Jack and I were to work together on an unusual very early morning duty on the Fakenham Branch in August 1985. The Queen and the Duke of Edinburgh were visiting Great Yarmouth and arrangements had been made for them to travel there by train.

On the Dereham branch with the Royal Train: left to right are Driver Jack Nelson, Signalling Inspectors Bob Thorpe and Basil Hyatt, and secondman David Tyson.

The Royal Train was a mixture of various types of coaches and as you can imagine it was accompanied by a massive amount of security. The Royal couple travelled down to Norfolk and the train was stabled overnight on the entrance to the Fakenham branch.

Both Jack and I, along with another driver, were taxied out to Wymondham at 2am to relieve the crews that were there. The Royal Train had a locomotive at each end, one to haul the train onto the branch and then detach, while the second locomotive had been coupled on at the Norwich end ready to haul it out for the onward journey to Great Yarmouth later that day.

We relieved the night crew, one of whom was a great lad also named David, who had not been on the railway long. All he kept saying to me was, "Do you think I look smart David?" Apparently someone had commented on his choice of uniform, a light weight blue jacket as opposed to the heavier dark coat. Once relieved, the crew disappeared into the night with the secondman still asking his mate the same question.

Given the hour of the day Jack and I went to jump on the locomotive for forty winks, but were prevented from doing so by the police and we were directed to the signal box. This wasn't so much a request, rather an instruction that it was best we stayed there. We were also warned not to wander off as the place was swarming with armed Special Branch officers.

We spent the early hours of that day in the signal box chatting, drinking tea and waiting for our chance to start the locomotive up and make our way to Norwich. There was also a high ranking British Transport Police officer with us. We hadn't been in the signal box long when his radio crackled into life and one of his Special Branch officers alerted him to the fact that there was someone wandering around in the neighbouring graveyard. "Where are you?" the officer asked….. "In the graveyard," came a rather strained reply…… "That's your relief," was the officer's curt reply followed by a rolling of his eyes and a shake of the head.

It seemed as though everybody was descending on Wymondham in the early hours of that morning – the traincrew, BTP, a signalling inspector, fitters and track staff and not forgetting Special Branch. Someone also said the SAS were lurking about.

I was told by the police officer that he had stopped an elderly track worker whom he seemed to think was close to retirement. He'd been walking along the side of the train with huge bags of sawdust and looked totally exhausted. When asked what he was doing the track worker explained that he had been given the job of putting the bags underneath the train's toilet waste outlets. Most trains dumped the effluent from the toilet directly onto the track, hence the notices in the toilets of coaches not to flush in the station. He must have lugged the bags up and down the length of the train four or five times only to be told that there were chemical toilets onboard which had retention tanks!

Around seven in the morning the paperboy, as he was referred to, arrived. The paperboy was another signalling inspector, Bob Thorpe, who carried a plastic box filled with three copies of every daily newspaper which ranged from the Daily Telegraph and Racing Post, I guessed for the Queen, to The Sun, obviously for The Duke!

Soon it was time to fire up the locomotive, a recently re-painted class 47 with its wheels all whitened and the cab roof painted silver, a Royal Train requirement so I was told. Firstly, we had some photos taken for posterity, and then a riding inspector joined us and gave us our instructions for the journey. He told us that we were to leave at a pre-determined time and were not to exceed 50mph so that a) we arrived at Norwich bang on time and b) because the Queen did not like going too fast while she was having her breakfast.

Soon the time came to make the eight mile journey to Norwich. The train drew slowly off the branch with Jack in the driving seat taking the utmost care not to snatch the coupling. The last thing he wanted to do was give the coaches a jolt thus spilling Her Majesty's morning cuppa. I was looking back to see if the train followed correctly. The riding inspector stood between the two of us with a sheet of paper which had the running times schedule in one hand, and a stopwatch in the other.

I was astonished by the crowds of people who had turned out early in the morning to wave to the train. They were on the platform at Wymondham station, on footbridges, at crossings and on embankments. It was a mystery to me how so many people knew this train was going to be leaving and how they knew it had been stabled over night at Wymondham. So much for security! I must admit – I felt myself well up with pride. I'm no royalist but it just highlighted to me the power and respect the monarchy had at the time. Within no time we were in Norwich. I jumped off the locomotive to untie and soon it was on its way to Great Yarmouth.

It was traditional for the driver to receive a letter of thanks from the Area Manager with reference to them having driven the Royal Train which was always accompanied by a £10 gratuity. The secondman would receive a letter and £5. I received a letter but no money! Feeling somewhat aggrieved I raised this with my manager and some weeks later I was handed a further letter with a crisp five pound note contained within. I know of one colleague who framed his letter along with the money, but I chose to pay a visit to the Plasterers Arms, a pub I frequented in Norwich. It was renowned for being the cheapest in the city and it also sold Scrumpy which was like drinking rocket fuel. Armed with the 'Queen's Booty' the first round of drinks for my mates and I was on Her Majesty. I don't remember much about that night for obvious reasons, the Plasterers being a very appropriate name for the establishment.

Over the years traffic on the branch declined and later it was referred to as the Dereham branch once the line closed between Fakenham and Great Ryburgh. In the new year of 1981 I parted company with Felix and was paired with a different driver called Charlie Bray. He was a completely different character to Felix and on this particular day we were on the early morning shift heading for Great Ryburgh. Vic was seeing to the Norwich Road gates at Dereham Central (as I believe it was once called). As we waited, Charlie told me that his previous mate would jump out while Vic dealt with the gates. He would run along the line to the next set of gates and have them open ready for the train to pass through without stopping, thus saving a few minutes. Keen to impress, I jumped out of the cab, ran past Vic, who gave me a puzzled look as I rushed along the line to the next set of gates.

From the locomotive they did not seem too far from Norwich Road but, given the slippery wooden sleepers, uneven surface and ballast stones, it was quite a distance. As I was running along I realised that the train was catching me up so I had to up my pace to get to the gates and have them open before it arrived. Fortunately I managed to get them open just in time. However by the second day after breathlessly climbing up into the cab I realised Charlie had been stringing me along and I had fallen for it hook, line and sinker!

Generally the volumes of traffic were quite light depending on the time of year with maybe no more than five or six grainflow wagons per train or a few fertiliser wagons, if the train ran at all. I was always disappointed if I arrived at work to find the train had been 'caped' (railway jargon for cancelled which goes back to the days when telegraph was used). During the autumn much of the grain would be kept in huge silos and then loaded into the wagons when there was a buyer. I believe a great deal of it was sent up to Dufftown (nothing to do with Homer Simpson), or Muir of Ord in Scotland. In the production of whisky Norfolk grain was considered to be of the highest quality.

During 1982 I was on duty with driver George Leman on the early Dereham shift. As the early morning Whitemoor train arrived at Wymondham we were surprised to see that about 30 wagons were being dropped off for us to haul to Dereham. It turned out that trials were being run with a company to haul solid bitumen to store at Dereham. If the trials were a success then there would be a regular service. This would have been good for the line as it was most likely loss making at the time.

After completing our shunting duties we made our way onto the branch and around to the first set of gates at Church Lane which were also known as Abbey Gates due to being in close proximity to Wymondham Abbey. I dropped down, opened the gates and George drew the train through. Not only did we have the bitumen wagons but several other wagons as well, so by the time we got through the guard was just a tiny figure in the distance. I must admit he was somewhat difficult to see. Soon I saw what I thought was his right arm held above his head which was the 'right-away' hand signal given once the guard had closed the gates and was ready for us to move on. "Ok George... right away," I said...."You sure about that?' he asked...."Yep," I confidently replied.

Off we trundled with the Class 31 locomotive struggling to get traction due to the weight and length of the train. Shortly we arrived at the next set of gates, Station Road, Kimberley. Again I opened them, we passed through and waited and waited....and deep down I knew that what I thought I had seen as right away, clearly was not.

"Best you go back and see what has happened," said George though I think we both knew. I did the walk of shame towards the rear of the train with me crossing my fingers hoping the guard would be there. Alas no one was in sight.... oh dear! I closed the gates so as to let the traffic through at the same time suffering the scowls of several passing motorists. Then I made my way back to see George. "Alright Hawkeye," were his first words!

We agreed to re-open the gates and reverse or 'set back' so we could pick up the guard. This took a little time but soon enough we were making our way back to the previous gates which were about two miles in our rear. I was in the brake van using the calling on hand signal to guide George back. Soon enough a figure appeared in the distance. 'I'm in for a right telling off here,' were my immediate thoughts as the guard and I came face to face. Fortunately for me he was just laughing about the situation. "Nice morning for a stroll in the country!" he exclaimed even though he was wearing sandals. "I was in the process of locking the gates, when I looked around you'd disappeared." Eventually we were back on track and continued on our journey.

On arrival at Dereham Vic was pacing up and down the platform. We were greeted with, "Cor 't' hell, where have you lot been?" George promptly filled Vic in who saw the funny side and said to me, "You'll never live that one down Spider,".... 'Spider', nobody had ever called me Spider and for the life of my I don't know why Vic called me that. For the rest of the time I visited Dereham I would be welcomed in that broad Norfolk accent, "Alright Spider," which was followed by his distinctive guttural laugh. If there was a joke there I would have loved him to share it with me. My friend and colleague, Chris Pearson, was known to Vic as 'Stones' which baffled him too!

The Dereham branch was fun to work on and a change from the usual tasks. Even when the weather was bad I always thought it was pleasure to be there. In the winter of 1987 I had to go over there with two drivers and an inspector on the snowplough. The inspector was Allan Waites who had trained me as a secondman and had progressed through the managerial grades. It had been a particularly bad winter and many of the main lines around East Anglia had been blocked by snow drifts for several days.

We had two Class 47 locomotives coupled together for double the power along with two drivers. The Class 47's did not have the necessary equipment to be coupled in multiple. Given that there was no form of communication between the drivers of the front and rear locomotives, they agreed that they would use whistle codes. This resulted in the driver of the leading loco sounding the horn when power was to be applied, and then sounding the horn when power was to be shut off. The code had no specific form, just a series of blasts, or as the leading driver described, "I'll just make a hell of a racket!"

We also had to make sure the snow plough had a red tail light on the rear. There is a golden rule that ALL movements must display a red tail light on the rear. This is still the case today and is to show that the train is complete and to act as warning to trains approaching from their rear in degraded situations—for example, if a failed train needs to be assisted in the rear with another locomotive. Tail lights seemed to be in short supply this particular day so there was some debate as to whether one was actually needed. The inspector began by stating it may not be necessary. However the lead driver refused to go without one. "Best you go find one, Allan," was his conclusion!

That was the power of the driver. If he said we were not going, then we were not going, his word was final... end of story! It was a lesson I was to learn on many other occasions. Never allow yourself to be coerced into doing something you believe to be

An example of locomotives working in multiple: 37116 and 37075 are seen on a Freightliner train in Ipswich Yard in 1992. (Alistair Barham)

fundamentally wrong or compromise on safety. Those lessons were to serve me well.

We were advised that once we got across the Dereham branch we would need to be careful clearing snow from rail lines close to buildings. Earlier in the week the snowplough had belted through Gunton Station on the Cromer branch line. As they passed through the station at high speed the force of the displaced snow had smashed the windows on the restored platform buildings that were now a private residence. The snow had also gone right over the top of the station buildings and down its chimney.

The formations of the snow across the branch line were beautiful. The icy northern winds had blown the snow into drifts but the plough cut through them like a hot knife through butter. We made it through to the end of the line with little trouble and returned to Norwich.

Not long after I finished my driver training I began my route learning over the branch but sadly I was never to drive over it as a fully fledged driver, as it closed in 1989. I'm glad to say that the line is open and running as a preserved railway known as the Mid Norfolk Railway and is run by volunteers. Not so long ago I was fortunate to visit with my friend and former colleague Chris Pearson. The restoration of the station buildings has been excellent. The old messroom is no longer the damp dingy room it once was in the British Railways period of decline but is now the station buffet. I will always have fond memories of the days working over there, characters such as Vic, the Royal Train and stopping to pick apples or blackberries during the autumn. Those happy days are now confined to the ghosts of the past.

Snowplough in use at Lenwade in 1981 with Inspector Eric Wilkinson on the left and Driver Edgar James on the right. (Chris Harkins)

Chapter 5—"Tom….. We're off the road"

I WAS BOOKED on an additional Sunday duty. I was looking forward to it even if it was a very early morning start, something like 3am, as it was the first ballast turn of my career. Sundays were paid at time plus three quarters and I had just purchased my first motorbike for getting about and needed to pay my parents back the money they had loaned me. Ballast or engineers' trains were generally scheduled to work at night or during weekends and they were there to supply materials and equipment for track work. Ballast trains would be made up of several wagons or hoppers that contained a particular type of stone that the track was laid on so that it would remain stable. From time to time the ballast was required to be either replaced or added to depending on its condition.

As it was an additional duty I was not working with Felix. My driver, Bob Dubbin, the guard and I were driven out to Gunton on the Cromer line to relieve a crew that had been on site all night. On arrival we were advised they had not turned a wheel since arriving, however it would not be too long before the engineers would require our services. We had a train of about fifteen hoppers, a Shark brake van and two Class 31 locomotives coupled together in multiple due to the weight of the train. A Shark brake was designed with two ploughs beneath it that could be lowered when required to push any excess ballast stones off the rails once the hoppers had laid them.

Soon the engineering supervisor advised us we were to be moving on—he would direct the movements from a wagon further down the train. We were going to push the train towards North Walsham rather than hauling it which seemed a bit unorthodox, but this was because the train had been hauled into the section and there were no passing loops to allow the locomotives to be run around to what would then be the front.

A Shark brake van in derelict condition at Shenfield—this one was put in a siding when defective and remained there for over thirty years until being cut up on site in 2024. (Alastair Holmes)

Soon the order came to propel and with both of us looking out we crept along. We could see the ballast stones falling out onto the track with Bob and I keeping a keen eye out for hand signals from the engineering supervisor as we slowly progressed. The Shark brake deployed its ploughs and as soon as it encountered the stones it began to bounce up and down as did the locomotives. This went on for some time and, being unfamiliar with the sensation, I turned to Bob and exclaimed, “Blimey, I thought we were going to come off the road!” He smiled and replied, “In all my years on the footplate, I have never been off the road.” Coming off the road is railway jargon for becoming derailed.

Once all the hoppers had been unloaded, we continued to push the train through to North Walsham where we were able to run around and attach the locomotives to the front of the train. We made our way back to Norwich at the breakneck speed of 35mph. Having only been on duty just a few hours it was looking good for an early finish which meant we would be paid a full day’s wage for maybe five or six hours work, just so long as the right foreman was on duty and he was in a charitable frame of mind.

On arrival at Norwich we were signalled into the goods yard and as we approached the boardwalks next to the shunter’s hut out came ‘God of the Goods Yard’ as I was later to name him, Billy Cook. He shouted up at me that we were to go down “Paris” as far as we could. The goods yard was made up of several lines that were referred to as roads and each of these were allocated a specific name. I can't remember all of the names, but there was Delhi, Paris and Sebastopol to name but a few. Several of the shunters referred to Delhi as Del-hi for some reason. I just think it was because they had not made the connection between the names of the roads and the cities of the world, even though they had worked there for thirty years plus!

They would back the pilot on to the rear of our train so the locomotives could be released for us to take to the loco sheds. I relayed the instruction on to Bob. The train was soon pulled away from us so our locomotives could be released and we were then signalled off on a route that I had not been on before. I was in what had now become the leading cab with Bob driving from the rear and I would operate the brakes if the need to stop arose. To get from the station or the goods yard to the loco shed, where all the locomotives were stabled, involved several moves as there were no direct routes. Generally the driver would remain in one cab and the secondman would be in the rear. The locomotive would then travel backwards and forwards on the various lines with the secondman operating the brake to let the driver know when the signal allowing the move was cleared.

We passed the goods yard signal box and then onto what was known as a 'reception line' where Bob brought the locomotives to a stand just to the rear of the signal which he would require to take him over the next set of points and on towards the side of the loco shed. As we moved forward I was now in the rear cab. We pulled up directly adjacent to the loco shed where we were to clear a set of points. These particular points were spring loaded– once the locomotives passed clear they would spring back to their original position.

Once clear of the points I leaned out of the rear locomotive to give the stop hand signal and we then came to a stand. The distance between the side of the locomotives and the shed wall was very narrow and I had difficulty in calling Bob back. Eventually Bob got the message and applied power to set back. We promptly went up the line we just come from. My immediate reaction was, 'That's not supposed to happen!!' I dived across the cab and shoved the brakes on as hard as I could. We came to a stand after there was a crash and a bump.

I didn't want to look back for fear of what I was about to see. Nevertheless I forced myself to peer out of the cab window back towards the rear locomotive. 'Oh bloody hell,' was my first reaction. What was now the leading locomotive with me in had travelled back up the way it came from. Unfortunately the rear locomotive had taken a different direction, the one both of them should have taken. This resulted in the derailing of both locomotives.

There is always someone who will make a wisecrack in a time of adversity and this was no exception to the rule as I was later to find out when someone asked me if both locomotives had developed an 'earth fault', a twist on a electrical malfunction that a locomotive can develop!

I walked back expecting to have my balls chewed off by Bob. I'm sure Felix would have been quick enough to heap the blame on me. He was standing there surveying the damage. He looked at me and said, "What was it I said to you this morning about never coming off the road?" Then he laughed. Both the locomotives were derailed and no longer connected, the coupling had sheared off, there were pipes and wires all over the place, and the dust that had been disturbed by the derailment was just beginning to settle. What a flipping mess. I also realised that both Bob and I could be in a heap of trouble. Although our actions were considered by most locomen to be efficient as well as custom and practice, propelling in this manner was against

A derailed Class 31 locomotive at Norwich—in front of the loco are Roy 'Noddy' Gambling and Ray 'Dinger' King. (Steven Dey)

the rules. Bob should have changed ends and driven from the leading cab at all times.

All sorts of thoughts were spinning around in my head. Was this my fault, did we clear the points correctly? Am I in trouble, will I get the sack? Bob, with a hangdog look, wandered over to a telephone on the side of the loco shed and called over his shoulder, "Shut both of the engines down, no need to put the handbrakes on!" I heard him call the foreman. "Tom, It's Bob Dubbin here, we're off the road on the corner of the shed."

Shortly after Bob's phone call the foreman, Tom French, came over from the messroom in his signature green cardigan, grey trousers, cream loafers and armed with a packet of Embassy fags. He stood surveying the situation, popped a fag in the corner of his mouth, lit it, took a drag and said, "Oh!" I guess he was working out how the hell he was going to sort out this mess. The derailment was blocking the southern end of the loco sheds so it was going to be a nightmare getting engines onto and off the shed over the course of the next day or so. Not only were the locomotives damaged, the track was in a poor way too.

Just before Bob and I made our way to the messroom for a cup of tea, Mac, one of the fitters who had been standing outside the shed, came up to me. "You did nothing wrong son, I was watching the locos come onto the shed, you cleared the spring points, I even heard them clunk back into place." I thought back and realised that if we had not cleared the spring points I would have not been parallel with the shed wall. I relaxed a little, but there was still a nagging worry that I had failed to check the points had actually sprung back correctly. Fortunately I had a witness who was happy to back me up. On arrival at the messroom Tom asked us to write our reports which we duly did.

For several days I was fretting about the consequences. Would there be some sort of inquiry? Would I get a grilling from an Inspector or hauled up into the Area Manager's office? But nothing happened. I did get a bit of stick off Felix when I went back to working with him a few days later. He had his own opinions as to what had happened and of course it was all my fault!

About two weeks later I was at the station tying a locomotive on to the 07:40 train to London when Norman Duggan, the Area Manager, came walking along the platform and was obviously heading in my direction. 'Oh no, he's on to me,' I thought. "Your name Tyson?' he said in his broad Welsh accent. "Yes Mr Duggan," I replied. "I haven't received your report, can you make sure I have one as soon as possible?" "Yes Mr Duggan." And that was it, I never heard another word about the whole matter. Some weeks later I saw Bob and he asked me if I had heard anything to which I told him no. "Me neither," he replied.

It was only some years later while I was reading about an accident at Bellgrove Junction in Glasgow that I found out the British Rail Board did not carry any insurance. Any damages would be repaired and self financed. I guess the insurance premiums would have been too high.

Chapter 6 : Breaking my 'Duck'...Let Loose at the Controls

THE RELATIONSHIP WITH my first driver, Felix, was not a resounding success and I soon found that other drivers were more talkative, friendly and happy to share their experiences. Some would even let you have a drive. The first driver to let me take the controls was Jack Whiting, a stocky chap with steel rimmed glasses and a nasally voice. He was also one for playing practical jokes on his colleagues.

I had met Jack on several occasions before I joined the railway as he lived close to our house and my impression of him was of an upstanding, rather straight laced type of person. I was soon to learn how different he was at work, always messing around in the messroom and winding up other drivers.

If a particular driver, Tony, was in the messroom, Jack would get the lid of a metal teapot and take it into the canteen, the door to which had a small round glass window. He would slowly rub the lid of the teapot over the glass in a circular motion. The noise really put your teeth on edge, very much like the sound of finger nails being drawn down a blackboard. Tony could not handle it and after a few moments he would clear off. Jack would stop and return to the messroom and sit on a bench next to the window sills which were made of ceramic tiles.

Eventually Tony would return. He would look at Jack and ask, "Finished?" Jack would nod. As soon as Tony had settled down he would proceed to rub the teapot lid over the ceramic tiles with the same effect as the canteen window. Off Tony would go again. Tony was in the later years of his career and I think had he been a younger man Jack would have had the lid inserted in a place where the sun doesn't shine!

Another of Jack's pranks involved the TV in our messroom. By coincidence it was the same model as the one he had at home. Several drivers were watching TV as Jack walked in. He made himself a cup of tea, got his lunch out and sat well away from the TV minding his own business. All of a sudden the volume went down. Those watching clearly thought there was a malfunction so they used their remote to turn the sound back up only for the channel to change. This charade went on for some time, channels changing randomly, volume up and then down, then the TV went off. All the while Jack sat there chuckling to himself.

As Jack lived just a stone's throw from my parents' home, the day before we

Arthur Nudds, Jack Whiting and Bob Rollands in the mess room. (Stephen Dey)

were to work together he told me to come around and he would give me a lift which I greatly appreciated. We were booked on duty quite late in the afternoon to work the Norwich to Birmingham service, usually with about five coaches and hauled by a Class 31 locomotive.

The Birmingham stock and locomotives were fitted with a vacuum brake which was much more difficult to operate than the more modern air brakes that were being rolled out. Once applied, the vacuum brakes were very slow to release, so it required a great deal of skill to judge where to brake and when to release it. This enabled the train to stop in the right place at the platform without a jolt. I had watched my regular mate, Felix, operate the brake on countless occasions making it look so easy. This is always the sign of someone who knows exactly what they are doing. Naively I thought getting in the seat would be a piece of cake.

Once we boarded our train in platform one, Jack turned to me and asked if I had driven one of these before. "Just a couple of times," I lied. He very generously offered me the chance to drive to March where we were to be relieved by a crew who would take the train on to Leicester. I tried to curb my enthusiasm but inside I was bubbling with anticipation as my regular mate had never let me drive. Not being over familiar with the route, I asked Jack to keep an eye on me.

After being given the right away signal from the platform staff, we set off with me looking back making sure the train was following in a timely manner. I was thinking to myself, 'This is fantastic,' as I opened the regulator or power controller (regulator was a term used on steam locomotives) just enough to make sure the diesel engine did not create too much electricity as I did not want to overload the generator.

There were two types of diesel locomotives in operation. Diesel electric which uses the engine to run a generator which in turn creates electricity to supply the traction motors to power the wheels. Diesel mechanical traction, generally railcars or diesel multiple units (DMUs), uses the power from the diesel engine to run a drive shaft to turn the wheels. That's about as technical as I get.

I was keen to impress Jack, so keeping my wits about me, I constantly monitored the speed of the train making sure I was not over-speeding, at the same time watching out for the signals ahead and hoping they were displaying proceed aspects. There were seventeen signal boxes between Norwich and Ely North along with their associated signals. At the time the vast majority of the signals on the lines in East Anglia were the older semaphore type as opposed to the more modern electric colour light. These days LED signals have been installed which can be seen from many miles away. Each group of semaphore signals were manually controlled by individual signal boxes.

During the day the signals were easy to see, but in bad weather such as fog, snow, heavy rain or darkness they were more difficult to locate. They were lit by paraffin lamps which were weak at the best of times and could either run out of fuel or extinguish in bad weather. It was vitally important to know exactly where they were located so route knowledge is key to finding your way around.

As the journey went on so I gained confidence. I was beginning to enjoy myself with the thrill of being in control of several hundred tons of train along with the throb of the diesel engines, the whine of the generators, the roar of the rails and track. By now we were speeding through stations and under bridges at 75mph as trees, telegraph poles and their lines flashed by. I was in control of this train and almost fresh out of school at sixteen years of age. I had only just got a motorbike which did a maximum speed of 45mph and used to overtake milk floats for kicks, so this was off the scale as far as I was concerned.

We passed over Croxton automatic barriers on our approach to Thetford, which was the first scheduled stop on the journey. On every route each driver would have his own landmarks. Generally these were buildings, trackside equipment or a bridge which they would use as a point to begin applying the brakes ready for the next stop. Some years later, when I was route learning the Cromer line, a driver advised me, “You know when you’re getting close to Salhouse as there is a white horse in the field with a huge cock.” As soon as I signed up for the route the horse disappeared. I guess it had been sent to the glue factory!

On every journey the driver is expected to perform a ‘running brake test’ at a point where the train is at its optimum speed and well before any stopping point or speed restriction. This is to make sure that the brakes are working and to get a feel of the braking characteristics of the train. Many trains would look identical but the characteristics of the brakes and the weight could be very different. The driver would also have to take into consideration the condition of the rails, whether they were wet, dry or contaminated, train speed and weight, gradients and line curvature as well as visibility. No two train’s braking characteristics were alike.

As we approached Thetford I applied the brakes at a footbridge where I had observed Felix do so. The train started to slow but I could now feel the pressure. ‘Have I put too much braking into the train? Will I stop short of the platform? Will I overrun?’ All these thoughts raced through my mind. I hit Thetford platform at about 25 mph and then thought I was going to stop short so I released the brakes. They seemed to take an age to come off. The train was slowing too quickly. Now it seemed I was going to over run. ‘Oh my God!’ I thought. I re-applied the brakes and then with a jolt we came to a stand pretty much in the right place. Jack didn't even look at me but just said, "We'll have a better stop at March." I felt I had been gently chastised.

The rest of the journey passed without incident and I enjoyed travelling through Breckland which led to the flatlands of the Fens. Over the years we would often see jets taking off from Lakenheath and Mildenhall airbases and marvel as the 'Blackbird' SR71 would do a vertical take off on its assent to the edge of space to spy on Eastern Europe. (This was before the advent of spy satellites.) A10 Tank Busters would belt across the Fenland at high speed at what seemed like just a few feet off the ground. Having read 'Tornado' by John Nichols, I have gained the utmost respect for any pilot who can fly an aircraft at speeds in excess of 600mph just forty feet off the ground!

I have been fortunate enough to witness some of the most stunning sunsets. The topography of the flatlands along with the huge skies allows nature to paint its massive canvas. At times I have been mesmerised by the sight of the sun slowly sinking in the west, a huge ball of fire reflecting off the clouds or casting enormous shafts of light across the golden fields of wheat and barley. High winds could create huge soil clouds after prolonged dry periods, the dust whipping up into the air and reducing visibility to almost zero. And I have marvelled at the flocks of starlings that would gather and weave across the dusky atmosphere. I consider myself to have been privileged to see such sights and regret not having a camera with me to capture nature's beauty.

Lakenheath Fen is adjacent to the railway and these days is an RSPB nature reserve. In the early eighties it was a man-made woodland with a particular type of tree that was used in the production of matches and was owned by the match manufacturers Bryant and May. The Bryant and May factory was located at Bow Junction near Stratford where we passed through on our approach to London. One driver told me Bryant and May went bust as the employees were "Always going on strike." It took me a minute or two to get the pun!

A rare bird would nest in the woods which would attract large numbers of bird watchers at certain times of the year. One particular day the Golden Oriole as it is known flew across in front of a crowd of twitchers straight into the path of a passing Birmingham train. No more Golden Oriole!

Our next stop was March in Cambridgeshire rather than Ely. Hauled trains would by-pass Ely as it involved unhooking the locomotive and running around the train. This was considered unproductive so we were routed around Ely curve from the up Cambridge line to the Peterborough line. Progress along the long curve was slow and it was important to make sure the correct signal had been cleared for you at Ely North Junction signal box. The last thing you wanted was to be routed into Ely by mistake.

'The Ship of the Fens' which is Ely cathedral stands majestically on a small hill casting its gaze over the area and on a clear day it can be seen from many miles away. As the train crawled around the curve we would take in its beauty while looking back to make sure all was well with the train. Once the very last coach had passed onto the Peterborough line I was able to wind the regulator wide open and hear the throb of the engine, the sound of the exhaust whistling and the generator screaming. Slowly the train increased its speed as we made our way across the Fens and into the darkness.

Being with Jack was a welcome change to the more mundane days I was spending with my regular mate. Felix's attitude towards me was one of reserved indifference. I found this was quite common within the industry but nothing compared to some of the abuse pioneering young footplate women were subject to at the time. Many of these men had a wealth of railway knowledge and experience; in some cases they would use their superior knowledge as a whip to beat you with which often left the recipient feeling stupid and undervalued. I vowed to myself that I would always do my best to help new colleagues and share what I have learned over the years to help rather than hinder them.

Class 31 hauled train arriving at Norwich. (Steven Dey)

Chapter 7—Secrets of the Loco Messroom

MESSROOMS ARE THE focal point of every depot throughout the railway network. Each has its own characteristics and is occupied by a wide range of characters. Situated next to Norwich City's ground, there was a permanent, very distinctive odour which would cling to your clothes. I first came across it when my father would return home from work. It was a unique combination of diesel fumes and tobacco. The messroom was the hub of the depot where we signed on for duty and spent endless hours. We also shared the accommodation with the maintenance staff.

If we were not allocated to a particular running job, we ate, snoozed, chatted, played games, watched TV and generally mucked about there.

I always knew if my Dad experienced a particularly bad day and had encountered a locomotive with engine trouble because the smell of diesel fumes on his uniform was quite strong and the messroom smell was quite different. My father had a reputation amongst his colleagues as being immaculately dressed while at work.

Some drivers looked as if they had been dragged through a hedge backwards. Arthur Nudds was a real character and would turn up for a day's work after carrying out his proper job as a game keeper at Poringland. One afternoon he brought a fox on a lead to work as it had been injured and he was nurturing it back to health. Arthur was a larger than life character, built like the proverbial brick shit-house with a lumbering stroll, hands like dinner plates, a shock of wild brown hair and a huge grin which revealed the large gap in his front teeth. He would frequently tease the secondmen, saying to one lad, "Michael, a young lady with a baby in a pram has been down the loco looking for you… what have you been up to?" followed by his distinctive roar of laughter.

Arthur was as strong as an ox. Occasionally I witnessed him untie a locomotive from a train and while it would take a fair bit of effort (as well as both hands) for me to lift the coupling off the hook of a coach, Arthur would do it with his right hand in a smooth flowing action as the locomotive 'squeezed up'.

One late Saturday afternoon Arthur and I had been to Ipswich. On our return to Norwich we were booked to carry out relief work, meeting trains on arrival at the station, uncoupling them, and preparing them for their next trip. It was about seven in the evening and Arthur asked me, "Do you have to be in the city to meet your mates this evening?" I had planned to ask Arthur if I could get away around nine and advised him of my hopes. "Best you go now," was his reply. "But what about all that tying on and off?" I asked. He just gave me a look and told me to "Bugger off." I didn't need telling twice.

Arthur was a one-off and I was proud to be associated with him. I attended his funeral in early 2019 and was gobsmacked when the former head of the British Army, General Lord Richard Dannatt, gave the eulogy. He knew Arthur who did most of the game keeping on his land.

The messroom, or 'loco' as it was often referred to, was not the cleanest of places. Each Sunday it would be subjected to a major swill down. As I approached the main doors one Sunday morning the phrase 'Inside for the lakes' had been chalked on the brick work by the entrance. I was puzzled until I walked through the sets of doors and into the main seating and locker area. It was as if there had been a flood. The floor was concrete and there was a small drain at the far end with a small hole in the floor which had an ill-fitting lid. The messroom cleaner, who was actually the time keeper, was slowly brushing the puddles of water down the hole at the far end of the room with a rubber contraption at the end of a broom handle, like a massive squeegee!

The time keeper's duties also stretched to emptying the tea slops from a huge bin situated adjacent to the hot water geyser in the old canteen area. The process involved dragging the bin towards the fire doors and emptying it outside. Unfortunately one morning the time keeper lost his balance and the whole lot flooded the messroom floor with a mass of stewed tea, tea bags and tea leaves. Rather than try to clean the lot up he just got the squeegee and worked the mess around and around until it all disappeared down the tiny drain in the corner of the messroom. Not the most hygienic solution as it created a blockage in the drain as a result of a week's worth of tea bags and leaves being coaxed down it.

As there were no full time cleaners at the loco it also fell to the time keepers to give the messroom and the toilets the once over each shift. The facilities were somewhat basic and the toilets were not much better. There was a line of urinals that had cracks, the porcelain was worn and stained, and the sinks were pretty much the same. It was some years before I summoned up the courage to use the toilets, or 'traps' as they were known. I had to be absolutely desperate on account of the toilet tissue that we were supplied with. Now I use the word 'tissue' somewhat loosely as it was more like tracing paper and did not really absorb what it needed to absorb. It was more like spreading things around, if you get my drift!

My father told me of the time he was in the toilets while one of the time keepers was carrying out his duties for the shift, something I think he felt was beneath him. This particular chap had a mop which he swilled the trough of the urinal with, in which my father had just peed, then he hooked the mop out and, to my father's horror, washed it out in one of the sinks! Frankly, it's amazing that there was not more illness

Mess room cleaner Graham Barrett. (Stephen Dey)

about. In some respects health and safety in the workplace was more of an aspiration than a reality when it came to cleanliness.

Eventually we did get a proper cleaner, a sweet little chap called Graham who was a carriage cleaner at the station and had been made redundant, so he was relocated to work with us. He was a quietly spoken man who dressed like a throwback to the 1940s and could have easily fitted into a Lowry painting. His hobnail boots were always immaculate and he wore light blue dungarees over a checked shirt, with a tweed flat cap out of which two rather large ears protruded. He was not the brightest of individuals and had a very limited range of subjects he would discuss; the weather, Norwich City, Speedway (he could do an imitation of a motor bike, a twist of his right wrist and a "rrrr... rrrr") and snooker.

Graham lived out at Melton Constable, an old railway town situated in North Norfolk. Sadly, there are very few traces of the railway today but back in the days of steam it was a large works where they built steam locomotives. The transport links were really poor so Graham would often travel in with one of two drivers who lived close by, or catch the bus to Norwich. This meant that his attendance was a little bit hit and miss given the infrequency of the timetable. Cleaning was non-existent at weekends which led to the rather unsavoury state of the toilets, bins and sinks!

Each day he would wait for the lunchtime news to finish on the TV and sit mesmerised as the weather forecast was predicted. "David," he said to me one day, "There's a low in the Atlantic, it's the lowest low they've ever seen," with a sense of extreme seriousness. This was the day before those famous gales of 1987! One driver told me he had witnessed a most bizarre 'conversation' between Earl (whom you will

encounter later) and Graham which went something like this;
Earl; "Hmmmm, tum tee tum.."
Graham; "Ha Ha mmmmm."
Earl; "He He He... Ha Ha."
Graham; "rrr rrr Hmmm Ha Ha."
And so on and so on!

Our messroom was situated close to the loco sheds, the railcar sheds, lifting shops and what was known as the back yard where redundant stock or wagons needing repair were stabled. It was also next to the main A47 Carrow Road and adjacent to Norwich City's ground. It was not unknown for some of us to pop over and watch a match if the opportunity arose while we were spare.

The accommodation was very basic and for a period we were relocated to Portakabins for about six months while asbestos was removed from the roof.

Once I walked through the main doors to be confronted by a man of some seniority squatting on one of the window sills. He wore a bright yellow plastic mac, hobnail boots, and a very old 'piss-pot' motorcycle crash helmet with goggles, while blowing on a duck caller! I did a double take, especially when he jumped down from the window sill onto the table, then the bench, and finally onto the floor. He then hopped off into the canteen. I was struck dumb at this spectacle but those present seemed unperturbed by it. This was my first encounter with Harold Francis, or 'Fiddler' as he was affectionately known.

Harold lived at Cromer on the North Norfolk coast and was a really lovely chap but was often late for work as he was careful with his money and wherever possible avoided using his motorbike. He would make every effort to use any other form of transport possible rather than his own. Sometimes he would get a ride with a Royal Mail van destined for Norwich, or he would hitchhike, or get a lift with other drivers who lived in the area. Hitchhiking was not ideal given its random success, and not conducive to good timekeeping bearing in mind the railway ran strictly to the clock. Alternatively he would flag down a Cromer to Norwich train at a bridge close to Roughton Road and get dropped off at the same place on his way home!

Harold would often be heard before he was seen due to the 'duck caller' or his impression of a pheasant's call. He did however have a short fuse as I found out one night when I decided to 'dress' him while he was asleep on one of the benches in the messroom. I used old bits of newspaper, Coke cans and the like to put on the brim of his cap and over his body while he blissfully slept. A little later there was a clatter of cans hitting the stone floor followed by mumbled curses along with a tirade of expletives hurtled in my direction. I think I heard the phrase, "If it wasn't for your father I would stick one on ya!" I made myself scarce until Harold had calmed down.

He did get reported to the train crew supervisor one summer's afternoon by a driver from March depot. We didn't generally see footplate men from other depots as the messroom was quite a distance from the station. They generally preferred to use the guard's messroom on platform 5 of the station. On summer Saturdays March crews, who worked predominately freight trains, would work some of the holidaymaker specials that ran from the Midlands and the North to Great Yarmouth. If they had a long wait for their return working or train home they would make their way over to the loco.

On this occasion the March driver clearly did not know what Harold was like. He could not believe his eyes when Harold turned a wooden chair on its side and started sawing the legs off. He was so surprised he went through to the foreman's office. "D'ya hear old mate, there's a bloke in the messroom cutting the chairs into pieces." He must have been dumbfounded when the reply came back, "Not to worry mate, it's only Harold."

What was actually happening was that Harold was creating the illusion he was cutting the legs off the chair. He was actually drawing his finger nails backwards and forwards across the bottom of the seat which made a rasping sound very similar to that of a saw. Once he got so far he then dropped a piece of wood on the stone floor which made that woody sound that convinced the March driver that he had really sawn the leg off.

Other drivers have recalled times when Harold would walk around the outside of a steam locomotive cleaning the windows..... while it was actually in motion on the main line!

There were times in my career when I could be accused of being extremely naive, trusting those who told what turned out to be 'tall stories', or being egged on to do something that I would later realise made me look a bit of a mug. You may recall my earlier reference in a previous chapter about opening the gates at Dereham.

One winter's afternoon I had been spare for several hours with little prospect of either getting away early or actually having something to do, so I decided to clean my motorbike which was parked in the bike sheds. The weather was cold and the evenings were drawing in so I wheeled my VF750 Honda (my pride and joy) into the messroom and borrowed some cloths from the cleaner to give it a good clean. I took pride in my motorbikes and liked to keep them spic and span; it was not unheard of for me to spend most of my day off cleaning the bike and then taking it out for a 'burn up' that evening only for it to rain and get covered in crap! It certainly helped to pass the time and she began to sparkle after a couple of hours.

A couple of older drivers began to admire my bike and were talking between themselves then asking me the occasional question like, "How powerful is it?" "How fast have you been on it?" (I lied just in case they passed the information on to my Dad, who would then tell my Mum - they hated me having a bike.) "What did it cost and how

much is the insurance?" which was met with a sharp intake of breath when I revealed what I paid.

After a short while they asked what it sounded like when it started up and they suggested I should turn it over in the messroom, so I fired it up and decided that I would take it for a trip around the lockers. Fumes soon started to build up. As I rode along the footplatemens' side of the messroom I noticed a driver sitting down on one of the benches looking daggers at me. I then rode around the far end of the lockers, back up through the fitters' side and killed the engine. Both drivers were laughing but I still hadn't twigged that they had egged me on. It was only when I took the bike out to the bike sheds and returned did I get a telling off from Harold Tasker who was none too pleased about having his tea disturbed and the atmosphere polluted.

Some days later I was contacted by the Area Manager and advised that my actions had been reported to him and he warned me about any future conduct. He went on to say that he hoped this would be the end of the matter. I was fortunate enough to have a good reputation (so he said) so the matter would not be taken any further. I apologised for my actions but, deep down, I was somewhat pissed off, firstly with myself for being led into such a situation and secondly for being reported for such a trivial matter. Although we never fell out, I didn't really see 'eye to eye' with Harold. I did bear a bit of a grudge over the time I bought a brand new enamel tea can which he chipped the very first time I used it. I guess that may have been petty and small-minded of me at the time!

The boredom of being cooped up in the messroom for hours on end, with little to do, along with the fact that many of us were still in our teens, led to pranks being played on each other.

One bitterly cold winter's night after a particularly heavy fall of snow a couple of secondmen, Bes and Jim, decided they would play a prank on Mark. Mark had a dark blue Mark 1 Ford Escort which was parked in the loco car park. He was on the evening Stratford tanks and was due back around two in the morning. Bes and Jim decided it would be a good idea to build a snow wall around Mark's car so he would have difficulty getting it out when he returned. There was plenty of fresh snow on the ground and soon they had built a wall a couple of feet high around the rear and sides of Mark's car. He would not be able to drive forward as the car faced a large pond of putrid water which contained God knows what.

As the hours passed, so the temperature began to drop. Bes and Jim became concerned that Mark had not turned up when expected. Obviously the train's arrival was delayed due to the weather conditions, so they decided that maybe it would be best if they removed the snow wall. Unfortunately the wall was frozen solid and their attempts to kick it down were utterly futile.

On their return to the messroom they waited coyly for Mark to return when, later than expected, he walked in. Bes and Jim sniggered nervously. They watched from the messroom window as Mark crossed the car park, walked past the blocked in Escort and glanced at the snow wall. He continued on and around to the rear of a huge advertising hoarding that had been erected at the edge of the car park. Soon Bes and Jim heard a car engine start up. Exhaust fumes came from the rear of the hoarding and Mark then drove out from behind it in an identical blue Ford Escort to the one they had blocked in. The smiles turned to frowns at the realisation that they had blocked in the wrong car, which actually belonged to one of the fitters who was obviously going to be none too pleased when he found his car at 6am after his night shift. Both of them made sure they were not about to face the music.

Over the years Jim became renowned for pulling the occasional stunt (some of which were spectacular) or making a comment that maybe nobody else would dare to say. I was in the messroom with him one summer's afternoon, both of us were spare and had pretty much exhausted all options available to us for relieving the boredom.

After a while Charlie 'Pokie' Dye walked in and began to lay out his tea. Charlie was a lovely man but infamous for being extremely frugal or 'tight' and, for some unknown reason, he would never wear his false teeth. Charlie laid out his sandwich box, then spread out a tea towel, made some tea and began to dine. From the sandwich box he produced a big ripe tomato and tried to bite into it but due to the absence any of teeth this proved to be an unsuccessful exercise. Jim and I sat there watching him as he continued to struggle with the problematic tomato. I could tell by the sparkle in his eye that Jim wanted to say something to Charlie, as again he attempted to bite into the tomato but still to no avail. Jim could take it no more. "Would you like me to start that tomato for you Charlie?" he asked, trying not to burst with laughter at the same time. Charlie looked up at him... "I tell you what," Charlie said. "There's too many bloody wags around the flippin' place, that's what there is!" We roared with laughter. I can't remember if Charlie ever got to eat his tomato.

On football match days the police would use the loco car park to park their vans and cars so that they had close access to the ground. Carrow Road was shut off to through traffic in the run up to matches and after the game to allow the crowds to disperse safely.

Now one day, Scratchy Jack, so called because of his short temper, was killing time with his mate Noddy Gambling (I kid you not), watching the crowds walk down to the match when a car pulled into the car park and a chap got out. "Look at that bastard," Jack exclaimed to Noddy, "trying to park in our car park, cheeky bastard!" With that Jack was off to remonstrate with the potential offender despite Noddy's warning that all may not seem what it appeared to be. Noddy did not hear the conversation but saw Jack confront the individual, a conversation ensued, the offender produced a wallet of some kind, Jack coloured up and backed off with a slow retreat to the messroom. On Jack's return, Noddy enquired as to what took place. Jack replied sheepishly with three words, "Plain clothes police". Sometimes its best to keep your snout out of things.

Trowse station closed in 1939 but reopened briefly in March 1986 when main line trains terminated there due to the swingbridge being replaced, thus preventing access to Norwich station . A London service is seen here at Trowse prior to departure (Stephen Dey)

Chapter 8 - Caught by the Short and Curlies

AFTER A YEAR or so I was beginning to get to know most of the drivers and assistants although there were a few I had not encountered due to the nature of shift work and the sheer number of people who worked at the depot. I always remember reflecting that many of these men seemed really old. I know I was just a kid but looking back, and comparing them to how many of us look today, there seems to have been a massive difference. Even so, many of the old boys who are now long gone lived to be well into their nineties. However those who were close to retirement did seem ancient, and I guess much of that was down to the fact that health and social care was not as good then as it is now. They also had to endure a World War and some of them left the railway and joined the armed forces to fight for their country. One driver was stuck in Burma and treated appallingly by the Japanese and another was a gunner on a Lancaster bomber (not Mr. Bullcock—more about him in a later chapter). Angus 'Dolly' Grey joined the Royal Navy.

Being young, relatively fit and active, as well as naive, I underestimated the strength and agility of some of my older colleagues.

There was one particular driver that many of the secondmen really enjoyed being with. Time spent with him was more like a day out rather than an actual working day. He was a really funny man who would let you do as much driving as you wanted. George, or 'Tio' as he was nicknamed, was the sort of chap who would be happy to share his experience and pass on information, and was blessed with the foresight that, although we were just 'kids', we were the future of the industry. The more driving experience we gained, the easier it would be to get through our exams later in our careers.

George was a stocky gentleman with rather bandy legs, short grey hair and a pencil-thin moustache. He also wore the silly driver's cap. If the weather was cold he would wear a flat cap although in all my years I knew him I never saw him wear an overcoat, even in the coldest of winters. One thing I was to find out was that not only was George quick on his feet but he was as strong as an ox.

One day I was in a mischievous mood as George walked into the messroom. "Alright George!" I said as I flicked the peak of his cap. Off it spun into the air and skidded along the floor. "Right you little sod," was his reply and he made a beeline for me. I decide to outrun him which I thought would be simple as he proceeded to chase me around the lockers that split the messroom in two. It was after a couple of circuits that I realised that George was actually catching me up so I thought I had better change tactics. I charged for the exit towards the foreman's office beyond which was a set of outside doors. Unfortunately for me I heard George shout, "Get him Jack!" just as Big Jack (and, believe me, he was bloody big) Sporle came walking through, blocking my planned escape route. I quickly changed tack and wrong footed George with a 'shimmy' and made for the fire exit.... which was locked!

With both George and Jack now bearing down on me my only alternative was to escape through the swing door into the old canteen, then climb into the huge sinks at the end of the room and out through the window. I nearly made it. I had the window open and was halfway out when a huge hand got hold of my testicles and gave them a very firm squeeze.... I froze.

The next thing I knew, I was lying in the sink with Jack holding me down (still applying pressure on my crown jewels) as George proceeded to take his false teeth out. "What the fu...." I failed to finish my comment as George gave me a love bite on my neck! After they had administered my punishment they both laughed like hell. However I had to readjust myself and try and regain my composure as well as my pride as I walked back to the messroom where there was much laughter at my expense.

I didn't think too much about it until I got home later that day. As soon as I walked through the door my mother took one look at me asked and what on earth was that on my neck. My reply which was the honest truth but must have seemed ridiculous. "Oh, a driver at work did it," as if it was a normal everyday occurrence, although my father just saw the funny side.

In these days of political correctness I guess I could have reported the matter, but then it was just part of everyday life. My pride may have been a dented but I thought it was just my turn on that day, and after all, I was the instigator of the 'banter' and perhaps it was a lesson not to underestimate the strength or agility of some of my older colleagues. What did get to me was when I was out with my mates the following night doing the pubs of Norwich, I bumped into a girl of whom I was particularly fond. I had been plucking up the courage to ask her out and knew she was keen on me. But once she saw the love bite her attitude towards me changed. She pointed at the offending marks. "Who did that?" she asked. Now I was in a bit of a dilemma. Did I tell the truth or should I make up some cock and bull story? I (wrongly) chose to go for the latter and sadly, never got to take her out.

I was not the only person to fall victim to some of George's capers as I witnessed one day when Ray Hill, known as 'Hilly Billy,' was giving him a load of 'lip'. Nothing nasty, just a general mickey take. George and Big Jack were playing the fruit machine when George turned to Jack and exclaimed, "Lockers." I had no idea what 'lockers' meant but I was soon to find out. They got hold of Hilly Billy by the arms so that his legs were dangling a few inches off the ground and then, with a heave and "Up you go", they proceeded to place him on top of the lockers that stood about six feet high and ran along the middle of the messroom.

The lockers were not the wardrobe type that stand about six feet high in which you can hang clothes and store bags, they were simply boxes or 'cube' lockers about two feet square that were stacked on top of one another in piles of three and must have run in a line of about thirty feet. In comparison to George, and especially Jack, Hilly Billy was like a bit that had dropped off them. He could not have been more than five feet tall, skinny as a rake, his clothes were scruffy and creased as was his driver's hat. He would wear a jumper with the tie on the outside rather than tucking it in. Generally he would have a roll-up fag dangling out of his mouth with most of the ash, along with burn marks, down his tie, jumper and trousers.

These were men in their late fifties, messing around like school kids with Hilly Billy parading up and down the length of the lockers while George and Jack carried on playing the fruit machine. It was indeed a bizarre sight and I'm not too sure how long they left him up there. Each time he walked the length of the lockers I was terrified they were going to collapse.

Despite being scruffy in appearance Hilly Billy was a lovely old boy to be with although his driving did leave a bit to be desired at times. I bumped into him in the city on my day off and could not believe the contrast; a smart suit and tie, a three-quarter length camel coat, brogues and a trilby with a small feather in it.

Billy was renowned for gambling on the horses and was extremely canny when it came to making a bet. It was said that he went into the bookies one afternoon to collect his considerable winnings but had forgotten to pay the tax on the original bet. This meant a large percentage of his winnings would go to the tax man. It was only when he received the money did he notice that the tax had been paid on the original bet. It turned out that the girl who took his bet had noticed his error so made sure it was calculated into the price of it. Without hesitation he gave the girl the money that should have been paid in tax as a thank you for her diligence.

There were several first aiders in the loco and from time to time they would provide training for their colleagues in the ambulance room which was situated in the messroom block. These lessons were agreed with management who even invested in a dummy to be used to demonstrate CPR and mouth to mouth resuscitation. One first aider was called Kenny who had been given the nickname 'The Flying Doctor' though I have no idea why. (Most nicknames of older drivers were a mystery as to how they had been conceived.) He was giving a lesson to a group of drivers one day and was explaining that the dummy had a false mouth that they could use to breath into to simulate mouth to mouth. He also explained that the dummy had been purchased at great expense and had cost the company over £100. Of course it was inevitable that one of the comics in the class stated , "If they put a crotch and pair of tits on it I will pay £500 for it."..... There's always one!

A scene from the mess room: far left, Kenny Sutton, 2nd left 'Gunner' Creed, partially in view (3rd left Cliffy Moore) centre, facing camera 'Fingers' Fred, to right of Fred just in view, Frank Ford. Others unidentified. (Steven Dey)

Chapter 9—The Curious Mr Strange

THERE WAS ALWAYS some sort of wind up or frivolity taking place in many a messroom and I guess most depots throughout the country had their fair share of pranksters. However one conductor took his high jinks almost into an art form. Many of his pranks were aimed at a little chap called Keith who also had an extremely short fuse. (My Father warned me that if you couldn't take a joke people would 'pull your leg' all the more as you were considered easy bait.) He always seemed to be on the receiving end of a stream of practical jokes from fellow conductor Gary Strange, a large chap with a great sense of humour. Keith was a little chap with hardly any neck and a bald head with just a few strands of hair on the top.

Gary walked into the guard's messroom with a sheet of blue carbon paper in his hand. This was placed in the conductor's excess ticket book which they used to issue fares to passengers with incorrect tickets. The carbon paper was used so a duplicate could be made for the conductor's records. Gary walked up to Keith and with the 'wet side' of the carbon paper rubbed it all over Keith's bald head.

"What the bloody hell do you think yer doin?" shouted Keith.

"Oh, sorry Keith, I slipped," came Gary's reply.

"Just mind what you're doin' will yer?" said Keith.

As far as Keith was concerned that was the end of the matter. Soon after he got his gear together ready for a trip to Great Yarmouth not realising that the top of his head was totally blue from the ink of the carbon paper. It was only when people started commenting on his blue head did Keith twig what had happened. Apparently it took several days of repeated washing to get rid of the stain! Gary had to spend the next few weeks avoiding Keith who vowed to get him back at some point.

Sometime later, when things had died down, Keith and Gary were again in the messroom and back on speaking terms. Gary kept going over to the cooker with a tablespoon and heating it up. No one really paid any attention until he crept behind Keith, who was concentrating on playing cards. Gary got the spoon, which was pretty hot by this time, and branded Keith on his bald bits. As you can imagine Keith went nuts, mainly because it flipping hurt. Immediately a chase ensued although I never found out what the outcome was apart from the fact that Keith was walking around with a red patch on his forehead and 'Made in England' just visible!

It's fair to say that Keith was not Gary's only victim; far from it. Nobody was safe from the practical jokes that were unleashed on anyone who Gary considered to be 'fair game' and there was plenty of choice. Numerous members of station staff received a soaking. As Gary's train would depart from a manned station, he would lean out of the coach window armed with a large receptacle of water which would be thrown at the victim.

I asked colleagues for examples of his pranks on the Norwich Thorpe station staff Facebook page and was inundated with comments and stories about Gary's antics. Many colleagues had either been victims of a Gary Strange 'sting' or had witnessed such events.

Steve Warren; 'Never leave him alone with your ticket machine. He used to write messages over the ticket stock, so when you issued them everyone had a special hand written message on them, thankfully just, 'Hello' or 'Have a nice day' etc.....'

Greg Watson; 'He would fart or meow like a cat when you were making a PA announcement.'

Cliff Knapp; 'Marmite, chocolate or some other dark substance on the PA handset in the guard's brake. Also he took great delight in microwaving your hat in the buffet cooker.'

Gary Strange on an InterCity service. (David Lacey)

Paul Nelson; 'Locking Emma in the guard's van at Norwich after she put a parcel in the 'cage' and only letting her out when they arrived at Diss.'

Kelly Mayes; 'Handfuls of ticket clippings at Diss (when I worked on the platform) ... or a bottle of water thrown over me as he was leaving Diss station. Bloody menace.'

Deborah Peart; 'I often found sugar in my till in the buffet!'

Tim Thetford; 'A full teapot of 'leaf tea' out of the joint signing on point upstairs window on my head after I pulled the old 'tie routine' on him.' (The 'old tie routine' being a very hard yank of the tie so as to tighten the knot to a point where it was impossible to undo and then cut the end off with a pair of scissors. A prank Gary inflicted on several victims.)

Chris Wright; 'When I worked in the buffet he once got one of the muffins I had on display, put it on the bar and flattened it with his fist and walked off as if nothing had happened.'

Paul Nelson; 'He used to set the alarms on all the guard's pagers to go off at 3am in the traincrew supervisor's office.'

Kate Brooker; 'When we had phones on the trains (before mobiles were issued to us), Gary would tell you a pager message had come out and for you to ring this number and ask for Liz.... I rang Buckingham Palace!'

Rachel Russen; 'I got soaked with the fire extinguisher as I came into the back of customer services! He would also fill my pockets and bag up with ticket clippings.'

Emma Poore; 'Cups of water on dispatch if I was lucky.... a carton of milk if I was unlucky.... he also threw my hat on Diss station roof!'

Chris Pearson; 'Some guards would store the Almex ticket machines in the guard's room cooker (God knows why).... One day Gary turned the cooker on which resulted in a red hot machine, dry ink, the plastic keys melted along with a load of crispy bank notes.... that led to a trip to the Traincrew Manager, Mr. Duggan's office!

A prank Gary played on two ticket inspectors, Len Tuck and Russell Burgess, was way back in the early 1980s. The most common trick employed by ticket dodgers was to lock themselves in a toilet in the hope that the Guard or TTI (as a Travelling Ticket Inspector was known) would not notice or ignore the locked door. This particular day Len noticed a toilet door was locked so he knocked and accompanied it with, "Tickets please," in a firm and commanding voice...... Nothing happened, he knocked again only harder with the same request......still nothing. This pantomime went on for a little longer and then Russell joined Len. Eventually a ticket was slid under the toilet door by the occupant. Both spotted that it was out of date so they began to threaten the occupant with the removal of the door. A few moments went by and they heard the toilet flush, the door opened and out came Gary with, "Ah, morning Len, morning Russell," and off he went to carry out his guard's duties... They had been stung and, I'm led to believe, they were not the only ones to fall for this prank.

Chapter 10—The Pheasant and the Roll Up!

THERE WERE NUMEROUS 'messing' facilities at Norwich, not just at the loco but there were the various shunter's huts in the goods and passenger yards. They were also on the station where the conductors were accommodated. The guards' room was situated adjacent to platform five and was used by those drivers who were in the top link or 'railcar gang', or as many called it 'the Old Man's Gang'. Railcars comprised of either two or three coach units with a driving cab at each end and a diesel engine slung below each coach. They would ply their trade on the local lines to Great Yarmouth, Lowestoft, Cromer and Sheringham as well as Cambridge.

The railcar drivers were the most senior men at the depot, hence 'the Old Man's Gang' label. There was little point in them making their way over to the loco for a break: by the time they had got over there it would be time to return to the station for the next part of their day's work. As with most loco men of such seniority in the early 1980s these railcar men were in the latter years of their career. They were all well respected by their colleagues but as secondmen we rarely got to interact with them unless they were booked on a particular main line or relief job on a Bank Holiday.

One of these drivers was a chap by the name of Reggie Reynolds who liked to keep up with the local railway scandal and would love to wind people up. Generally one of his stories would begin with the phrase "They tell me....."

A conductor, Gary Watts, relayed a story to me that Reggie had got hold of in relation to an incident that took place on the Cromer to Norwich line late one weekday evening. Gary confirmed it happened as he was involved.

Gary was on the last train from Cromer to Norwich with a driver by the name of Tom who was renowned for being easy to wind up and had a bit of a short fuse. On arrival at North Walsham a regular traveller got on with his bike: Gary was aware he generally got off at Worstead. This particular evening the individual was travelling to Wroxham. Gary told Tom only to stop at Worstead if there was anybody on the platform as they had just the one passenger on board. They passed through Worstead without incident and then pressed on to the final stop before Norwich which was Wroxham.

The line between Wroxham and North Walsham was a single line with trains travelling in both directions. To prevent head on collisions a 'token' system was in operation. To proceed onto the single line the controlling signal had to be in the 'clear' position, the signalman also would hand a brass 'token' to the driver. Without both the train could not move onto the single line. The driver would hand the token back to the signalman at the other end of the single line so that the next train could be allowed to proceed.

As the train approached the exit from the single line at Wroxham, Tom was supposed to stop and hand over the token to the signalman. However Gary offered to sit in the secondman's seat as they passed rather than coming to a complete stand. With this done and with no passengers on the platform they passed through the station without stopping. Moments later there was a knock on the door of the driving cab. Tom and Gary realised they had forgotten the passenger with the bike!

It was not possible to set back to the station so Tom took the executive decision to stop the train at the Norwich Road bridge, approximately a mile from the station, let the passenger out along with his bike and agreed to say no more about the whole incident. "Keep quiet about this Gary," were Tom's instructions. Unfortunately for Tom, some days later the passenger spilled the beans to Reggie's conductor who, in turn, passed the information on.

Over the coming weeks Reggie was itching to wind up Tom but had to be patient and wait for the right moment. Eventually the opportunity arose when Reggie was in the guard's room having a cup of tea and in walked Tom. He settled down with his sandwiches and a cup of tea and started chatting with those present, including Reggie. Fortunately for Reggie he was on the last Cromer to Norwich train that night and by coincidence Gary happened to be the conductor too. In a louder voice than normal Reggie said..

"Now then, young Gary, you're on the last Cromer with me tonight?"

"That's right Reggie," Gary replied.

"Well," said Reggie. "They tell me.... there's a special stop order on the last one out of Cromer tonight!"

"Really?" asked Gary.

"Indeed there is Gary, but it's not your normal every day stop. No, this one is an extra special stop, second cornfield on the left past Norwich Road Bridge after leaving Wroxham, so I am told."

The penny dropped and Tom exclaimed, "How the bloody hell did you find out about that?" and there followed a tirade of expletives and questions as to Reggie's parentage. It was minor errors such as Tom and Gary's that went only as far as the messroom so no real harm was done. For Reggie it was all part of the game!

Personally I thought the most welcoming messroom was on the platform at Lowestoft; not the present one, but the one that was there prior to the station being remodelled and renovated. The current messroom is functional but uninviting, and with no traincrew stationed there is characterless and solitary. After the traincrew depot closed there in the late 1990s I had little need to actually visit it. Most jobs to Lowestoft involved being stationary there for just a few minutes before heading off back to Norwich.

The old messroom had character and a beautiful open fireplace that would always be kept roaring in the winter months. We would generally have an hour or so there after bringing in the early morning newspaper train from Norwich. Working the Lowestoft or Great Yarmouth paper trains meant crawling out of bed at around 03:30 for a 04:30 start. In the depths of winter it was no fun climbing onto a freezing cold locomotive and working it across the marshlands to the UK's most easterly point. If the wind was coming from the north, it was not the best place to be, so the open fire was a welcoming sight.

One particularly cold morning we worked the papers from Norwich with an Ipswich crew in the rear cab. They were booked to travel from Ipswich to Lowestoft to work the Lowestoft to London train. The only way they could get there by rail was via Norwich. In the winter we would pipe the steam heat through the paper vans of which there were two, maybe three at most, so the guard would have heat.

Before we left Norwich the Ipswich secondman offered to turn the boiler off for me on our approach to Lowestoft as it was situated next to the rear cab in the locomotive engine compartment. I thanked him for this. For some reason best known to himself, he chose to turn the boiler off as we passed Oulton Broad station which was only a few minutes away from Lowestoft. Generally it was custom and practice to turn the boiler off in good time to allow the steam pressure to drain away from the pipes.

As soon as we arrived at Lowestoft I climbed down to uncouple, split the vacuum brake pipe, then shut the cocks off on the steam pipes. As soon as I split them I was showered in steam which covered my face and neck. To begin with I didn't feel any pain, however as the minutes passed, my skin started to burn. I managed to get to the messroom to wash cold water over my face, which was beginning to redden, and my left eye was stinging and watering. I was none too pleased. I am glad to say that the damage was superficial and soon passed but it proved to me that I needed to be more careful in future.

Once the papers had been unloaded from the vans the pilot would haul them into the goods yard and we would back the locomotive onto a set of coaches in platform one. As soon as we could we would supply steam to the train to pre-heat it for its journey to London while we waited to be relieved by the Ipswich crew.

I also recall working the Great Yarmouth paper train one winter's day. This was a bit different to the Lowestoft formation as it consisted of the paper vans, and a combined passenger coach and brake to cater for several drivers travelling to Great Yarmouth who were booked to travel 'pass' to work the early morning trains from Yarmouth to Norwich.

In most circumstances, once the boiler had built up a head of steam, we would open the supply cock and stick about 70psi through a nine coach train; on much shorter trains we were supposed to limit the amount of pressure. On this occasion I opened up the supply cock on the boiler and put 70psi of steam pressure straight through to the three coaches. As we left Norwich I observed the steam pressure gauge build up, then in the space of a second it dropped to zero. I had blown the stream pipe off the rear carriage..... that is why we were supposed to limit the amount of pressure on trains with just a couple of coaches! I was not particularly popular with the drivers by the time we arrived at Great Yarmouth after they had endured a stone cold journey!

One of the Lowestoft drivers, Roy, was very particular about the cleanliness of the messroom. He took a personal interest in it and would get extremely animated if anybody left a mess especially if the Baby Belling cooker was left in a state. It got to the point where he would check inside the cooker every time he came into the messroom.

There was also an ex-Great Yarmouth driver who, after being made redundant, had transferred to Lowestoft. Peter was a real character and would travel over from Great Yarmouth each day. He also had a rather strange hobby, or maybe more of a fetish, for collecting dead birds that had been killed on the railway. If he got the chance he would stop his train on the return from spotting it on the outward journey so

Lowestoft station in 1975, before the removal of the roof over the concourse.

that he could retrieve it. Generally it would be rare birds such as owls and the like. He would take them home, chuck them in the freezer and then have them stuffed. I can't recall if Peter did the 'stuffing' or whether he sold them on to a local taxidermist.

Roy entered the messroom one day and flew into a rage. He'd carried out his usual inspection only to find a dead pheasant sitting inside the Baby Belling looking out at him with a used 'roll up' fag in its beak. I imagine there were no prizes for guessing who the culprit was.

I walked into the messroom at Liverpool Street one quiet Saturday afternoon as was usually the case at weekends. Towards the end of the 1990s the depot was quite small with only a handful of drivers and conductors. They were a close-knit group and ran their own Welfare Association, as did many depots, which was funded by profits from a fruit machine located in the messroom.

I settled down with a cup of tea and a newspaper when, out of the corner of my eye, I noticed something rather strange. On the opposite side of the room there was a table with a safe beneath it. The safe door was ajar and on the table top was a green cloth money bag. I was intrigued at this bizarre situation so I took a look inside the bag. I counted £500 in notes and when I looked in the safe there was even more money. I found this a very uncomfortable position to be in and was struggling to think what to do. Eventually I closed the door of the safe but was unable to lock it. I picked up the bag with the money in and went in search of someone in authority.

I walked along platform nine towards the main station concourse and soon bumped into Malcolm who was the Senior Railman on the Anglia side of the station (this was a time when BR has ceased to exist and we were in the private sector). I explained the situation and he suggested we should make our way around to the Station Supervisor's office and hand over the money.

I thought no more about what had taken place until the following Monday morning. Shortly after boarding a train at Norwich to travel up to London to begin the week's ASLEF executive session, my mobile phone rang. It was Seth, one of the Union reps at Liverpool Street... "I believe you found some of our money in the messroom on Saturday. Where is it?" "Correct Seth," I replied. "It is with the Station Supervisor at Liverpool Street"... "Right," and with that he hung up.

'Thanks Dave,' I thought to myself. To this day I do not have a clue as to who left that money out for all to see and I am sure it was a genuine mistake. I believe I did the correct and honourable thing. I am sure there were others amongst our fraternity who would have pocketed the money and possibly whatever was in the safe too. A 'thank you' would have been more than sufficient but I did not even get that which irks me to this day.

Chapter 11 - "Snow, Snow...Thick, Thick, Snow!"
Working with Large Hearted Arthur

IT WAS ON one particularly cold winter's day I was with Big Arthur Allen, a rather large gentleman and a bit of an eccentric. He would generally have some merry quip or odd comment to impart during a conversation. One of which he was renowned for was, "D'ya hear... you're doin' that all wrong!" which generally turned out to be an incorrect statement. I had tied the locomotive onto a train, climbed up into the rear cab, started the boiler and begun to supply the steam. During the time I had carried out my duties it had begun to snow.

It was snowing like mad with the thickest flakes I had ever seen and by the time I climbed up into the leading cab a couple of inches of snow had laid. Arthur was sitting in the driver's seat. "Bloody hell, Arthur, its snowing like mad out there!" I exclaimed. Arthur looked at me, pulled out a cigarette, placed it in his mouth, produced his Zippo lighter, flicked the lid open, and struck it. This produced a flame so big that Red Adair would have had a job putting it out. He lit the fag, took a long draw and just said, "Snow, snow, thick, thick snow," a play on the ballroom dance saying 'slow, slow, quick, quick slow'. I said nothing and just thought to myself, 'Bugger me...this is going to be a long day."

Big Arthur was indeed a most peculiar individual. He was single, lived with his parents, and must have weighed something like thirty stone, hence the nickname. He would also randomly make rather odd noises. It would not be unusual to hear a "Ping, tiddle, boing," to alert you that Arthur was the vicinity. I was climbing off my motorbike one morning when all of a sudden I heard a "Honk Honk" only for Arthur to hove into view. "Morning Sword!" he exclaimed.

Arthur's mode of travel to work was a specially reinforced bicycle and it was on one of his journeys to work that he was involved in a road accident that led to him being hospitalised. He received several injuries which kept him in for quite a while so Harry Phillips, the ASLEF Branch Secretary, paid him a visit. As Harry was leaving the ward a nurse approached him and asked if he wouldn't mind seeing the doctor as there was some concern about Arthur's health. It turned out that they thought he was suffering from a prolonged spell of concussion as a result of the accident given the sporadic "Ping, tiddle, boing," outbursts. They were relieved to know that this was 'normal' for Arthur.

Being a middle-aged single man, Arthur was a regular reader of several 'mens' magazines' and would often pay a visit to the W.H. Smith bookstall on the station platform to purchase the latest edition of his favourite publication. Although he was happy to share his wisdom and freely offer advice such as "De y' hear old mate.... etc etc," he was not so generous with a read (if that the best description) of one of his treasured mags.

Arthur lived next door to another driver by the name of Albert Rackham who could not have been more of a contrast. He was a slim, short man and loved to spin a story which he would articulate with passion and skill. Albert popped into his local newsagent's shop one evening to buy the local newspaper, the Eastern Evening News, as Arthur was leaving with a collection of his 'gentlemens' monthlies'. When it came to Albert's turn to pay for his paper, he asked the newsagent if he wasn't a bit embarrassed by Arthur's racy purchases to which he replied, "Actually Arthur's my best customer!"

Albert recalled that there were times when Arthur needed to have a 'clear out' of the accumulated magazines and every now and then he could be seen carrying a stack of them to the bottom of the garden to have a bonfire. He would have a look at each one, sometimes lingering as he unfolded a centrefold picture, shortly after which he would toss it on the fire.

Getting a locomotive from Norwich station to the loco shed was quite a drawn out affair. There was no direct route and it involved the following process. Firstly leave one of the platforms at the station and pass the Passenger Yard Signal Box up to a dead end known as 'the engine spur'. Once released from the spur the locomotive would reverse, generally with the secondman in what would now be the leading cab (which is against the rules). The secondman would release the locomotive 'straight air brake' which was the signal for the driver to apply power once he saw the brake pressure fall.

From the spur the locomotive would take one of two routes which led to another dead end road known as 'old four'. The driver would then lead again and on the clearing of the relevant signal, the locomotive would pass over to the control of the Goods Yard Signal Box and across to the entrance to the loco shed. The secondman would alight from the rear of the locomotive to pull a pair of hand operated points then, once he checked the points had switched correctly, he would call the driver back onto the loco shed. This process could take some time especially if the signalmen were not in a hurry which always seemed to happen if you were in a rush to get finished or were on a square up job. Square up jobs were not necessarily your last booked job, but could mean getting away early as somebody else had agreed to cover the last job for you.

I was with 'Big Arthur' on a relief turn as we trundled down onto old four. I sat there for a few moments when all of a sudden I heard Arthur call up to me, "D'ya hear?" ... "What's the matter Arthur?" I asked as I looked out of the cab side window at him on the ground having walked back from the other cab. "Nothing matey, we just need to hook up to the steam heater van and take it to the shed for fuel." "I wasn't aware we were supposed to to do that Arthur," I responded. Generally a crew that were sitting spare would be asked by the foreman to carry out this task. This particular van was equipped with a boiler and used on early morning trains to pre-heat them in exceptionally cold conditions. Within the van along with the boiler were fuel and water tanks.

Class 31 locomotive with the steam heat van at Norwich. (Steven Dey)

It was a pain in the backside to hook a locomotive onto the van as the handbrake was almost ineffective. So it was a delicate exercise getting the locomotive to back just enough to 'kiss' the van's buffers and then slip the coupling on. After several attempts I managed to achieve this and off we went to the loco shed.

As we passed the shed I noticed a puzzled looking fueller looking at us. Within a few minutes we were backing into the shed to fill up with fuel and water. The fueller came over and asked me, "Why on earth 'ave you brought that over here? We sent it over to the station an hour ago after it had been fuelled?" This pleased me no end. Had Arthur checked the fuel and water gauges on the van he would have seen they were both showing full!! After informing Big Arthur I then had to call the signalman up and eventually we made our way back to old four and then back to the loco shed again. I was not happy as we had just wasted a good chunk of our break. This was typical of Arthur though, big hearted, harmless.... but nuts!

Chapter 12 - The Passenger Yard and Station

THERE WERE VARIOUS domains under the railway umbrella of Norwich station. The station with its concourse, platforms and distinctive dome were linked to the passenger yard, goods yard, loco sheds, back yard and diesel shops. Then there was the Victoria pilot used to shunt the freight traffic at the old station on the southern edge of the city. All of these domains had individual groups of workers allocated to them. The passenger yard would have two shunters on a three shift system who were responsible for the passenger, parcel and postal trains along with an additional shunter who was allocated to deal with railcars (for railcars see photo on the next page). They had their

Cravens Class 105 railcar arriving in platform 4 at Norwich, with Driver Bertie Haysted at the controls. (Steven Dey)

own hut parallel to some sidings and almost opposite the passenger yard signal box. It was a grey wooden construction with a window at each side and a felt apex roof. Inside there were several lockers, a sink, hob and a pot belly stove in the centre. Also it had tables, a few chairs, and benches that ran along two outer walls that had windows. There was also a telephone.

As I got to know some of the characters that worked on the railway I came to realise that not all you were told was necessarily the truth. Some individuals loved to spin tall tales, others had very vivid imaginations and some were just complete and utter bull-shitters. One shunter whose name was Bullcock was nicknamed 'Bull-shit' due to his wild yarns.

Bullcock tried to convince his colleagues that he had been a gunner on Lancaster bombers during the Second World War which may have been true. He was renowned for a tale about the time he was in the gunner's turret during an attack by the Luftwaffe while over Europe on a bombing raid. He explained that he was firing the guns continuously which led to barrels getting so hot they drooped because the metal over heated!

Years after the war, Bullcock returned to work from a very enjoyable holiday in the south of France. I'm not quite sure if a shunter's wage stretched to that, but let's give him the benefit of the doubt. He explained that he and his wife found a nice spot on the beach, so they hired a pair of deck chairs and began to enjoy the Riviera's temperate climate.

Sometime later, he explained, a chap sitting close by kept staring at him. At first he did not pay much attention to the individual but as time went by the staring became more intense. Bullcock exclaimed that the person did look rather familiar. In the end curiosity got the better of him so he went over to the chap, who happened to be German and asked, "Do I know you?' "Well, in a way, yes" he replied in broken

(Above) The Passenger box.
(Below) John Shepherd and Wiggy in the Passenger box in the 1980s.
(both photos Steven Dey)

English, "Last time we met I was in a Messerschmitt 109 over France, you shot me down!" Bullcock went to explain to his colleagues that "It took me a little while to recognise him, as the last time we saw each other he was wearing a flying helmet and goggles, but I knew I had met him somewhere before." I think it is fair to say that the story expands the truth somewhat.

Many of the drivers who worked within the various yards were individuals who had been restricted from mainline duties. This was generally for health reasons such as heart trouble, hearing loss, poor eyesight, back problems or in one particular case not having the capacity to be let loose on the travelling public.

The passenger yard hut was considered to be a happy hut and there were times when it was standing room only if all three shunters were there as well as the pilot driver and his secondman and the two railcar shunting drivers. Much depended upon who was on duty at the time but if you clicked the right shift then all hell could break loose and there would be much laughter and high jinks.

There were two particular shunters, Nobby and Micky, who were partnered for many years. They had a nickname for just about everybody and if there was any scandal or gossip they would be in the thick of it. They had two nicknames for my father, 'Pockets' on account of the fact that most of the time he would have his hands in his pockets, and some time later when they found out that he had a boat, the nickname changed to 'Pugwash' after the cartoon character Captain Pugwash! It's those little things you find out about your parents only through such work connections: he had never mentioned this at home. Later I became 'Split Pin' on account of my skinny legs.

The great thing about these two individuals was that it was all for a laugh and there was never any malice in whatever they said or did. One of the other shunters in the passenger yard, Peter, was nicknamed 'Slop Pot', the origins of which are a mystery.

You could pretty much guarantee that if there was any spare time then there would be a card school in progress, either cribbage, rummy or a game called 'knock'. Knock involved being dealt four cards and then trying to match them up. Once you had a winning hand, you would knock on the table and the other players had one more round to try and get a decent hand. You would then show your cards and the person with the worst hand had to put five pence in the kitty. Each player had four lives at five pence per life ..... unless you were Earl.

Earl was a really lovely old boy. He came through the footplate in the same manner as all other locomen, starting as a cleaner, which involved cleaning out the fire boxes of steam locomotives, then progressing to passed cleaner so he was able to act as a fireman when required. Then he became a fireman, later a passed fireman and finally driver. For some particular reason it was deemed that Earl should not drive on the mainline. He may have been perfectly capable, but when you went with him as a secondman it was clear that there was something not quite right. There were times when he would be talking to himself, mumbling away or not really paying attention to what was going on. Or so it seemed, until it was time to go home or get away early, then he would disappear like a rat up a drainpipe!

Earl was a stockily built chap, quite short with dark hair. He had very bushy eyebrows and always wore his full uniform with that silly driver's cap. Most men would tell you that he was a real ladies' man in his younger days, and there were one or two rather racy stories that would be told about his encounters with the opposite sex.

One of these stories involved Earl taking a young lady to her home after an evening out. She invited him in and while her parents were upstairs in bed asleep. Earl and the young lady proceeded to get friendly on the sofa. Things went a little bit further and suddenly footsteps could be heard coming down the stairs so Earl who was, shall I say ...

standing to attention, put his trilby over his manhood just as the girl's father came in the room. Which, funnily enough, is what Earl then did into his strategically placed hat! I did wonder if he wore his hat when leaving for home after the episode.

Four of us including Earl were playing knock in the hut one afternoon. He kept putting in his 5p when he lost a round but for some reason he kept on winning the kitty. After about three or four wins questions started to be asked. It transpired that rather than just keeping four 5p pieces to hand, he had a pile of coins and just kept putting in! No wonder he was winning, he had an unlimited supply of lives. Suffice to say we had to keep an eye on him and explained the rules to him... again. "Oh, ah, hmmmmm," he said with a broad grin on his face and a twinkle in his eye as he shrugged his shoulders as if to say 'Who... me?' Sometimes I think Earl was more canny then we gave him credit for.

Earl was always happy to have a laugh at his own expense. One of the funniest things I saw him involved in was with another driver, 'Big' Jack Sporle, a giant of a man with hands like dinner plates who was always laughing. I entered the hut one day to find Earl sitting on Jack's knee with his silly driver's hat on back to front and his teeth clenched. Jack was operating Earl as if he was the ventriloquist to his dummy. These were two blokes, well into their fifties, messing around like a couple of kids. "Gottle of gear....gottle of gear," Earl kept saying while being pushed around from left to right and back to front. 'If the travelling public could see this,' I thought through my tears of laughter.

Much of the work in the passenger yard was done with a Drewry class 03 pilot. These were small locomotives that were designed specifically for the purpose of shunting. In some ways they looked a little like a steam locomotive as they had a cab at one end which overlooked its snout with an exhaust chimney towards the far end. There was also a low wagon fitted to the front of the pilot called a runner which helped activate the track circuits*, as the Drewry on its own failed to do so due to its short length. One individual fitted a Christmas tree to the runner and after a month or two all the pine needles fell off. However the tree remained on the runner for a few years after with just a piece of tinsel for decoration. Nobody could be bothered to remove it and it looked quite comical trundling around the station during the summer months.

The London and Birmingham services would often need shunting for run-a-rounds. This would happen every hour with the London services and less frequently for the Birminghams. A hauled train would run into the station pulled by a locomotive which would be detached on arrival. The pilot would attach to the rear of the train and haul it out by about a quarter of its length so that the locomotive could be released via a set of points into the adjoining platform. The pilot would then push the train back onto the stops of the platform, detach from the train, and the locomotive would then back onto what was now the front of the train ready for its journey back to London.

At the end of each day, as the service was coming to an end, the trains would be worked to Great Yarmouth where most of the coaches were stabled overnight and cleaned. Occasionally if there was a faulty coach it would have to be removed or 'knocked out' from the formation. From time to time rolling stock in the passenger yard had to be shunted. The newspaper, Royal Mail and parcels trains had to be marshalled ready for their late evening return to London and across to the Midlands. This work would be carried out by the Drewry pilot.

**Track circuits: a low level electrical current is fed through the rails. The wheels of the train make the circuit which sends an electrical signal to a panel in the signal box, indicating to the signalman that the track is occupied.*

I was with Earl one day on the run-a-rounds, or relief as it was called, when he commented, "Bit of a rough job this one today David!" He then went through everything we were scheduled to carry out where he finally came to the conclusion that it wasn't such a bad job after all. Relief work involves relieving arrivals hauled by locomotives and running them around onto the front of the incoming train ready for its next departure. It may also involve swapping locomotives, or taking them for fuel and water at the loco sheds.

We had completed a couple of run-a-rounds when we relieved a Birmingham train which was hauled by a Class 31 locomotive. It was autumn so it meant that I would need to operate the boiler to heat the train once we had completed the moves. The Class 31's boiler was situated in the engine compartment directly behind No.2 driving cab and could be seen though a small window in the door that led from the cab. After the locomotive had been released we set it back onto the train and I coupled up, then made my way into the engine compartment to fire up the boiler.

Soon it was building up a head of steam so I left it to run merrily away on its own. After a few minutes I could smell smoke so got up and looked though the engine room door window. To my shock and surprise there were flames licking up the side of the boiler. "Earl... we're on fire!" I exclaimed in a heightened voice of anxiety. I turned

A view of Norwich station from the cab of a Drewry Class 03 diesel shunting locomotive. The Class 31 locomotive on the left would probably have been to work a Birmingham train, while the Class 47 locomotive in the centre would probably have been to work a London train. (Steven Dey)

Cyril Mobbs in the Passenger Yard shunter's hut, with the infamous stove in the foreground. (Steven Dey)

off the boiler from a switch in the cab, grabbed a fire extinguisher and entered the engine room. By this time the flames were more intense and dancing up the side of the boiler. I pointed the extinguisher hose at the fire, pulled the safety pin out and squeezed the trigger. To my relief foam shot out of the nozzle and the fire died out almost immediately.

I exited the cab backwards, extinguisher in hand exclaiming, "Blimey that was a close one Earl ..... Earl... Earl?" Earl was nowhere in sight, the engine was still running and the cab door was open. I recall thinking 'Where the hell has he gone?' ... then 'Maybe he's gone to call the fire brigade'. I shut down the locomotive as a precaution and looked out of the cab window towards the rear of the train but Earl was nowhere to be seen. I alighted from the cab and walked back down the platform towards the Station Manager's office as I thought it best to phone for the fitters to come across and sort out the problem or arrange for a replacement locomotive. As I passed the coach nearest the train one of the doors opened and out came Earl. "Where have you been Earl?" I asked. "We were on fire, I wasn't hanging around on there old mate," came the reply.

It turns out he panicked and did a runner rather than help me. It was a good job one of us stayed to sort out things! Eventually we detached the locomotive and it was swapped for a replacement from the shed. I even got commended for my actions, no thanks to Earl though.

I was allocated to work with restricted driver Wally Dey who had been taken off mainline duties as a result of a heart attack. Wally was a comical individual who never seemed to get upset or stressed and was always up to something. I remember climbing up on the passenger yard pilot one afternoon after Wally had been on the morning shift to find the cab was knee high in scrunched up newspaper. Apparently he had been working on this particular project all morning, collecting newspapers from trains as they arrived then scrunching up each individual page and flicking it onto the floor. It took quite a while to offload the offending paper.

We had completed the first few run-a-rounds and made our way back over to the messroom where we had a leisurely afternoon tea. He pumped a few quid into the one armed bandit and, with a good hour before our next job he called over to me, "Time to go, come on young man." I wasn't quite sure what he meant but willingly followed as Wally took a carrier bag from his pocket. "Now then," Wally said, "We have a little job to do." I must admit I was somewhat puzzled. He went on to explain that we were on a mission to collect as many rubber gloves as possible in the time we had before our next job. I questioned as to why he wanted to do this but all I got out of him was, "You'll see." We made our way to the goods yard where I began to scour the area. It wasn't too long before I piped up, "Found one Wal." "Good lad, pop it in the bag".

We were issued with thick orange rubber gloves which we would use when coupling and uncoupling locomotives as the air pipes were dirty and the couplings greasy. After about half an hour we had almost filled the carrier bag. I kept quizzing Wally as to what we were actually going to do with the gloves. Was there a drive to clean up these things? If there was I hadn't seen a letter— I certainly hadn't been told about such a campaign. I kept wracking my brains as to what was on Wally's mind. As the time passed we made our way through the various yards, then we crossed the rails to the passenger yard shunter's hut. Wally opened the door and peered in. Nobody was about, so in we went.

As it was early autumn, someone had decided to light the potbelly stove ready for the night shift. Wally was renowned for having a penchant for starting fires – I believe the appropriate term is pyromaniac.

By now I had been given charge of the plastic bag and as we stood by the stove Wally carefully lifted the lid with a driver's cloth covering his hand. One by one he proceeded to drop the gloves into the fire with a just audible chuckle. I still didn't quite understand why we were doing this. Once the final glove was dropped into the fire Wally carefully closed the lid and said, "About time we relieved that London, it's due in shortly." We left the hut and made our way across the lines to the station platforms.

It was only when I looked back at the hut did I noticed a pall of thick black smoke pouring out of its chimney. The gentle autumn breeze carried it directly across the lines and headed straight for the Passenger Yard signal box. The signal box was at times manned by a particular odious individual who I guess Wally was none too keen on. As the smoke drifted across to the box loud cursing could be heard and the large sliding windows of the signal box began to slam shut.

Finally the penny dropped. The perfect weather conditions, nobody about in the shunter's hut, an abundance of discarded gloves, and the victim on duty in the signal box. I guess Wally had planned this all along and waited for all the right conditions to fall into place. As the cursing continued and the windows slammed Wally chuckled to himself. Another good day at the office.

Chapter 13 - The Goods Yard

LIFE IN THE goods yard was somewhat more mundane. The characters were very different to the passenger yard, as was the work. When I joined the railway we were still in the days of loose coupled and partially fitted trains. A loose coupled train meant that the only brakes were on the locomotive and the brake van at the rear where the guard would be. If required he would screw down the brake to assist: the brake van was also needed just in case the rear portion of the train became detached from the front. Partially fitted trains were a mix of wagons marshalled directly behind the locomotive which had brakes controlled through the driver's automatic train brake along with unfitted wagons behind. A brake van would always be at the rear.

In the early 1980s there was still a fair a mount of freight in and out of Norwich yard: coal, heating oil, bitumen, wood, bricks, aggregates, chemicals, grain and engineers' materials. However, the industry was in decline due to lack of investment and in later years the BRB's policy to offload ad-hoc traffic in favour of bulk trains decimated rail freight. (*The BRB was the British Railways Board, responsible for the railways in Britain until the onset of privatisation.)* The BRB was only interested in one train hauling large bulk loads of coal, fuel, aggregates and shipping containers. Freight trains that picked up and dropped off wagons at ad-hoc places that had a variety of wagons of various materials were eradicated as a result of the BRB's 'Network 90' policy.

Trains would be allowed into the yard and met by the Yard Supervisor or Head Shunter who would advise the driver which 'road' he was to be sent down. The train would proceed down to the buffer stops and the locomotive would then be uncoupled and the crew would wait for the wagons to be pulled out so the locomotive could be released. In some cases the locomotive would be shut down and left behind. The pilot (or 'Gronk' - even some of the locomotives had nicknames) would back onto the rear of the train and draw it, or part of it, out and commence shunting the wagons onto various other roads. Much depended on what type of wagons they were and whether they were to be unloaded or shunted into a different formation for a train which would go out elsewhere.

On arrival in the yard, wagons that were fitted with air or vacuum brakes were 'bled' in readiness for loose shunting. Loose shunting involved a process of drawing the relevant wagons off the incoming train then, when given the appropriate hand signal by the shunter, the driver would apply full power to the pilot, the coupling would slacken, the shunter would de-couple the coupling then give a stop hand signal to the driver. He would apply the brake thus bringing the pilot and part the train that was still attached to it to a halt. The wagons that had been uncoupled were left to trundle down the relevant road and would come to rest, either by running out of force, or by bumping into the buffer stops or any other wagons that were stationary on that road. Sometimes there would be more than a bump, more like a loud clang followed by a cloud of dust. It was not unknown for both wagons to bounce up, off the rails, and then land back and wiggle from side to side.

Given that the mantra of 'safety first' was drummed into us, this type of shunting was extremely dangerous. Tons of metal and goods trundling along, out of control, with only a hand brake situated at the side of the wagon that had to be manually applied to slow it down. Sometimes the shunter would apply a couple of these brakes before loose shunting the wagons.

I never ceased to marvel at the skill of the shunters, especially the way they would use their shunting poles. These were about six feet in length and had a curved metal hook on the end. The shunter would gather a coupling up from the front of a wagon and as the pilot squeezed up to it they would rock and swing the coupling onto

(Above) The Class 03 Drewry shunter trip pilot on the swing bridge over the River Wensum awaiting the signal to go into the goods yard.
(Below) The Goods Yard box on the right, with locos stabled behind the Passenger Yard Box. (Both photos Steven Dey)

the hook. They made this practice look very simple, yet it was a bit like getting a good golf swing right: grip, balance, timing and force. This was all done on an uneven surface while the vehicle was moving! I tried to use the pole on several occasions and failed miserably!

It was in the goods yard that I came across the bad old ways of the railman's establishment. Some used their knowledge and experience against a new member of staff who they resented. This manifested itself one day when a lad who was maybe only about seventeen years of age, and new off the street, was in the yard to learn about shunting.

Mike was not the sharpest pencil in the box but he had a heart of gold and was keen to learn. Unfortunately he was up against the establishment. Some individuals resented new colleagues and much of this was due to the fact that their rate of pay was so poor that they relied on overtime and rest day working to make their wages up to a decent level. Many railmen would work twelve hours a day, seven days a week, so it was in their best interests if the new boy failed. It was my view that they went out of their way to make sure he did.

They would expect Mike to know the various roads and how to use the pole from day one. If he put some wagons down the wrong road he would be berated and sworn at. There seemed to be very little training and he was doomed from the day he walked into the yard. His ultimate downfall came when he went to put the hand brake on a 'Grainflow' wagon. Unfortunately what he thought was the handbrake was actually the handle that opened the hopper beneath the wagon. Consequently he dumped several tons of prime Norfolk grain destined for a Scottish whisky distillery onto the ground. I'm sure if he had been deployed in the passenger yard he would have lasted much longer. In the end the bigots got their way and kept hold of their overtime. Some months later I saw Mike painting a bungalow. I guess he was self employed with no benefits such as sick pay and pension.

I was disgusted by the actions of some of these men. The fact that they used their wealth of railway knowledge and experience to beat someone up and get them the sack was a lesson for me. I have always believed in sharing information and experience with those who are new to the industry so that they may succeed. I am pleased that most of these old ways are now consigned to the dustbin of history.

Although the atmosphere in the goods yard was more mundane, it's not to say that there weren't any laughs. There were, and the characters were unique. There was a pair of shunters who worked on the Victoria pilot. This was a shunting locomotive with a crew that were designated to ferry wagons between Norwich goods yard and the old Victoria station where there was a coal yard. Their names are lost in the memories of the ghosts of the railmen who have since passed away, but these two individuals were always up to some sort of mischief. Whenever you saw one, you knew that the other was sure to be close by and trouble was brewing. This was in the mid seventies and they had been given the nick names 'Starsky and Hutch' after the American TV cops.

One winter's day, they were out and about shunting in the yard. Once their work was completed it was time for lunch and maybe forty winks by the pot belly stove in the brake van. All brake vans were kitted out with a stove that sat in its middle with wooden benches around the outside. The stove would be stoked with coal and had a chimney that went vertically through the roof and protruded about a foot out of the top.

One guard, Ray 'Socky' Mattin, had decided to take a nap in the brake van and was making the best of the generous heat from the stove which was so hot the metal was beginning to glow red. Ray was a tall slim individual who wore a crumpled guard's hat with a full length railway coat and would often be seen with a roll up fag on the go.

Soon he was fast asleep in the brake van, wrapped in his coat and dreaming of his first pint at the railway club on his way home from work.

Little did Ray know that Starsky and Hutch were about. They had managed to get hold of some fog signals or detonators as they were known. Detonators were disc shaped explosive devices that were used in an emergency and were placed on the railhead. When a train passed over they would explode thus alerting the driver to danger ahead. He would then immediately apply the emergency brake.

The two mischief makers sneaked up onto the van, climbed up on to the roof, and over to the chimney. They popped two detonators down the chimney which rattled down into the stove. After only a matter of a few seconds there was a massive bang as the detonators exploded. The stove lid blew off showering Ray with cinders and almost deafening the poor chap. He emerged from the brake van white as a sheet with a smouldering hat and coat.

Starsky and Hutch were treated to a tirade of expletives, not only for putting the fear of God up Ray, but also disturbing his beer filled dreams. This incident went down as part of the legends of the goods yard. However the damage to the stove and brake van probably took some explaining.

Billy Cook was king of his domain, a very regimental individual who had an opinion on many things. He also had a very distinctive walk that came from almost fifty years of working in the yard and having to step over rails all the time. Billy was all bluster and would shout and bawl at certain people until they took him on.

I hadn't been passed to drive very long and was allocated to the afternoon goods yard pilot which at the time was not a particularly busy job due to the decline in freight traffic. We were shunting a train and he gave me the signal to move away from him or to set back. However I had omitted to change the direction lever on the pilot so we briefly moved in the wrong direction which led to him bawl at me, "No you twat, I said set back!!"

Most people who know me would say I am a mild mannered, easy going individual, but it was a comment such as that which I could not let pass. I had made a slight error which resulted in a move of no more than a metre in the wrong direction with only a couple of wagons attached. I brought the pilot to a stand, climbed down and stood in front of Billy then stared him directly in the eye. "Never speak to me like that again," I said, then I climbed back onto the pilot and that was the end of the matter.

From that day until the day he finished on the railways he was no problem at all. I think he forgot that I was no longer a lowly secondman. I had now made the grade and was a driver, even though I still had silver buttons on my jacket... they should have been gold!

My great friend and work colleague Michael Lloyd was somewhat miffed when he picked up his new uniform after becoming a driver: the buttons on his jacket were silver rather than gold. Not to be deterred, Michael contacted his manager to complain. Some weeks later he picked up a letter from the timekeeper's office only to find some gold buttons within. This wound him up even more, they were too tight to exchange his jacket!

Other characters in the yard included Hatch, Chunky, Paul and Stanley who at times were supervised by Claude. There was also a TOPS office next to the shunter's messroom. (*TOPS—Total Operations Processing System, the computer system used by British Rail for managing locomotives and rolling stock.*) In the summer Claude would wear a lightweight cloth jacket which the shunters dubbed as his 'Ice Cream Man's jacket', much to his annoyance.

Chunky was a particularly volatile individual at times and you knew if he was on the afternoon shift that he would have had a couple of pints on his way to work which could lead to the odd mistake and the inevitable ceremonial throwing down of the shunting pole. One particular day a new employee must have misheard Chunky's nick name and kept calling him 'Crunchie' much to everyone's mirth.

There was an old saying that you could smash up a train and not reap any consequences, however if you were caught stealing then you were gone. One individual took the art of pilfering to a much higher level, turning up for work at the goods yard in a Ford Granada. After a day's work he would leave but the car would be weighed down with all sorts of bits of wood, engineering materials and anything else he could lay his hands on. After several weeks of this the individual was summoned to a meeting with the management where photographs were produced showing the car arriving, clearly unladen, and then leaving with the suspension groaning under the weight from what was in the boot as well as with piping and wood strapped to the roof rack. It was an open and shut case.

One sad event that occurred in the goods yard messroom involved Melvin Goodrum or 'Bright Eyes' as he was known to his work mates, a really lovely chap who would do anything to help out a colleague. Melvin was an acting driver and was what was known as a protected man as a result of the 1965 manning agreement which had been struck between the BRB and the unions that protected their earnings no matter what turn of duty they were on. They were driver assistants but could be called on to drive at any time. Melvin was booked on the yard pilot with Mick Woods who was a driver who had been transferred into Norwich but was far junior to the old hands such as Melvin. This caused some resentment among some of the protected acting drivers (Spawny Elvin would carry a chip on his shoulder for many years), but not Melvin.

Bright Eyes was in his mid fifties, single and he loved the finer things in life. He enjoyed a few beers, was a very sociable individual and loved to smoke cigars. While he was in the goods yard messroom he began to complain of chest pains. Woody kept on at him to go hospital, he even offered to run him there himself but Melvin insisted he would be ok. Within the hour he had collapsed and died. RIP Bright Eyes.

Two Class 37 diesel locos stabled at the south end of the loco shed. (Steven Dey)

Chapter 14 - The Loco Sheds, Back Yard and Diesel Shops

ADJACENT TO THE goods yard stood the loco sheds. This was where the locomotives were fuelled and watered and various examinations and minor repairs carried out. A driver and secondman were allocated to the loco shed which generally involved moving the locomotives onto various 'roads' depending on the requirements for that locomotive.

Early morning and late afternoon shifts were particularly easy jobs, but the night shift was the busiest time when most locomotives were at the shed and had to be placed in a specific order ready for various jobs the following day. The locomotives for the early morning paper trains had to be placed last on any particular road as they were first out in the morning. The driver would be given a list of locomotives and which jobs they had been allocated to. Depending where they were and when they arrived on the shed could potentially lead to a lot of shunting around to get them in the right place. Although secondmen were not qualified to drive most drivers expected his mate to help out.

One afternoon I was with George Marshall Nichols or 'Wing Commander Nichols' as the younger lads called him. He was a tall elegant man with slicked back grey hair, a small moustache, immaculate in appearance, and he smoked a pipe. If you dressed him up in a RAF uniform he would have fitted in perfectly.

We had been released from the goods yard and trundled across to the loco shed, George was in the rear cab and driving, I was in the leading cab as we backed onto the shed. I was using the set back hand signal and was aware that we needed to stop outside the shed as there was a locomotive occupying the inside. I gave George the slow down signal but we kept on moving at the same speed. The stationary locomotive was getting closer and closer so I gave the stop hand signal and shouted that internationally known warning to stop.... "Whhhoooooaaaa!!!!!"

There was a deafening clang as we smacked into the stationary locomotive and I was thrown across the cab. 'I'm in for a military style bollocking here,' I thought as a cloud of rusty dust started to settle on the ground. I walked back towards the rear cab. George put his head out of the cab door, puffed on his pipe and exclaimed, "Reckon there's one in there!" And that was it. I'm just glad nobody was working on the stationary locomotive at the time.

Located between the loco sheds and the railcar sheds were the stores. I had been on the railway for several months and did not even know they existed until I had been on night shift with Peter Price. Peter and I were to spend a week on the night shift. When I told my father who I had been paired with he said .... "Oh, you'll be paying a visit to the stores at some point this week then."

Peter was what I can only describe as a very jovial, positive individual, balding and stout with a rather large belly. He was a pleasure to be with for the day or night as the case may be. On our first night together we took a locomotive over to the station for one of the late trains to London and then carried out some other duties. Around two in the morning we made our way back to the messroom for a cup of tea. "We'll just have a little detour," said Peter.

Off we went on a route around the back of the loco shed and down some dark passageways which I had not seen before. We passed through a set of doors that opened up into a glass and wood panelled corridor that led to a wicket where there was a bell buzzer that stated 'Ring'. Peter pressed the ringer and kept his finger on the button... "Come on Jacko," called Peter. After a few minutes a white haired old boy with a stoop, wearing a grey cardigan and rubbing the sleep away from his eye, appeared from the rear of the stores .

Two Class 47 diesel locos stabled at the north end of the loco shed. (Steven Dey)

Peter opened a side door and said, "What have you got for me today Jacko?" All I could see was Jacko standing there with his hands on his hips while Peter cast his eyes over the various shelves, which were amply stocked with equipment used in the running of a depot the size of Norwich. I came away with batteries of all sizes, gloves, cloths and a tin of Swarfega which was used to remove grease from our hands. It felt a bit like my birthday had come early. Once we returned to the messroom I had a real job getting everything in my locker.

Over the years I have seen drivers use Bardic lamp batteries to power their radios and men walking off with bags of toilet rolls (that greasy Izal paper that did not absorb). Cloths would be taken home and were used in many a driver's shed or garage. My father had a boat and I noticed that the fire extinguishers stowed in the cockpit were very similar to those on a railcar! I was told that in the steam days some men would put lumps of coal in their bags to take home to put on their fire.

Situated at the side of the loco sheds were the back yard and diesel railcar shops. This was where railcars were maintained and fuelled. There were also sidings where redundant wagons and coaches were stored either while they were waiting to be scrapped, pilfered for spare parts or awaiting repairs. I did not have an awful lot of experience around the back yard and railcar sheds. This was due to the impending commissioning of Crown Point depot which would take over all rolling stock maintenance in 1982 and led to the closure of the sheds including the locomotive sheds.

I was never really comfortable working in the back yard as it seemed a place where you could easily slip up and have an accident. The back yard operations were a bit different to the other yards, as they had a team of shunters along with drivers who would carry out the duties required of them. This did not apply here, and it was a driver and secondman who would carry out all the shunting: the duties of the shunter were carried out by the secondman. I often wondered whether this was really correct, but it had become custom and practice and we never questioned what was required of us.

Frank and Paul were instructed to release a coach which had been buried in behind some other stock in the back yard. They had to start up a Class 03 Drewry pilot and shunt some old stock before they could get to the coach that was to be repaired. This meant moving the wagons on to other tracks and then releasing the require coach. This could prove to be a bit of a pantomime with a lot of toing and froing. Each road had what were know as hand points. (see photo opposite) The movements in the yard were not controlled or signalled by a signal box, it was down to the crew to make the moves vigilantly and carefully. Hand points were heavy to move and generally had a metal handle about four feet long and stood at a 45 degree angle that would allow the user to pull the handle towards them when the points needed moving over.

Contrary to what we were told not to do, Paul was riding in the running board of the pilot rather than climbing up in the cab or walking alongside the pilot while it was moving. The pilot was moving as Paul dropped off the running board to pull the points. By some freak accident the point handle travelled up the inside of his trouser leg and he became stuck. Fortunately Frank witnessed this and laughing at such a freak incident he halted the pilot and climbed down to help Paul who was stuck. It was only when Frank got close to Paul did he realise the seriousness of the situation. The handle had not travelled up the inside of his trouser leg, it had penetrated Paul's back passage and he was in serious trouble. Fortunately Frank was a trained first aider, he made him as comfortable as possible, then dashed off to call for an ambulance. Paul was rushed to hospital and operated on immediately, he survived the incident but if I recall correctly his bowel was damaged which led to him having to be fitted with a bag.

A Bardic lamp, which was carried by most operational staff and had a knob on the top that operated a shade that allowed the lamp to display a white, green, yellow or red light.

Hand points.

Paul was a very quiet, shy, individual and as a result of the awful accident he was off work for many months. Once he retuned he was a completely different character, being more talkative and confident. Later I became quite friendly with him when I did my driver training. He tried to claim compensation from the BRB but clearly he had been breaching the rules even though the locomotive was equipped with running boards specifically designed to allow employees to ride there.

Paul was on a mission and when it came to him attending his driver training, he made no effort to pass the exams and spent something over two years training, taking his exams, failing and then re-training again. This happened three times and on the dates of his last exams he just did not turn up, in the 80s we were allowed three attempts to pass our driving exams. I spent many hours with him travelling to and from London when I was training, but I was not surprised when he failed to turn up for his 'last chance saloon' exams. Eventually his employment was terminated.

One driver who was what could only be described as a 'character' or some may go a bit further as a 'likeable rogue' was Peter. This particular evening Peter was working in the back yard, while he was pulling a set of points he had a sudden urge. He found a quiet spot, dropped his trousers and unloaded into a newspaper that he had spread on the ground. After he was finished he wrapped up the evidence and decided to dispose of it in the toilets.

It being Friday evening, it was a traditional that the fitters on the night shift in the railcar shops would get fish and chips before they began work. As Peter was walking along the inside of the shops with his newspaper package one of the fitters stopped him in his tracks... "Oh that's typical of you Peter, go off and get fish and chips without asking if anyone else wanted some", despite Peter's protestations the fitter took the 'fish and chips' from Peter and proceeded to unwrap them. I can only imagine what his reaction was once he discovered the contents.

There are several events involving Peter which I guess could be described as 'urban myths'. My favourite being the time Peter decided he would attend the Boxing Day football at Carrow Road the home of Norwich City FC. The loco car park was situated directly opposite the Barclay End stand of the ground and Peter presented himself at one of the side gates that was manned by the police. He explained to the police officer that he had worked the football special from the away teams station and wondered if he would be able to slip in to watch some of the match. The officer duly obliged after Peter flashed the BR buttons of his uniform at him. I wonder at what point the officer realised that no trains ran on Boxing Day and that he had fallen victim to one of Peter's many scams!

Chapter 15 - Crown Point.....The Bermuda Triangle

IN OCTOBER 1982 Crown Point depot was opened to traffic. It had been under construction from the time I had started on the railway, and had been built as a maintenance depot so that the loco shed and diesel shops, along with the carriage sidings at Great Yarmouth, could close. The theory was that it would be more efficient to run trains the short distance from Norwich station to Crown Point rather than the twenty miles to Great Yarmouth. The depot was opened with a great deal of publicity: even the Chairman of the British Railways Board, Sir Peter Parker, attended the opening ceremony.

Unfortunately the planned efficiencies did not come to fruition for a very long time mainly due to its design. Many of its twenty four roads were on a curve. Each move from one road to another or, to exit the depot, were tied to signals which meant that every single move had to be controlled by the signalman. In the old loco and back yard the crews had the freedom to work out what needed to be where and were free to move engines and units at will. Crown Point's design put a stop to anything like that and efficiency suffered as a result.

From day one the depot was plagued with delays and rolling stock shortages. I recall walking down platform 3 at Norwich one morning and seeing my father getting ready to work the 11:42 to London with four coaches, a train that would generally have a rake of nine or ten on any normal day. There came a point where some coaches actually went missing. This was more down to an administrative error than them actually disappearing but it did earn the depot the nickname 'The Bermuda Triangle' and not long after 'Crown Paint'. Crown, the paint manufacturer, had an advertising slogan that their non-drip paint 'did not run.' So Crown Point became 'Crown Paint ....where nothing runs!'

When on the night relief turns, which had been a doddle prior to its opening, crews were diagrammed to work trains from the station to the depot. This would involve spending hours waiting around for a guard to turn up for the short journey, as driver only operation had not been agreed in the Norwich area, so every trip had to be fully crewed. Once the guard turned up crews could wait hours for a slot to make it to one of the two reception roads. More often than not the guard would clear off, tired of waiting for the signal to clear or his shift had finished. Once cleared onto reception it could take just as long to haul the train through the washer and then back into one of the stabling roads or the sheds. It was not uncommon for trains to come out of the depot having not been cleaned at all. I was with a driver who was based in the railcar link and took "Great pleasure" in shutting down the engine and leaving it as his hours of duty were finished. He was sick of the sight of "Twat's Playground" as he called it.

The efforts of the shunters and other staff to get the place working properly should not have gone unnoticed: they were up against it from day one. Everything was expected to go out to the depot from as soon as it opened, so the combination of its design and sheer volume of traffic was a recipe for disaster. I guess in hindsight there were things that could have been done much better. Having said that I think the creation of the depot helped protect jobs in the area.

As with any concentration of staff, Crown Point had its fair share of characters who would play pranks on each other or do things that deserve honourable mentions. One such incident occurred not long after the depot had opened and was executed by one of the shunters whose name was Ray, or 'Shaggy Dog' as he was nicknamed. This was on account of his longish hair which if the truth be known was grown to conceal a spreading bald patch. Ray had a distinctive Black Country accent and would begin most walkie talkie conversations with "Shunters 't tower" which translated meant "Ray to

Signaller." (Crown Point had its own signal box known as 'the tower' to control all movements.) He carried a fair bit of weight and would wear a bright orange boiler suit when engaged in shunting duties.

Ray called a shunting move to the tower, then hopped on the running board of the 03 Drewry pilot that was generally used for shunting moves. As with Class 08 pilots they had a purpose built recess with handrails at sole bar level to allow the shunter to ride on the pilot without getting up and down from the driving cab, although a rule change banned such a practice.

The pilot drew the set of coaches out of the shed and made its way up the washer road so as to be able to clear the points that would allow the train to be set back into one of the other roads in the yard. Generally the washer was switched off for moves such as this and would only be operated when trains came onto the shed prior to maintenance. The first move through the washer would apply a detergent called 'X-mover' which was extremely caustic so getting it on your skin or in the eyes was not recommended. As the pilot passed through the washer it burst into life spraying the pilot, the train and of course Shaggy Dog with a coating of X-mover. Shaggy Dog decided to make the return journey through the washer, this time with a blast of cold water to wash off the detergent. I could see his logic and I guess he was none too pleased at getting soaked twice in one shift. I'm not sure if the washer had been switched on in error or if it was a prank.

The old loco was now closed and we had to make our way out to Crown Point to pick up any locomotives, trains or units. This was a longer walk than going to the old shed, but most of us used an unofficial route which cut across the main line. The official route was considerably further which most drivers considered to be a hindrance, especially if you were on the last part of your job and wanted to get away.

The trials and tribulations of Crown Point continued for many years to come and it was rumoured that the British Railways Board were becoming increasingly frustrated by the performance issues to the extent that the offer of an open cheque book was made to try and resolve the issues. Sometime later the yard was split by the addition of some signals in an effort to allow more moves to be made simultaneously but that did not seem to work. The operating supervisors were provided with a Portakabin that allowed them to do their work in the warm and dry rather than wandering around the yard in all weathers.

One particular driver, Mick 'Slippery Elm' Woods, was placed at Crown Point very much against his will and he became rather resentful. This had transpired as a result of some changes to the link structure at the depot. Rather than working trains on the main line Mick was now confined to movements at Crown Point.

From time to time he would have a difference of opinion as to how a particular shunt should be carried out, or something would aggrieve him. This would result in the 'Woody slow trot' and would bring operations at the depot to a near standstill. The maximum speed at the depot was 15mph and this was the speed at which all shunting movements were carried out at. But this was actually incorrect. All shunting moves should have been carried out at 3mph, which is exactly what Woody did. As a result of the slow trot trains of nine or ten coaches that had to be hauled around and re-marshalled, or have coaches replaced for repair, took three or four times longer than normal. This meant trains were released late thus causing delays to the early morning departures from Norwich. Woody could not be touched as he was applying the rules.

One afternoon a different Mick had to shunt a Class 86 locomotive into an unelectrified road. To negate the need to shunt with a pilot, he decided he would take a run up to the shed and drop the pantograph (86s were electric and took their power from the overhead power lines) and coast into the shed while dropping the 'pan' so that it would not catch on the brickwork above the shed doors. 14 road was the fuel pad for diesel locomotives and so did not have overhead power lines. Mick took a run up with the 86 and pressed the pan down button. It coasted into the shed beautifully, but unfortunately the pan did not come down as quickly as he anticipated so there was a crash as it became detached from the roof of the 86. More explaining to do.

Others have fallen victim to the curse of the fuel pad and more than one driver was christened with the nickname 'Gusher' after moving a locomotive with the fuel pipe still attached!

Some time later Mick was to redeem himself while working two railcars empty from Ipswich. Each evening a set of several railcars were booked to be brought back to Crown Point for cleaning, fuel and maintenance. Mick was almost at Norwich when he noticed there was a problem with one of the units as the engine lights had gone out on his instrument panel. He dropped the cab window and was shocked to see that the rear railcar was ablaze. He immediately brought the train to a stand and without any assistance managed to split the leading railcar from the rear one which by now was an inferno. He summoned the emergency services and advised the signalman to switch off the overhead power lines. He was later commended for his actions although someone in high office did comment that it would have been better if he had let both railcars burn as the one that he protected was 'a pile of crap'!

In the mid 1990s the industry was privatised which led to the creation of more than thirty different train and freight operating companies. As the boundaries became more defined, so did the various companies' train liveries which became a train

Class 86 electric loco No. 86 234 (named Suffolk Relax Refresh Return) at Norwich station in Anglia Railways livery on 11 August 2002. (Alastair Holmes)

spotter's paradise with all the various colours and designs, some of which were quite vibrant.

Crown Point came under the Anglia franchise and they adopted a light green livery. There came a point when the ethos of all working for the same organisation such as British Rail began to break down with staff identifying with their company rather then the industry as a whole. Maybe Eric had this in mind when he decided he was not going to move a Class 86 locomotive. The supervisor asked Eric, "Would you get the 86 off the reception road and put it on road seven please Eric?" There followed a short pause then Eric replied, "No". The supervisor was a bit surprised by Eric's response and asked him again, he also questioned as to why he had refused to move it, to which he replied... "It's red." Again the supervisor asked Eric to which he expanded that the reason for not moving it. "It's red... I don't move red ones." The locomotive belonged to Rail Express Systems, the mail and parcels haulier, not Anglia. So it stayed on reception until someone less awkward than Eric could be found to move it. Privatisation had a lot to answer for.

Chapter 16 - "Tell Jock Henderson to Kiss my Arse!"

JANUARY 1981 AND I was with a new mate in the B1 link who was a complete contrast to my previous one being tall, smart, talkative and generous with his time as well as allowing me to take the controls from time to time. Even though my footplate career got off to a rocky start with my first regular mate being a challenge to work with, I did learn a great deal from him in that period from August to December 1980 for which I was grateful.

My new mate, Charlie, would often come to work on the late pm shift once he had spent the morning and early afternoon in the Fiveways Pub in Earlham. He loved to play cards for proper money rather than the pennies we would play for at work, and if he had won you would certainly know about it. Depending on what job we were on and the time of day, we would pay a visit to the alternative messrooms, or railway clubs, at places such as March and Cambridge, or some of the numerous pubs that were dotted around Liverpool Street. I was still only 16 but this did not seem to bother any of the landlords. Generally it would be Charlie who would get the beers in and much depended on the time we had between trips although we never had more than a couple of pints.

There were some drivers who would come straight onto the afternoon shift after spending several hours in their local pub. As soon as they got to their first destination of the day, if there was a pub close by that was open, they would be in as soon as possible to top up from the lunchtime session. I think that was pushing things too far. BR had a policy of no drinking on duty but it was not enforced until the mid to late 1980s when drugs became more widespread and a formal drugs and alcohol policy was strictly implemented.

Charlie would often bring cream cakes to share. We were on an additional duty which involved picking some tanks up at Parkeston and sitting in the yard at six in the morning on a cold, grey winter's day when he produced some cakes. It was certainly quite novel to be eating them at such a time. The guard was in the cab with us and likened me to a seagull due to the manner in which I scoffed the cake down.

During 1981 changes were proposed to the rosters at Norwich. The practice of having a regular mate, a throwback to the steam days, was to come to an end which in some ways for me was disappointing, but for others it was a blessing. Some drivers and secondmen just did not get on. There was one particular incident where the secondman made a formal request to be released from his driver. This particular driver disliked the secondman and refused point blank to speak to him which, after a while, drove the poor lad crazy. These days, it would be considered a form of harassment, but this was a different time where bullying, sexism, homophobia and racism went unchecked and was rife in some parts of the industry. The secondman was good at his job, he was a likeable chap who had no issues with anyone, yet this driver just would not engage with him on any level whatsoever.

The new link structure altered the manner in which the driver and secondman were to be paired. Rather than working together for the whole year, the B1 drivers and secondmen links differed in size which led to the secondmen completing their roster cycle before the driver they were shadowing.

This was due to the replacement of the older Mark I coaching stock with the more modern Mark II coaches which were equipped with electrical train heating and air conditioning. As a consequence most London services would be manned by a driver only, thus eliminating the requirement for a secondman. It was a worrying time as it was mooted there was the possibility of redundancies: however this soon passed when additional traction trainees were recruited. Nonetheless the size of the secondman's link was reduced to cater for the loss of work.

Once I had completed the roster cycle I parted company with Charlie and ran parallel with George. He was a revelation to be with, always winding up other drivers, making fun of me, and insisting that I do all the driving, which I revelled in. Work was becoming far more entertaining and I was enjoying my role.

George and I had a week's work on a particular turn of duty where we relieved a crew on the Wensum curve just outside Norwich which had brought the North Walsham tanks in. We would then work them through to Parkeston.

The tanks conveyed a highly flammable condensate which was a by-product of the extraction process from the gas fields in the North Sea. Once we arrived at Parkeston we would then travel passenger back to Ipswich where we would pick up the London to Lowestoft train and work it across the East Suffolk line. The first day on this turn George offered for me to drive from Ipswich to Lowestoft. This was the first time I ever declined an offer but I had not been across this line many times and was not particularly confident. We agreed that I would observe him on the Monday and drive the rest of the week.

What George was not aware of was that my father had tipped me off about something that had happened when George was learning the East Suffolk route and my Dad was the driver. Somewhere between Beccles and Oulton Broad the railway runs parallel with the A146. There was a petrol station situated on this particular stretch which was lit up at night and to the untrained eye could be mistaken for the next station. This is exactly what George did when he was learning the line with my Dad, even to the point that he started to apply the brakes to stop at the phantom station.

It was dark as we left Beccles so I kept a sharp lookout. Sure enough, on the right hand side of the line, through some trees in the distance, I could see the petrol station. As we got closer I turned to George and exclaimed, "Bloody hell George... I thought for a minute that was our next stop!" There was no response.

The next day it was my turn to take to the controls. George was there to guide me along the line giving me advice as to which landmarks to take note of and its various characteristics. Soon we were leaving Beccles and again I made the comment about the petrol station, again there was no response. This went on every night that week, and every night there was no reply, but I suspect George knew exactly what I was getting at!

I had so many laughs with George, but he could take a good ribbing as well as

North Walsham to Parkeston tank train seen with a pair of Class 31 locomotives (31231 leading) on the Wensum Curve at Norwich. (Martin Steele)

give it out. One winter's afternoon we were on a relief turn and were making our way across to the station through a thick layer of snow that had fallen that day. As we got close to the rear of the Passenger Yard signal box we bumped into driver Denis Brown and secondman David 'Belly' Bellchamber. We stopped for a brief chat but before anyone could say anything Belly said, "Hello George," and knocked his driver's cap off and into the snow it fell. Quick as a flash I jumped in and said to David, "That's no way to treat my driver." David was a bit taken-aback by my comment as I quickly bent down and picked George's hat out of the snow and plonked it back on George's head. "Why thanks......." George stopped halfway through his sentence and then, "You bastard..... Yooouu bastard." He took his hat off to reveal a pile of snow on his balding head. He also had to shake his hat to remove the rest of the snow I had placed in it. Denis and David were pissing themselves but I was left wondering what the payback was going to be later that day.

We parted company and made our way over to the station to relieve a London arrival which we were to shunt in preparation for the early evening mail train to London. This involved using the locomotive we had relieved, and backing it onto some coaches along with the travelling post office vans and shunting them into the station. As we were backing the train into the platform, with both of us looking out each side, I became aware of George making some muffled cries. "Oh....Aw.... Oh....you bastards." As we came to a stand I turned my head to look at him only to see his face and hat covered in snow. I looked out of George's side to see shunters Peter Dawson and Micky Pearce bombarding him with snowballs from ground level. I have to say, the pair of them were pretty accurate, in particular Micky, as he was an accomplished darts player. Poor old

George got hit twice in one afternoon.

Back in the steam days, drivers were described as 'Gods' by those who worked with them. In some respects, the power they wielded carried through to the days of dieselisation. This influence rubbed off on many of us as young men and continued as in later years we too became drivers. No more of a stark example of this came to light when George and I were on the weekday morning area civil engineer's turn.

The crew and train would be at the disposal of the engineer's department and were allocated work pretty much on a day by day basis. The work was very random. It may be hauling hoppers to a particular depot, or picking up flatbed wagons loaded with track ready for laying in a specific area later that week or over the weekend. We were the ACE (Area Civil Engineer's) department's 'bitches'!! We climbed onto our locomotive up in the goods yard attached to a few wagons and a guard's brake van with instructions to take the train to Chesterton Junction. Chesterton was just outside Cambridge where track was constructed and the numerous engineer's materials were stored.

In the early eighties many of the trains were fitted with vacuum brakes, and some of the wagons had no brakes just a manual hand brake lever located on the side of the wagon. On this day we were working a partially fitted train meaning that the wagons nearest the locomotive had fitted brakes controlled by the driver, but the ones at the rear had no brake hence the requirement for a brake van. These trains were limited to a maximum speed of about 35mph so getting anywhere of distance could take quite a while. Often slow running trains were shunted into a passing loop to allow faster trains to get by so they could keep to time.

Once the pre-journey duties were completed and the guard was in his brake van we set out for Cambridge following the Birmingham service that had just departed from Norwich. We had been pretty fortunate, managing to avoid being shunted into a loop and were soon passing through Brandon. As we approached the next section controlled by Lakenheath we noticed its distant signal was against us showing a caution which meant the associated home signals would be at danger. As we slowed, the distant signal showed no evidence of being cleared to the proceed position and as we passed it we could see that the crossing gates were still across the main line. This did not look too good.

We came to a stand at Lakenheath's first home signal. George sounded the horn just in case the signalman had dozed off but this was to no avail. The signal stayed at danger. "Looks like you're going to have to take a walk to the box," said George. And that is exactly what I had to do. Many of the signal posts were not equipped with telephones which allowed direct contact with the signal box that the signal was associated with.

I made my way to the box, knocked at the door and went in. I signed the book after which the signalman informed me, "I have a message for you from Jock Henderson. You are ORDERED to return to Norwich immediately to pick up some more wagons, then take them to March after you have dropped your current load off at Chesterton." "Oh," I replied "I'll go give my driver the good news."

I wandered back to the train and climbed into the cab. "George, we've got to return to Norwich, pick up some wagons and take them to March once we have dropped off our load at Chesterton..... by the orders of Jock Henderson." George looked at me as if I had just beamed down from Mars and said, "Well, its like this David, you must go back to the box and tell the signalman to tell Jock Henderson to .... kiss my arse!!" "Anything else?" I asked. "Yep. Make sure the signalman tells Jock Henderson to KISS MY ARSE!!"

Once again I made my way to the signal box and thought that if this carried on I would be on a mileage payment. Again I climbed the stairs, knocked on the door and went in. "The driver says to tell Jock Henderson to... and I quote 'Kiss my arse!' and he would like to you to use those very words." There was a brief pause. For one second I thought the signalman was going to chastise me but he rolled up his sleeves and as he reached for the telephone, he said, "Right... I'll give him the good news."

I didn't hang around for the conversation. By the time I got back on the locomotive the gates were open, the signal was in the clear position, and we were on our way, not back to Norwich, but off to Chesterton as originally planned.

The Power of The Driver.

One particular night duty involved signing on around 23:00 so the crew could catch the last train to Ipswich where they would pick up a locomotive and travel down to Parkeston to pick up some empty tanks to work back to Norwich. Generally, as soon as the crew arrived at Parkeston they would establish if the tanks had been unloaded. If released, they would prepare the train and could be ready for departure to Norwich by 02:00. Although it was not booked to leave until 04:20, if the right shift was on duty at Anglia control then as soon as the train was ready for departure it would be allowed to run. This was not really a problem as there was very little other traffic about at that time of the morning. It also meant that the crew would get back to Norwich around 4am and leave the train on the Wensum curve next to Crown Point depot ready for the morning relief to come on at around 05:30.

However, there was one shift in Control that simply refused to let the train run early. If you were on the wrong shift then you were screwed, especially if it was winter as the train ran every day due to the increase in domestic gas consumption (the train transported a condensate from the North Sea gas fields from North Walsham to the refinery at Parkeston). I 'enjoyed' a week with Big Arthur Allen on the night tanks. We clicked the wrong shift so had to wait two hours before departure. Once I had eaten my sandwiches and had a cup of tea, I would put my feet up and say, "I'm going to have a snooze Arthur," to which he would respond, "Right-ho sword." A few minutes would pass and he would begin whistling..... he would stop whistling when we arrived at Norwich some four hours later... I had a week of that in the run up to Christmas and he drove me bloody nuts!

I was warned about one particular individual who was based at Parkeston and went by the dubious nickname of Whiplash. Like so many nicknames, I had no idea how this came about, but I guess it was something to do with his unusual sexual exploits. I never came across the man, but was told that one secondman entered the messroom at Parkeston late one night. Whiplash was present and engaged the young lad in conversation as he waited for the kettle to boil. "Oooo, you look like a fresh faced, young secondman!" he exclaimed. The lad was a bit embarrassed by such attention. "Tell me....." said Whiplash, "...were you ever caned at school?" The lad, who hadn't been caned, thought he would big himself up a bit and replied, "Yeah, I was!" After which Whiplash asked in a menacing tone of voice, "Did ya' enjoy it?" This question prompted the secondman to make a hasty exit.

Ray 'Dinger' King was on the night Parkeston tanks which for some reason ran every night even though it was summertime. Each night the crew advised the signalman that they were ready to depart and each night they were told by the signalman, "Control says you must leave at your booked time".

This went on all week until the early hours of Saturday morning. However, even without informing the signalman that they were ready to depart the crew noticed the outlet signal had been cleared. It was 02:00. Dinger contacted the signalman only to be informed that Control had agreed to let the train run early as the locomotive was needed at Norwich for another train later that morning. Dinger was incensed and advised the signaller that if they could let them depart early that morning, then they could have done so all week. They were booked to leave at 04:20 and that was when they were going to leave. He may have been cutting off his nose to spite his face but it sent a clear message to the controller!

The first few months of my footplate career didn't go quite as I expected but as time went by I came to enjoy the job. I made many new friends and soon found that there were other aspects to the industry that I had not considered being part of.

The future was looking good.

Guards completed their journals with details of the freight trains they worked. Here is an extract from Guard Donald Murdie of a train of oil tanks from North Walsham to Lindsey Oil Refinery, near Immingham. It is unusual in that the train developed a hot axle box which resulted in a wagon being detached and shunted into a siding at Lakenheath: this process taking a very creditable twenty three minutes. With the removal of so many sidings and increased concerns over trains of dangerous goods such as this one, if the situation were to arise today the delay would likely be in the order of several hours.

BRITISH RAILWAYS OD. 1310 Off. 2110

FREIGHT TRAINS WORKED

B.R. 87221

ON Thursday 28th December 1978

Train No	Time	From	To	Date	Brake Van No.	Driver's Name	Depot	Loco No.
6D43	1455	N. Walsham	Lindsay ORT	28/12	—	Begley	Norwich	37 096

WTT No. or Trip No. or Special	Yard, Depot, Siding, Passing Point, Boundary Point.	Time of Takeover and Arrival Times	Time of Departure or Handover and Passing Times	Mins. Shunting	Wagons Detached			Wagons Attached			On Departure			Delays	
					No.	No. of SLU	Tonnage	No.	No. of SLU	Tonnage	No. of Wagons	Length in SLU	Tonnage	Cause	Mins.
6D43	N. Walsham		1456					16	25	720	16	25	825		
	Wroxham		15/10												
	Wensum Jn.	26	34												
	Trowse		37												
	Wymondham		51												
	Attleborough		58												
	Thetford		16/16												
	Brandon		27												
	Lakenheath	1647	1710		1	1	45				15	24	780		
	Ely North Jn.		27												
	March Down Yd.	1754									15	24	780		

Remarks: Gave red light to signman. Brandon Stopped on HBH 1 tank det. at Lakenheath —

Additional Brake Vans: Brake defect No. 56006

Weather: fine

Chapter 17 - The Early ASLEF Years—The Lighted Flame

AS TRACTION TRAINEES, if we wanted to pass the exam at the end of the course, we were encouraged to 'sign here' on an ASLEF application form. The years of the closed shop, where to fulfil your contract of employment you had to be in the trade union that was relevant to your job, had just come to an end. The Unions were very sensitive about the end of this arrangement and were worried that membership would decline and their power base eroded. In the 1980s the TUC had a combined membership in excess of twelve million, compared to three and a half million some thirty years later due to cuts in public sector jobs and the decline of manufacturing and mining in the UK. However, it appears that trade union membership is now on the increase.

As a new member of the fraternity I never really had anything to do with the local representatives although I do recall one of them coming over to introduce himself during our training. We were told if we had any trouble we were to contact one of them. At the time the main character on the Local Departmental Committee or LDC was Chairman Harry Phillips who was also the Secretary of the Norwich branch of ASLEF. In addition to Harry, the committee was also made up of Roy 'Noddy' Gambling, Derek 'Moss Evans' Bridges and John Pipe. I never had any recourse to call on the support of the LDC, even after my derailment disaster.

The first time I really became interested in the power of the Union was when we were called out on strike in the summer of 1982. The British Railways Board attempted to introduce a more flexible way of rostering various grades within the industry. This led to a fall out over the proposals that would reduce the working week but meant moving away from the guaranteed eight hour working day. It was proposed that we could be rostered between seven and nine hours each day. When I look back and see the changes to pay and conditions restructuring achieved some fifteen years later in 1995, the BRB proposals seemed insignificant. At the time the ASLEF leadership considered the eight hour day to be sacrosanct with its leader, the formidable Ray Buckton, stating, "My eighty thousand members simply will not stand for it," and that was that.

In July 1982 the railways came to a complete standstill with most members of the Union respecting the instruction not to come to work. Stations fell silent and the rails soon began to rust over, freight stopped moving and the travelling public had to find other ways of getting to work.

The country was facing a huge cost to the general economy and questions were being asked in The House of Commons. Some of the comments of MPs and the Secretary for State are recorded in Hansard. One thing that struck me was a comment made by Dennis 'The Beast of Bolsover' Skinner who asked the Secretary for State; *'Perhaps the Hon. Gentleman can complete a little more of the story and tells us, in his capacity as a supposed full-time member of Parliament, picking up £14,000 a year, how many clients he has had as a non-executive director of Cutbitt Advertising Ltd. How much money does he make there and how much does he make from his moonlighting at all the newspapers? Perhaps he will lay it on the line instead of attacking train drivers'?*

The minister's response was contemptuous. Some things have not changed, forty years later!

I also noted that there were comments where the debate declined into a farce;

Mr. Dobson. "The Hon. Gentleman has a lovely voice."

Mr. Skinner. "Yes, it is absolutely beautiful - and he has a knighthood too."

Mr. Deputy Speaker. "Order. This is a debate about the travelling public and British Rail, not about knighthoods or beautiful voices."

You really could not make this stuff up but later in the debate Dennis Skinner hit the nail on the head;

Mr. Skinner. "At a time when 4 million are on the scrap-heap mainly as a result of the Tory Government's economic policy, I do not see why ASLEF members or any other wealth creators in the economy - they are the real workers - should sacrifice thousands and thousands of additional jobs. That is what the Tory Government are asking them to do. They are using Sir Peter Parker and others to bludgeon ASLEF. They want to smash ASLEF and throw more railway workers on the scrap-heap. I stand behind ASLEF and the NUR in trying to save jobs and not destroy them, which is what the Government have been doing ever since they came to power."

At the time I was not quite eighteen years of age, it was summertime and the sun was out and I was mobile having purchased a motorbike, so as far as I was concerned it was an additional holiday.

There were daily reports on the news with the focus on talks about resolving the dispute and sporadic cracks where members were coming into work because they had bills to pay or they were close to retirement and were worried about their pension. The Sun newspaper also ran a story about drivers going out on the booze and night clubbing when they should have been at work. As far as I could see this was all part of the propaganda war to show us as a bunch of work-shy Union Luddites who were holding the country to ransom. What did not help was the fact that the country was also at war in the Falklands.

On a local basis we were solid at Norwich with not one member of ASLEF breaking the strike. This was not the case at the other end of the main line in London where a few strike breakers, or 'scabs' as they were known, began to come into work. I can remember a photo in the local Eastern Daily Press showing a London service arriving at Norwich station and the driver being berated by Harry Phillips who was duly escorted from the station by the police. The wounds of that two week strike would run deep, especially at depots such as Stratford where one driver would bring his bike on the train with him and put it in the back cab of the locomotive. If he left it in the bike sheds at his depot the tyres were guaranteed to be slashed.

Several years later, I was talking with a colleague who had transferred to Norwich from the Southern Region where the dispute had been particularly bitter with a high concentration of members breaking the call to action. Not long after the strike he was route learning, which often involved riding with drivers from other depots. He waited on the platform at a particular station, the train ran in and as he approached the driving cab the driver opened the window. "Hello mate," said Neville "I'm route learning this stretch of line, can I ride with you?" The driver asked, "Are you an '82 scab?" Neville was somewhat taken aback by this, being a loyal union man he replied, "No way mate." The driver's response rendered Neville speechless.... "Well I am ... so you can fuck off!!" With that the driver slammed the window shut and the train moved off.

Some time into the second week of the strike a meeting was organised by the local branch of ASLEF at Norwich Labour Club which was attended by the District Organiser, Albert Atkinson from Cambridge. I have attended many branch meetings at depots all over the UK, with sometimes only a handful of members being present. But this meeting must have had the best part of eighty drivers and secondmen in attendance and was the biggest gathering of Norwich ASLEF members I have ever witnessed. The majority of members were solid in their resolve although some commented that they were not sure how much longer they could hold out. Many men had mortgages to pay, families to feed and other financial commitments but I was impressed by Harry Phillips' resolve. He stated he would be "....out no matter what, and would only return to work when the executive of ASLEF told me to do so!"

I left that meeting feeling we had the moral high ground but was soon brought

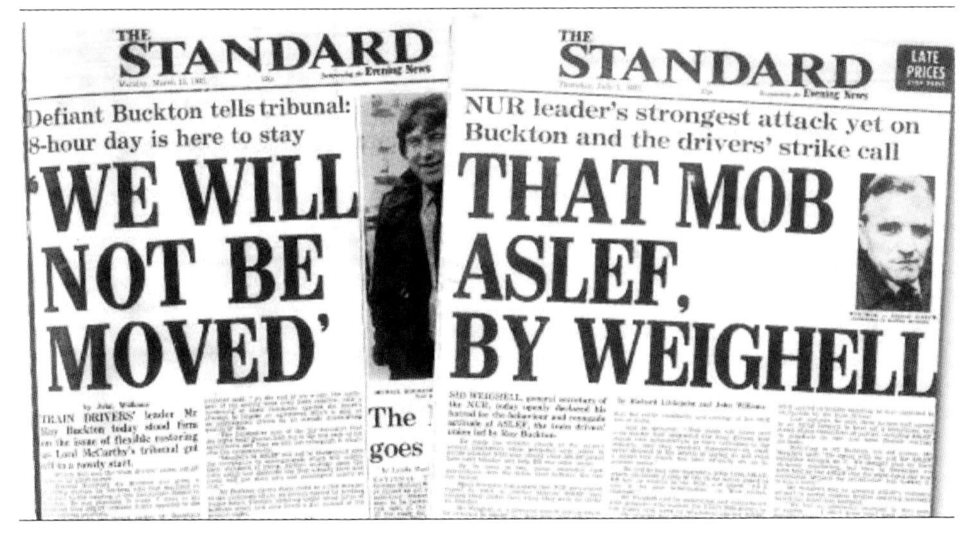
THE STANDARD

Defiant Buckton tells tribunal: 8-hour day is here to stay

'WE WILL NOT BE MOVED'

THE STANDARD

LATE PRICES

NUR leader's strongest attack yet on Buckton and the drivers' strike call

THAT MOB ASLEF, BY WEIGHELL

Press reports from the London Evening Standard during the dispute. (Author's collection)

down to earth when my Dad and I returned home to face my Mother who was working part-time and finally snapped saying, "Why don't you two get back to work?" I am sure many men faced similar pressures, however I was young and angry so I ignored the outburst.

Within a matter of days my Mother's wish was granted. We were advised by our executive and the TUC to return to work and face the imposition of the flexible rostering agreement. The Union and its members were given an ultimatum by the British Railways Board who, no doubt, had been instructed by the Thatcher government. If we did not return to work by a deadline, then we would be deemed as sacked. Looking back there is no doubt that this was the beginning of the Thatcher government's policy to break the power of the unions and we were amongst the first to crack. Later it would be the turn of the miners and the infamous dispute of 1984/5.

I have nothing but admiration for the miners and their families who went on strike for a full year. I know ASLEF and its members proved to be a big help in providing financial and charitable support as well as industrial assistance wherever possible. One driver at Norwich was chastised by his colleagues for moving some coal wagons in the yard. The purpose of moving the wagons was to prevent the wheel bearings from seizing up. That was the first time the wagons were moved for a full year. It was only when the strike came to an end did the wagons leave the goods yard.

Some years later when I was on the Executive I recall one of my colleagues telling a story about himself and a fellow ASLEF activist. Both travelled up to one of the pits that his branch had adopted with a van load of donated supplies. They had intended to travel back on the same day but the miners were so grateful that they were taken to the local working men's club where they spent too many hours and got to the point where travelling home was impossible. My colleague did the right thing and rang his wife to tell her he would not be home. It was only when she replied, "Well you haven't been home for the past fifteen years!" did he realise he had actually rung his ex-wife!

I think it was the bitterness and the sense of injustice I felt after the '82 strike that, as a young man, stirred something in me. Not long after, the Norwich branch of ASLEF passed a resolution that basically told the Union not to call us out on strike again. 'We should invite our EC member to the next branch meeting' somebody stated after the resolution was carried by a majority. "I think you've already done that by passing that resolution," the Chairman replied ironically!

I began to attend branch meetings more frequently. These were held at the railway club on Thorpe Road and I could listen to the reports from local reps and hear the correspondence which would be sent to the Secretary from ASLEF head office.

A notice went up at the depot advertising the attendance of a guest speaker at the monthly meeting, one Lew Adams. I had no clue who Lew was and not much idea about how the union worked or its structure. As I was on a rest day I decided to pay the meeting a visit. It was also a chance to have a few cheap beers as the railway club was renowned for offering cheaper booze than most of the pubs around the city.

Today there are very few railway clubs, in the main due to the implementation of the BRB drugs and alcohol policy which had a zero tolerance to employees being under the influence while at work. Prior to its implementation it was not unusual for a crew to pop into a railway club for a couple of beers while in between trains. Generally a blind eye was turned to such practices as most rail staff would have no more than a couple. However there was always the odd exception to the rule.

I made my way to the club expecting it to be standing room only given our Executive Committee member would be addressing the branch. I was a bit taken aback when I arrived to see that there were no more than about fifteen colleagues at the meeting which included the top table consisting of the Chairman, John Pipe, Secretary, Harry Phillips, and the Vice Chair, John Martin, as well as Lew. Over the years I came to accept that a packed branch meeting room was not always a good thing as it generally meant there was trouble. When I eventually rose to the position of EC member it was not unusual to attend a meeting with five or six members. I never complained even if I had travelled a long distance as I knew much of the information I shared would be passed on.

Nevertheless I watched and listened to the proceedings and when it came for Lew to speak I was all ears. My overriding memory of his speech was his passion, oratory skills and his demeanour. He cut a striking figure with his debonaire looks in a dark suit with the ASLEF tie, and that smooth accent that owned the room. I was won over and totally impressed. Lew finished his address and the Chair asked if there were any questions. I had several but I was far too shy to put my hand up.

Although there were fewer men at the meeting than I had expected it was when I returned to work the next day that I was surprised by the number of colleagues asking, 'what happened at the branch last night?' to which my immediate reaction was, 'I made the effort to go, why didn't you? You would've heard it from the horse's mouth.' I have no doubt, even with the days of Zoom and Teams meetings the same question is asked by members even though they don't have to set foot outside their front door to attend a meeting!!

The seed had been sown, I was an angry young man and wanted to change the world. However world domination would have to wait for the time being.

It was not too long before I was noticed by the Branch Secretary as one of the younger members of the ASLEF fraternity who had taken an interest in matters relating to the union and relations with the employer. At some point Harry approached me and asked if I would like to attend a weekend school run by the union at Cambridge. I responded positively, and Harry advised me he would "Make the arrangements", whatever that meant. I had no idea what went on at these weekend schools but I speculated that it was just as it said... a school where we would learn about various aspects of the union. I was somewhat surprised when Harry said that he would be going and bringing his wife Thelma along with him.

We caught the train across to Cambridge on a rather dull and foggy Saturday afternoon. Once we had arrived we made our way to New Hall College where we were allocated rooms and told to meet in the canteen for lunch and drinks. I made my way up to the canteen and was struck by the amount of older ASLEF members who were there. None of those I knew at all. I felt a bit intimidated by the noise and was still at this time rather shy with people who I did not know, so I was somewhat out of my comfort zone.

Harry soon appeared and began to introduce me to several people including one Tony West who was the newly elected District Secretary for our area. My first impression of him as I shook his hand was that if he squeezed it much harder I would never be able to use it again. Tony, like Lew, had presence, with his suave mannerism in his dark suit and ASLEF tie, he too made a lasting impression upon me. I did not know it at the time, but both Lew and Tony had been at Stratford depot together as well as being local reps at the same time. They were as thick as thieves you could say.

Harry also introduced me to a manager whose name I cannot recall. I believe he would have been a high ranking Regional Director or something like that. All I can remember is Harry stating that, “It won’t be too long before he’s (me) a thorn in your side!” Which I think was a compliment.

Soon it was time to begin the school and we were all ushered into a hall where the chairs were laid out in rows, not quite what I was expecting for a school. There was a stage with a top table. This looked very much to me more like a large scale branch meeting. Tony began by making opening introductions and then the Regional Director made a presentation but my overriding memory is of the question and answer session afterwards.

After a couple of questions, Tony pointed at me. Surely not. I had definitely not raised my hand to speak. I felt myself redden and then there was what I can only describe as an explosion of anger and shouting from the member sitting behind me. Indeed, Tony had not pointed at me, he had actually pointed at the chap sitting behind me whom I later discovered was the infamous Martin Samways from Doncaster.

My God, did he get stuck into the Regional Director. I was to come across Martin on many occasions in the future. He was ably assisted and supported, in equal volume, by a young Mick Rix of Leeds who started where Martin left off: again we would work together in years to come. Both put the Regional Director on the rack and I noticed that he had started to colour up after the twin assault from Doncaster and Leeds respectively. Both men exuded passion, anger and knowledge about the subjects they were attacking the manager on. Initially I was shocked by their outburst. It was never the way in which I portrayed myself, and if I did ‘set sail’ people generally knew it was not for show. In the coming years, both Martin and Mick would hold two of the most privileged and high offices within ASLEF.

As with so many of these things there is a social side to the weekend and this was no exception. I remember spending a few very pleasant hours at the Cambridge railway club where I met other members of the union from within the district along with the likes of Terry Wilson from Ipswich and Denis Cadywould with whom I would work closely in later years.

It was back to the college for a Sunday morning session and when it came to questions I braced myself. However I had made sure that I was sitting a bit further away form Martin and Mick. Not that I didn’t agree with what they had to say, it was just that I wanted to make sure I didn’t get deafened again! I need not have worried. When Martin did get up to speak, I think he may have had a hangover, as his comments were somewhat more subdued compared with the previous day.

I had made some new acquaintances. Admittedly I had not got over my shyness, so while I knew them they may not have remembered me. More importantly the fire had been stoked just a little bit more.

When we arrived back at Norwich Harry told me that I needed to submit a secondman's pay ticket so that I would get paid for both days. How the hell he swung that I will never know as I had assumed I had to take lieu leave for both days.

As the months went by I slowly became more involved with the activities of the union. At the annual general meeting I was elected onto the Branch Committee and took a closer interest in what was occurring at the depot. It was not long before one of my mates, Steve McLean, successfully put himself forward and got elected on to the LDC or as it jokingly became known, the lieu day club. Steve's success was a grand achievement in itself as the LDC's at most depots were dominated by the older drivers.

While I had begun to have aspirations for making progress onto the LDC my ambitions would have to be put on hold for a while as driver training was to be my top priority for the next twelve months.

Chapter 18 - Rules and Regulations (MP12)

NORWICH WAS TYPICAL of most depots when it came to recruitment and progressing through the grades. In the main, recruitment onto the footplate was via internal applications from grades such as signal box and messenger boys, or station staff who would apply to become secondmen. Once seniority allowed, they would be sent for driver training or MP12 as it was known. Myself and my four colleagues who joined the railway straight from the street were an exception to the rule. I am led to believe this did cause some resentment from some of those at Norwich who would have liked to progress to the footplate but were, in their view, overlooked.

Soon I would embark on a course that lasted a minimum of six months which would, if all the exams were passed, lead to me being passed out as an acting driver.

The age profile of the drivers at Norwich was very high and there were acting drivers who were still in their early sixties with little chance of them actually progressing to driver. All progression was based strictly on seniority. Many of the younger secondmen could not see more than a short while ahead, and felt that it would be many years before they would actually make the grade. Some decided to relocate to other depots, and several Norwich men transferred to the likes of Ipswich, Stratford and even depots on the Southern Region to get their driver's check.

It was something that I did consider. I even had the application form in my hand, but my father persuaded me not to make the application as he reminded me that many of the drivers were like him, in their early to mid sixties and would be retiring within the next five to ten years. I gave the matter a lot of thought and looked at those colleagues who were travelling to London every day. They had to travel two hours each way, then do a full days work which could amount to a fourteen to sixteen hour day. I tore up the application form.

I was chatting to Colin Fisk in the messroom one morning. Both of us were getting close to our driver training courses but were frustrated at the prospect of having to wait several more years before attaining the grade of driver. Colin then commented, "Well, a lot of these drivers are getting old now. Hopefully we'll have a harsh winter which could see a couple of them croak. That'll get us a bit closer to getting our driver's jobs." He actually made this statement with a straight face.

Many drivers look back on their MP12 course with some affection. If you were at a large depot there was most likely a training school. Generally you would turn up at your depot at 9am and would not have to work the awful shifts scattered around the 24 hours of the day, unless you were booked to work the occasional Sunday.

I was the senior untrained secondman and I was looking forward to the moment when I could achieve the goals I had set myself. I estimated that the course which was running at Norwich would finish towards the end of 1986, then I would be allocated a position on the next available one.

In the meantime I had decided to book a holiday to Malta with two other colleagues, Ian Johnson and Tim Bannon, which was arranged and paid for. We were going in June/July of that year, so I was somewhat surprised when I received a letter from the Area Driver Manager advising me that I had been allocated a position on a course at March in Cambridgeshire which was to start within the next few weeks.

I remember my initial reaction was that it was a pain in the backside to get to March each day and of course it would clash with my already booked and paid for holiday. I contacted Mr. Duggan and explained the situation: however he informed me that my holiday would have to be put on hold as I could not miss two week's training. I politely declined the offer and asked if I could be on the next course at Norwich. This meant that poor old Steve McLean was placed on the course. I don't think that bothered Steve at all as it meant he would achieve his ambition of becoming an acting driver sooner than he anticipated. So Steve went on the course, I went to Malta. It could be described as a win, win situation!

After returning to the UK from a great holiday with my two partners in crime, I was soon to receive a bit of a shock. I received a letter instructing me to report to Ilford driver training school to commence my course. Ilford.... this certainly was not what I had been banking on, I had hoped for six months of regular day shifts on average earnings at Norwich. (Average earnings were paid so staff did not lose out financially whilst being on training courses.) I was somewhat put out by this news and rather apprehensive not really knowing what to expect. It was also going to involve a great deal of travelling. I was used to a day's work being London and back, not London, a day's work in the training school and then travelling back.

To make matters worse the journey time between Norwich and London had been significantly increased due to the overhead electrification construction programme which was in full swing between Norwich and Colchester. For some reason it had been decided that a diesel locomotive would haul the London train from Norwich to Ipswich where it would be detached and swapped for an electric locomotive to then make the onward journey to London. Clearly, any gains the electric locomotive made were lost in the time it took to swap at Ipswich. Furthermore the journey was at least two hours to London with a further trip back out to Ilford along with a fifteen minute walk from the station to the training school.

My only solace was that I would be working a minimum thirteen hour day which would certainly boost my earnings at that time. Not being a money monster this was of small comfort. However there was also the plus that this was the next stage of my career progression to the position I had wanted ever since I was a young lad.

The day came when I would travel to London for the first day of the course and would also meet the other secondmen with whom I would spend the next six months. Ilford training school is no longer there. It was bulldozed some years ago to make way for a state of the art Tunnelling Training Academy for the Euro Tunnel and other projects such as HS1 and Crossrail. I had passed the school many times and had even spent a few days there on my boiler training course. It was also a dormitory for railmen who worked in the London area and crews from places such as Newcastle who were on lodging turns. Several of my colleagues at Norwich had worked at the London depots such as Stratford and King's Cross and used the dormitory or 'hostel' as many railmen who stayed referred to it.

The hostel was at the front of the building which was built in the late 1950s. You

Ilford training school and hostel. (Author's collection)

walked through the middle of the dorms and along a corridor which opened out into a seating area where there was a canteen with classrooms leading off. The hostel was closed in the early eighties due to a failure to meet fire regulations. Those whom I have spoken to who stayed there had many happy memories although one or two said the food could be a bit rough at times, one colleague citing sheeps' hearts as being on the menu. Others recalled that they would even be provided with a packed lunch each day they were on duty.

Fortunately I was not to be alone in my daily journey to Ilford and back as another lad from Norwich had been allocated to the course. Graham had transferred to Norwich from Scotland and was the next senior man to go forward after me.

It really was just like going back to school in some respects. However there was a distinctly laid back attitude, something akin to the messrooms we all used at our various depots. Lads would be smoking, reading the paper, chatting or playing cards. There were no mobile phones or iPads to distract people.

On that first day Graham and I sat in the canteen area along with several others. Eventually a group of us were called up and we were allocated our classroom. I remember walking in and bagging a desk towards the front next to the window which had a radiator under it. 'Excellent,' I thought to myself. 'When it gets cold I shall be able to keep nice and warm.' It was a classroom just like any other, twelve desks with a large desk at the front facing the students with a huge blackboard behind. There were also various bits and bobs laying around: later, I found out what they were.

The first five weeks of the course concentrated on rules and regulations, then a nine week basic traction course based on the Class 47 locomotive. This was followed by a three week theory of route learning course. I felt this was pretty pointless as most of us knew the routes we worked over like the back of our hand. Finally, ten weeks brake handling where we would put our rules and traction training into practice.

Our instructor was an absolutely lovely gentleman by the name of Bert Pell who lived and breathed rules and regulations as we were soon to find out. He was a stocky chap with dark swept back hair, a real Brylcreem boy, with dark skin and eyes that bulged slightly. He would also change into a dark blue overall smock that he wore all the time when teaching.

There was a distinct nervousness in the room apart from one individual with whom I would strike up a good friendship. He seemed quite confident and also gave the impression he already knew his way around the course. Neil, who was from Parkeston depot, was a large lad with a confident swagger and a mullet hairstyle which was very popular in the mid to late 1980s. He had a distinct Parkeston accent which was a cross between Suffolk and North Essex, you really have to hear it as I couldn't possibly describe it! It turned out that Neil had been on a course previously but suffered a severe leg break while playing American football. As he had fallen behind on his original course, it was decided he should start over again.

There was myself and Graham from Norwich, Neil from Parkeston, several guys from King's Cross including Colin and Colin (yes two Colins - not the same person twice) along with Phil, Steve from Ilford, then there was 'Smiffy' from Southend, Roy from Shoeburyness, Andy from Barking, Bob from Ipswich and Paul from Hitchin. For some strange reason Smiffy kept referring to Hitchin men as 'Bacon Gobblers', I have absolutely no clue as to why!

We were advised that lunchtime visits to the pub were unacceptable. However Smiffy and one other member of the class would slip away at lunchtime to a hostelry where they would partake in the activities that generally goes on in pubs.

Smiffy was never quiet or shy in coming forward, and this was certainly the case as I walked with him and Roy from the training school to the station to catch our respective trains home. It was a Friday lunchtime and we always knocked off early for some reason. As we walked along the road the traffic was snarled up and travelling at a snail's pace. Soon we caught up a hearse that had clearly just been to a funeral as Forest Gate cemetery was close by. There were two funeral directors sitting in the front seats and Smiffy commented, "Ere Roy, jump in the back and get a lift!" What Smiffy hadn't bargained for was the fact that the passenger side window was open. The funeral director in the passenger seat turned and gave Smiffy a cold, hard, thousand yard stare. As the car moved along keeping up with our walking pace he dourly retorted in a very slow, gruff voice.... "We'll get ya one day lads."

That was way back in 1987. Unfortunately his prediction came true in 2021 when sadly Smiffy succumbed to cancer after a distinguished career on the railway. After moving from Southend he spent many years at Colchester depot. He was a true character and I would bump into him from time to time, be it while I was on the executive of ASLEF or up in the messroom at Colchester when on the Thunderbird standby locomotive. RIP.

As the weeks passed we got into our routine of catching an early train up to London, into the classroom, taking in all the rules, tea break, lunch break, afternoon tea break and then home. We would leave Norwich in the dark and return in the dark and it was only at weekends that I would see my home in daylight.

One of the great things about MP12 was that you got every weekend off which, for an unattached lad of my age was great. I was able to catch up with either my fellow secondmen, or my mates outside of the railway. The long hours meant I was earning great money so I would be out as often as possible, and on many occasions I would stagger home in the wee hours of the morning after fully immersing myself in whatever beverage I happened to be keen on at the time.

Being part of the railway family meant that even if you had not made arrangements to meet up on a Friday or Saturday night, all you had to do was turn up. You were guaranteed to bump into someone from work in the George and Dragon pub on the Haymarket in Norwich city centre and a good night on the lash would follow. A tour of the pubs would generally be followed by a visit to Zaks, a large caravan situated on the edge of the old cattle market in the shadows of Norwich's historic Norman castle that even today dominates the city's skyline. The burgers they served up were legendary. If it wasn't Zaks then it would be off to one of the numerous nightclubs in the city.

It was on one of these nights out that a crowd of us were making our way down to the Tudor Hall, a nightclub situated at the bottom of a hill that led off the old cattle market. I guess there must have been about eight or nine of us on that night and as we made our way down the hill we passed a group of about twenty lads who were going in the opposite direction towards the Woolpack pub. As we passed each other there was some banter and piss taking but nothing that any of us considered serious. As both groups parted from each other, one of the louder, more cocky members of our crowd turned around, opened his arms wide, and shouted at the top of his voice, "Come on you twats...!!" There was a slight pause then they all turned around to face us. The instigator of this was off like a rat up a drainpipe along with most of us. Unfortunately I slipped over and fell and narrowly missed getting kicked in the head. One lad received a smack in the nose and a fat lip while the rest were about two hundred yards down the road shouting abuse at our attackers, whom one of us had foolishly provoked for absolutely no reason at all.

The altercation was over in seconds. Poor old Mark was bleeding from his nose and lip, I had grazes and a ripped shirt. The instigator, whom we thanked profusely for being such a gob-shite, was untouched. Mark made his way home to clean up and the rest of us carried on to the club,

For the duration of the course footplate work was almost non-existent apart from the odd Sunday turns. But I would often have to be booked off with pay if the Sunday turn was late so that I could have the right amount of hours off duty before coming back to work on Monday morning.

The daily routine continued for five weeks and the extended hours along with lively weekends took their toll on me so I was always glad when we could take a break from the classroom and have a chat about all those things young men do. The majority of us who were on the various courses (there were several going at one time all at various different stages) were all in our early to mid twenties and single.

Each day we would leave the classroom and queue up at the canteen for a cup of tea and a biscuit or whatever was on sale. The canteen was staffed singlehanded by the infamous Beryl, a lady of Caribbean descent with a thick accent which she would raise to a shrill level when someone produced their own mug that did not meet her personal standard of hygiene. "You need to wash dat mug out or else yu'll get de diareerer," were the immortal words that would embarrass the offender. There was also an occasion when Bob ordered a Cornish pastie which Beryl expertly zapped in the microwave only for him to cut into it to find it was frozen in the middle. On another occasion the shutter was down when we went for tea. Eventually a more senior Clacton driver rattled the shutters and politely asked if she was going to open ..... there was no reply and we all went without.

It was during one particular lunch break that I witnessed an incident that put me off playing cards for some considerable time. I was accustomed to playing for a few pennies so any losses were minimal. However on this particular day the loss incurred by one individual was what I considered to be very large.

After lunch, and with half an hour or so to spare before resuming our class I looked around and noticed a group of my colleagues huddled around one of the tables in the corner of the seating area. Being somewhat inquisitive I sidled over to take a look and see what was occurring. A brag school was reaching its climax. There was a considerable amount of cash in the pot for whoever was to claim victory. Each player was sure his hand was the one that was going to take the pot and every time the player put something like ten pounds in the pot he would say, "£10 in and I'm doing you a favour... call up." The other participant would retort with the same comment until they reached the point where both men had put what was equal to a week's wages in the middle.

The lad from Stratford turned up a cracking prial of three cards. He was confident that he would win the pot which must have been somewhere near £300. It was then the turn of Andy. He slowly turned his three cards up and revealed a pile of threes which in the game of brag is unbeatable. I watched the colour drain out of the loser's face as Andy scooped up the winnings. It was indeed a life lesson for me, never to get embroiled in high stakes card games.

It was also during these breaks that Smiffy developed a knack of clandestinely vandalising people's mugs. Most of us would use the small green cups that the school provided, but several colleagues would bring their own larger mugs (hence Beryl's hygiene campaign) so that they could have more tea. Many mugs were personalised, displaying a football team or a smart-arse comment on the side.

When the victim was not looking, Smiffy would casually sidle up to where the individual was sitting: maybe they were concentrating on a card game or reading the paper. He would get out what was known as a T-key (*see photo on the left*) and whack the handle of the mug with the pointed end of the key. In most cases this led to the handle falling off the without the victim suspecting anything was wrong until they came to grab hold of their mug which had been rendered handle-less!

All operational staff were issued with T-keys. They would unlock a whole range of things but predominately carriage doors and the electric train supply on coaches.

Smiffy thought his prank was a tremendous laugh which I guess at first it was. Neil and I were sitting in the canteen chatting one tea break when there was a familiar chink as another victim fell pray to Smiffy's prank followed by his distinctive chortle. "If he does that to my mug," Neil said... "I'll bloody kill him," and that was how we left it. It was only a matter of time before Smiffy, with fewer and fewer mugs to pick on, spotted Neil's. Not being party to his earlier comments Smiffy went in for the kill. He instantly regretted it!

Even though many of us attending the course were easy going and genial there were odd occasions when unpleasantness would arise. This was 1986 and more than four years after the infamous 1982 flexible rostering dispute but, in the case of one particular lad, the label of 'scab' still remained to the extent that all his so-called workmates referred to him as 'Scab' rather than his surname. I naively asked one of the guys on another course why they kept calling him this so brazenly and I just got, "He was an '82 scab at Stratford... once a scab always a scab, you can't wash it off you know." I'm pretty sure that if that sort of language was used today then the perpetrators would be severely dealt with. At that time, nothing was done.

Bert Pell lived and breathed rules and regulations and it was very difficult to trip him up. However, occasionally someone would ask a question that would leave him flummoxed for a few seconds with a kind of vacant look on his face and he would then state, "Phwaoorr .... you got me there!"

Each day we would trawl through the rule book along with its various appendixes dealing with matters such as signalling, working of trains, freight loads, speed restrictions, engineering work and single line working. Single line working was one of the more risky practices. It was something that drivers would encounter rarely so it was vital we knew the correct instructions and regulations which were drummed into us on a regular basis as there was a higher risk of collisions or what are known as a conflicting moves.

Bert would take us though each subject step by step in a methodical and easy to understand way. Neil commented to me at one break, "Uncle Ken hasn't been in as yet, you can guarantee he will pay us a visit and when he does, no matter what subject we were dealing with, he will start going on about the automatic warning system*." I thought this was just one of Neil's tall stories and didn't think anymore of it until one afternoon the classroom door swung open and in breezed Ken, the head of the training school.

Ken was a man in his mid to late fifties, in a very smart dark suit and a waistcoat with a chain hanging from it. He was grey and balding and had 'half-moon' glasses over which he would peer when addressing people. "Ah Bert, these your new boys?" asked Ken, knowing full well we were the latest bunch to grace his training school. "Yes Ken," Bert replied. "And what are you doing today?" was Ken's follow up question. "Section 'H' working of trains Ken".... "Ah excellent.... let me tell you all about the AWS system!" exclaimed Ken with a glint in his eye.

I wanted to burst into laughter but managed to keep a lid on things as he took us through the workings of the AWS system. How the track mounted magnets worked against the magnet fitted under the traction unit, how the system should be used and what to do if it failed. All very interesting.... but of no use to us as we were not that far advanced in the course and a total and utter distraction from what we were doing at the time. Obviously Bert was far too polite to interject.

Once Ken had finished blinding us with his wisdom he turned on his heels and swept out of the classroom.

From time to time Ken would pay the occasional visit or stop and chat to us while we were having a tea break or lunch. If he did come into the classroom he would generally impart some words of wisdom or share some anecdote that for some strange reason always involved Norwich men making a balls of things. Quite why he had it in for us Norwich men I never really knew.

**The AWS - Automatic Warning System is track equipment mounted at signals which will sound an audible warning in the driving cab. The driver has two seconds to react via a button on the driving desk. A bell sounds if the signal is green (no action required), a horn sounds (action required) if the signal is at caution or danger, and at temporary speed restrictions. Failure to react will result in the train being automatically brought to a stand.*

He recalled a tale about a warning horn that suddenly started sounding on a Class 47 in Liverpool Street station. The fitters attended and could not make out what was causing the fault. Later it came to light that the Norwich secondman had been putting toffee wrappers down the gaps where the horn handle was, thus creating a blockage that led to the horn jamming.

Ken would also generally advise us that is was best to knuckle down and pass the exams first time around as things generally got harder on the second and third attempts, and if we failed on the third try then we would be out of a job. "You Norwich boys have plenty of time on the journey to and from London to revise, so you should pass first time," were the words that were ringing in my ears when we faced the Regional Traction Inspector on our exam some five months later.

Neil later told me about a Parkeston driver who was sitting in the cab of a Class 47 locomotive in the platform at Peterborough waiting to be given right away to work the Manchester boat train to Harwich. All of a sudden the cab door burst open, a man (Ken) in a suit climbed into the cab without saying a word, planted his briefcase down on the cab floor and cleared off into the engine room. A few moments later he returned to the driving cab and seeing that his case had disappeared he asked the driver, "Where's my briefcase?" The driver curtly replied, "On the platform.... where you're now going .... now sod off!" And that was the end of that!

Chapter 19 - The Beloved Class 47 Locomotive

FIVE WEEKS OF rules and regulations had almost come to an end and it was our last few days with Bert. He introduced us to our instructor who would tutor us on basic traction, a chap by the name of Peter Martin who Bert commented was an excellent instructor. The school was then to close as it was Christmas so we were released back to our depots until it re-opened in the new year.

I have never been a particularly mechanically minded person so although I was looking forward to the next stage of the course, it was with some apprehension. Again we began the new year after a couple of weeks of being back in the roster and doing some actual footplate work which came as a bit of a change with shorter days and more time at home.

What I did not bargain for was the amount of colouring in we would have to do. Yes that's right, there we were a group of grown men being issued with coloured pencils and diagrams on the cooling, oil, fuel and air systems and told to colour them in.

As each of the nine weeks passed, we would be given detailed instruction on the various systems that were installed on the Class 47 locomotive. We also learned the location of equipment right through to the principles of basic electricity which, to this day, I have never managed to get to grips with. Don't ask me to explain back electric motive force!!

For me, and I think the rest of the lads on the course, the best parts of the nine weeks traction training were when we actually got to mess about with the Class 47s at Stratford depot. Rather than remain in the classroom we would locate to a Portakabin on the far reaches of the massive Stratford depot which, incidentally, is now where the Olympic Park stands. We would turn up a bit later in the day and would be gone earlier as there were no prying eyes checking us in respect of time keeping and we were, as most railmen, happy to work through our break so that we could get away a bit earlier.

It was while we were at Stratford that we were introduced to the delights of the greasy spoon cafe close to the freight terminal where many of the lorry drivers would pop in for a fried breakfast. It was not the most hygienic establishment and made the canteen at Ilford look like a Michelin star restaurant. I'll never forget a notice on the wall of the cafe stating 'PLEASE DO NOT THROW FAG ENDS ON THE FLOOR.... THE COCKROACHES ARE GETTING CANCER!" Things got even worse if you needed to pay a visit to the toilet block close by with graffiti on the wall of one cubicle that stated 'PLEASE FLUSH THE TOILET.... THE FITTERS WILL EAT ANYTHING'.

After we had dined at the cafe it would be down to the day's work which usually involved locating various items of equipment on the locomotive, looking at the systems, isolating cocks, learning how they functioned, what to do, and what not to do which was followed by fault diagnosis. These days really helped put the theory into practice.

We had only been a few days into the first part of the basic traction module of the course when the south east of England was hit by a very cold spell with over 50 centimetres of snow falling, coupled with high winds where deep snow drifts were commonplace. The whole of Norfolk was effectively cut off from the rest of the UK and our first attempt to get to Ilford on the Monday morning was utterly futile.

I had actually been at work on the Sunday and should have finished in time to get my 'hours off' for the next day. Due to the heavy snow I was deployed on a Class 31 locomotive to operate the boiler which provided steam for two inspectors who were using a 'steam lance' to clear snow out of the point work around Norwich station so trains could run. As soon as one set of points were cleared we would move forward to clear the next set only to find the ones we had just cleared were snowed up minutes later. This proved to be a futile exercise and I recall having to stand by the cab door in the rear of the locomotive to look out for the signal to apply steam pressure and when to shut off. I was soaked and frozen and it was quite sometime before I was relieved by a colleague.

Eventually I was able to make my way home. Given the hour and the weather conditions I decided to walk which took about two hours due to the snow drifts. I found myself struggling through snow drifts that had buried abandoned cars up to their roofs.

Each morning we would arrive at the loco messroom to sign on and were told there were no trains to London. One of us would then ring the training school to advise that we would not be in until things cleared up. By the Wednesday we were told that training had been cancelled for the week and we were to sign on at our home depots and await instructions.

By this time, not only had Graham and I been travelling from Norwich, but two other lads from the depot—Paul and Steve— had joined us. They had failed their exams and were on their second course. This meant that we travelled together and would play cards and chat; revision was not even considered!

Once Friday came we were all pretty fed up with turning up for duty at 8am, then hanging around until we were eventually allowed to go home. Friday was always known as POETS day so we unilaterally decided to 'piss off early tomorrow's Saturday'. We jumped in Graham's car and made our way to a pub that was a suitable distance from the depot. It was 11am and it had just opened. I think the landlord was somewhat taken aback when we walked in as he hadn't been particularly busy all week. We proceeded to have a few beers and then after a couple of hours decided to make our way home so we all went our separate ways.

Paul's house was on my way home so we trudged through the snow and sludge chatting as we went. When we arrived at his place he asked me if I wanted to come in. He had recently acquired some rather tasty hifi equipment so I accepted. He put a few discs on the turntable, a Linn for those in the know, and then broke out a bottle of whisky. After an hour or so I made my excuses. I had recently got a puppy and needed to get back to take her for a walk before it got dark.

I trudged along from Paul's to my parents' home, which was about a twenty minute walk, then I began to giggle. I just couldn't stop: clearly the mixture of lager and whisky was taking effect. I arrived home and announced to my horrified mother that "I'm pissed!" and was then given a severe dressing down about coming home in such a state at this time of the day.... as if any other time of day would have been ok. I also received a lecture as to why I should have been home earlier as the dog needed walking and I had responsibilities to her now, all of which went in one ear and out the other.

So, still smiling to myself I uttered the magic words to the dog, "Come on... walkies", and off we went into the cold late January afternoon. The snow was still thick in many places and Rosie was still full of fun and excitement. Being only six months old and she was keen to explore this white wonderland that had appeared a few days earlier. As for me, being a bit unsteady on my feet and having a strong young golden retriever pulling me along, it was only a matter of time before I fell face first into the snow..... and then repeated the process four more times!

We went for a long walk over to the fields and I was hoping that maybe we could stop off at the local pub for a warm up. This was before the days of all day drinking, unfortunately the Blue Boar was closed as we passed it, as if I hadn't had enough! Rosie was soon to become a regular as my mother would testify some months later. She was walking the dog one morning only to have her arm almost wrenched out of its socket as Rosie made a beeline for the public bar entrance... as far as I am aware, dogs have no grasp of UK licensing laws.

The following week we were able to get to Ilford for the resumption of the course which involved talking about all the various parts and systems of the Class 47. One of the best pieces of advice we were given was 'Clear the driving desk first.' Simply,

Class 47 No. 47460 with the unofficial name Great Eastern is seen at Norwich at the head of a London service in 1980. (Alistair Barham)

this meant that it maybe something you had done or forgotten to do that had led to a problem. If there was no power it maybe that the main reservoir had not built up enough air pressure to allow the brakes to work. It was this advice that kept me out of trouble on several occasions.

Many of the instructors had their own methods of teaching. They would try and simplify things for us, but there were times that I found their efforts just confused matters. In one particular compartment on the Class 47 there was a row of electro pneumatic valves which resembled Guinness bottles, so rather than call them EP valves, they were called Guinness bottles! There was also a piece of equipment known as the TMV7 or the Starship Enterprise, a reference to Star Trek. In my view it looked nothing like it at all and was of no use to us. The only thing I recall being told was, "If the EP valves stick... given 'em a clout with your lamp".

We would be constantly quizzed as to what various faults looked like and how to put them right, or what constituted a complete failure and what do in its event. Smiffy had a default answer to any question that had him stumped. "Whar..... DFR innit". The DFR being a diode fault relay which was a little green box situated down one side of the engine compartment.

One particular day Peter asked us to get back earlier from lunch break. The message did not get to Smiffy. On their return to the school, he and his colleague were passed by Peter in his car (Peter would generally go home for his lunch). Clearly they were concerned that they were going to be missing from the classroom so they ran as fast as they could to be in the classroom before Peter got back. We were all seated as Smiffy's accomplice snuck into the classroom so as not to draw attention to himself.

Shortly after Peter entered and taking stock, noticed that Smiffy was missing. Just as he opened his mouth, obviously about to enquire as to his lack of presence the door burst open and Smiffy staggered in. He was out of breath and sweating, although not so out of breath as to broadcast .... "Well I've seen blokes run to a pub... but never run away from a pub!" You could hear a pin drop as there was a collective sharp intake of breath and Smiffy's accomplice, who sat directly behind me, just put his head in his hands. Fortunately for Smiffy, Peter said nothing but just gave him a frosty look .

The nine weeks course soon passed and it was pretty much the last time the group of the twelve of us would be together. I recall sitting in the classroom back at Ilford one afternoon on the last week of the course during a lull. We sat at the far end of the room where there was another blackboard and various cartoons of class members and instructors were being drawn by Andy, who had a talent for that sort of thing.

Bob offered those of us that smoked a fag. We all took one and lit up. A few moments went by and then there was a bang and Graham sat there with the frayed ends of his fag which had just exploded. He looked like something out of a slapstick film with the fag smouldering and its tip bent. Bob had slyly put a joke explosive in one of the fags but wasn't sure who the victim would be... we were all in fits of laughter when our instructor walked in who clearly did not get the joke. We were then told we were free to go.

Chapter 20 - Brake Handling

WE WERE SPLIT up into various groups for the third part of the course which was known as theory of route learning. To me this was a bit of a sham as most of us knew the routes we worked over like the back of our hands. Nevertheless we made our way over to King's Cross route learning school to be given our instructions. This is where we came across the infamous King's Cross instructor Dicky Dunbar whom you generally heard before you saw due to his very loud voice. I had very little to do with him apart from on the ToR course but had a headache after the first day!

Each group was given a section of line to learn and instructed to make up a drawing that could be followed by other members of the various groups. Graham and I were given a stretch of line between Cambridge and London which was a pain in the backside as it meant travelling to Cambridge before even making a start. This was not really my best part of the course but I entered into the spirit of things and made up a worksheet that could be read by all the others.

One event that did stick in my mind was when we were travelling between Great Chesterford and Whittlesford. All of a sudden we spotted the vapour trail of an aircraft travelling vertically. We were amazed and could not fathom out what the hell it was. It was only a couple of days later, when I was talking to one of the guys at my depot who had an interest in aircraft, that I found out we had seen the SR71 or Blackbird US spy plane taking off from Lakenheath. These were the most awesome looking aircraft and I was fortunate enough to see one do a flypast at the infamous USAF Mildenhall airshow sometime later. These were fantastic days out where many, many Budweisers and burgers were consumed.

During my entire time at Ilford, Ken and the instructors would drum into us how it was so important to pass the course first time. The course was structured so we spent up to six months training which would cumulate in three days of exams at the end. These were predominantly oral exams except for the practical driving on the third day. If you passed all three then you were qualified, however if you failed the rules exam, you would have to go back and do the five weeks course again and re-sit. The same applied to the basic traction module. If you got to the end after three attempts and had not passed all three modules, you could no longer progress to the driving grade. Either you left the industry or applied for some other position within British Railways.

The instructors would recall stories of how hard it was to get through on a second attempt and the pressures of facing the exams for a third time. "Fail on your first attempt and it gets harder and harder," would be their mantra. It did strike home with many of us but I think there was also a deep rooted pride in getting through at the first attempt. There were others who saw the courses as a licence to print money. Average earnings known as L215 were paid as a result of an agreement struck between the unions and the BRB that paid an average of the previous twelve week's earnings or what you earned on the day/week. Many would work as much overtime and as many Sundays as possible in the run up to a course to purposely increase their average.

There were others who just were not cut out to be drivers. One particular secondman transferred out of the footplate grade a matter of weeks before he was due to go for driver training. This was as a result of an older driver having a fatherly chat with him. The guy was a driver instructor and had an honest conversation with him. I'm not so sure this was the right decision as a secondman from Stratford was also told he would... 'never pass out while he had a hole in his arse'. He confounded everyone and passed. I remember one of our Instructors commenting, "His arse must have sealed up!"

After the three weeks of theory of routes was up it was finally back to my home depot for what I considered the easiest part of the course and probably the most enjoyable too, brake handling. This consisted of ten weeks, Monday to Friday, of travelling around the network on various trains where we were expected to put the theory we had learned into practice. Graham and I were advised that our instructor was Des, a driver at Norwich who had been passed out to take trainees on their practical handling course. Des was not a native Norwich lad, he was an Essex lad and had plenty of the chat and banter you would expect along with a good deal of self confidence. I was friendly with Des and had no issues with him being my instructor for the duration of the ten weeks but I'm not so sure Graham was over impressed.

Nevertheless Des was keen to get us out there and made sure that we got to go on a variety of routes that neither Graham or I had worked over. He took us over to Peterborough one day where we boarded an InterCity 125 for a trip into King's Cross. These trains were manned by two drivers as a result of a longstanding agreement with the union due to the high speed and the length of the round trip which was King's Cross to Newcastle and return. I recall that both drivers were helpful and informative on our journey into London and pointed out various quirks of the route. I also remember passing over Welwyn Viaduct where my uncle and aunt lived close by. I had been under the viaduct many times but never over it. I recall one of the drivers pointing out the factory in Welwyn that made the breakfast cereal 'Shreddies'.

Once we got to Liverpool Street we were on home turf and managed to jump on a Norwich bound train which was driven by Arthur Edwards. Arthur was a jovial chap and had a bit of swagger about him. He wore a nice gold watch, always had a top of the range Ford car and used to bring his sandwiches to work in a briefcase!

We soon set out from Liverpool Street for Norwich but were unable to drive as

InterCity 125 set 254031 at Helpston—just north of Peterborough—with the 09:45 Leeds to King's Cross on 10 August 1979 .
(Stephen Swingwood collection, East Anglian Railway Museum)

the new Class 86 locomotives were in operation after the completion of the electrification of the entire route. Also this was to be Arthur's second trip after being passed out as he explained to Des, the first being a non-stop record breaking speed run on the Norwich to London journey in a time never achieved before. He also wanted to get the true feel of it as this train was a stopper rather than a fast 'express' service. I could understand this as the 86s were electric locos. They were very powerful and a different beast to the diesel locos that had been on the London route ever since the shift away from steam in the 1960s.

Unfortunately once we got to Colchester the 86 lost power and Arthur was scratching his head as to what to do. He kept asking Des for his advice despite the fact that Des told him that he had not been trained on the 86s and, in Des's words he knew "sod all about them." It was because Des was an instructor that Arthur thought he should have a heightened knowledge of all traction over and above what Arthur had been taught. So after pressing the pan-up-reset button for the 50th time and wandering into the transformer compartment and looking at not a lot, Arthur declared the loco a failure.

After a while a Class 31 locomotive was brought out of the engine shed at Colchester depot by a driver and backed onto the 86. The intention was to haul the train to Norwich which consisted of the dead 86 and nine coaches. Arthur had several things to isolate including the pantograph. There was very little either Des, Graham or I could do to help. All we could do was watch as the whole episode descend into a farce as it was clear neither the assisting driver nor Arthur really knew what they were doing. It got to the point where Arthur was leaning out of the cab window of the 86 shouting and waving at the driver on the 31 who was looking out the other side of his cab. As soon as Arthur moved to the other side of his cab, so the other driver moved to the other side of his. This went on for a few minutes until thankfully Des stepped in and the 31 was hooked up to the 86.

Des, Graham and I jumped into the rear cab of the 31 and Arthur rode with the Colchester driver. The plan had been altered so the train was to travel to Ipswich where a Class 47 would attach.

The Class 31 was a far less powerful locomotive and not suited for hauling the 86 plus nine coaches. Upon leaving Colchester we crawled up the incline at a snail's pace. Once the train was over the summit and through Ardleigh we began to pick up speed. The train continued to gain speed down the hill towards Manningtree which was built on a bend and has a junction that leads onto the Harwich branch.

There is a maximum speed of 70mph rather than the 100mph due to curvature of the line and point work in Manningtree station. This seemed to be lost on the Colchester driver, who we later learned was driving. We belted through the station at about 90mph. The three of us were thrown from one side of the cab to the other. I honestly thought the train was going to topple over! Eventually we arrived at Ipswich where the 31 was detached and replaced with a 47. Arthur was looking rather ashen and Des mentioned about the excessive speed through Manningtree. "Tell me about it," said Arthur, "I told him to slow down but he wanted to make up some time!" he exclaimed. Given that we were the best part of an hour late, almost turning the train on its side to make up the odd minute did not strike any of us as the most sensible thing to attempt.

The structure of MP12 meant exams were taken at the end of the entire course, rather than taken at the end each module. We had to wait until the end of the entire course which could be almost as much as six months. This meant having to constantly revise. Things are very different these days, but at that time we just got on with it and I would spend time going through various books and employing revision methods that would hopefully help me when the time came for my tests.

The ten weeks passed pretty quickly and we got into a routine of working a variety of trains from passenger to freight. We were never refused a cab ride or not allowed to take the controls. In many cases the drivers were only too pleased to let us take over as this meant they could have an early day and clear off home. One particular week we were assigned an instructor from Ipswich as Des was on leave. He took us down to Felixstowe docks where we drove some Freightliners. I had worked some heavy trains as a secondman, either ballast or tank trains, but these were in a different league altogether. There were something like 1500 tonnes of containers and these proved to be a hell of a job to get moving. Stopping was an entirely different kettle of fish compared to passenger trains which in general weighed no more than 400 tonnes.

There were occasions when things didn't go according to plan. I was waiting for Des in the messroom one morning ready to go out on a trip somewhere. I waited and waited and then around 10am he rolled in looking somewhat dishevelled and not in his usual uniform. He signalled for me to meet him outside and asked if it was ok if we had an early day .... now. I was a bit taken aback but realised that he was clearly not fit to go out on a service train. By the smell of his breath he had been out the night before and well into the early hours of that morning. I agreed not to mention anything and we made ourselves scarce. However my Father sussed something was up when I arrived home about five hours earlier than expected and was less than impressed by this.

Chapter 21 - Exams

IT WAS SUMMER and the days of our examinations were upon us. I had done all I could but I was not confident in my abilities on locomotives and struggled with certain elements on subjects such as basic electricity. When it came to rules and regulations I was generally happy, but knew if I got questions on a couple of certain elements I may struggle. The day before the first exam I was a nervous wreck and had trouble eating and did not sleep. What hadn't helped was a phone call I had received a couple of days previously from Neil. He told me that out of nine in our class who had gone in front of an inspector only two had passed so far. Much depended on who we would get as an examiner. All those who had failed had been in front of Geoff Mansell who was renowned for being an absolute stickler. My heart sank at this news as Graham and I were to have the very same man take our examination.

We had to be on duty early that day as our rules and regulations examination was to be held at March training school. I made sure I was in my full uniform and with all the books I needed for the day just in case we were asked to present them. I also checked the late notice case and the weekly operating notices as a matter of precaution, bearing in mind it was something we should do automatically anyway.

The journey to March seemed to go really quickly. I kept looking at my books, but after six months of training I told myself if I didn't know it now I never would, so I put them away and tried to relax. Soon the train pulled into March and it was only a short walk to the training school. I remember looking at the cloudless sky with the sun shining down but somehow I felt an impending doom.

My feelings were confirmed. We were told to wait. A good while later we were led to a classroom where Mr. Mansell was sitting. Neither Graham nor I had seen him before and he was an intimidating figure behind a desk. He told us to sit down and fill in a driver's report form. There was no welcome or trying to put us at ease, in fact quite the opposite. My mind froze for a few moments as I struggled to come up with a scenario that was easy to report without making things too complicated or lead me into any difficult questions. I can't recall what I wrote about but I do remember being pulled to pieces by Mr. Mansell which just increased my state of anxiety.

As the hours went by we settled in a bit and got through various aspects of the sections of the rule book. After about six hours of questioning we came to the end of the exam and Mr Mansell summed up. I will never forget his words.... "Well as you will no doubt be aware, you've both failed." That was pretty much it, he didn't really highlight what we had got wrong although we knew we had got off to a bad start and things didn't really improve much from then on.

I had time to reflect on the day during the journey home which seemed to take for ever. I was not relishing having to face my father and tell him how badly it had gone. Soon I was home and gave my parents the bad news and followed it with a character assassination of the inspector which carried no weight with my father. I felt bad for him. I think the majority of my colleagues thought I would breeze through as they had been very encouraging and I guess I had believed them.

Day two promised to really be no better but we did had a familiar face taking us for the next two days in the shape of Allan Waites. He had taken me on my traction trainee course and was now an inspector.

I must admit I surprised myself as we went around the locomotive at Stratford. Things went really well. We nailed location, as well as faults and failures. However when it came to my question on 'back electric motive force' I stumbled, in fact I made a complete balls of it. This unnerved me as we moved on to the air system. I got asked a question about assisting a particular type of failed train with an air leak. What should I do? I gave the wrong answer. Again, I had that feeling of impending doom which was confirmed when Allan gave me a chance to answer the two questions again. I still failed to give the right answer: my mind had gone blank. Reluctantly he failed me but he was good enough to tell me exactly where I had gone wrong. He did state that I would have to go back and do the whole nine weeks basic traction course but only to cover the two points I failed to address in the exam.

We were to have Allan for the practical brake handling exam the next day and he advised us that he had spoken to Des some months back and told him he would be taking us on the 06:25 out of Norwich. This was the service that went to London via Cambridge. This was news to both Graham and I. We had only been on that train once during the ten week course and Des had never mentioned anything to us about it. To make things more tricky the train was equipped with a vacuum brake which was notoriously more difficult to use than the air brake system. The pressure had just been ramped up for the third and final day.

Again I had to face my father and explain the details of where I went wrong. I didn't expect him to give me a hard time. That was not in his nature but he did not really console me either. He could be a man of few words and this time was one of those moments. He just told me that he had always struggled with the mechanical side of the exams.

Finally we were on to day three and I was in the seat of the 06:25 to London. All went well with the pre journey checks, the brake test and checking our stops for the journey which included stations such as Wymondham and Attleborough. I recall driving through Eaton just outside Norwich and blowing the warning horn for the crossing there. It was before 7am and Allan asked why I had done that in the 'hours of darkness.' The honest answer was that I forgot, but I told him I thought I had seen something that made me want to blow the horn. He just shrugged his shoulders.

I made sure I did a running brake test in good time before our first stop at Wymondham and then approached with what I thought was a good technique. However the stop in the platform was a bit of a lump which prompted Allan to ask me how many

The view from the cab of an Up train approaching Broxbourne on the line between Cambridge and Liverpool Street. (Author's collection)

times we had been on this train on the ten week course. I answered honestly and I could tell he was not pleased. As things turned out the next few stops were text book and the rest of the day went without a hitch.

By the time we got back to Norwich he advised us we had passed the driving which was some small comfort. I did have a conversation with Allan about how badly I felt I had done in the rules which I put down to nerves. In truth I know that during the time I had to revise I had failed to address those various areas I was weak on. I would quiz myself on what I knew rather than tackle the harder elements, some would say a 'schoolboy error'. Allan was supportive and repeated his comments of the previous day that on the whole our knowledge of the Class 47 was good, I just needed to focus on the areas I had failed on. This did give me an element of confidence but I guess the biggest issue I faced was my pride. I really wanted to get through first time and get out driving and earning a bit more money.

I would just have to wait a bit longer.

Chapter 22 - Take Two

AFTER GETTING OVER my initial disappointment of failing I was eager to move on. I was pleased when I found that the course would be held at the Norwich training school with some very good mates, Tim, Gary and Colin, who had joined the footplate grade a couple of years after me.

Mike Hoban was to be our instructor for the five week rules course, and we crammed into a small classroom along with some secondmen from Ipswich one of whom was Bob. He had been on my course at Ilford and had encountered the infamous Mr. Mansell on his rules exam too! Despite the rivalry between the two depots which mainly was due to the football and the associated hatred between the opposing fans there was a great camaraderie and a sense of fun.

I had known Mike for a good while and I had been his secondman on several occasions before he became a full time instructor. We came to a stand at Brundall one day with a Class 31 and nine coaches: the locomotive was losing air pressure and the brakes had applied. We managed to locate the leak and used Mike's driver's cloth (drivers were issued a cloth every week) to wrap around the pipe to stem the leak. We were both amazed when it actually worked well enough for us to get to Great Yarmouth thus preventing the train from blocking the main line and causing further delays.

Each day was filled with the usual banter and messing around that you would expect from a close group of workmates, and the five weeks rules course passed pretty quickly.

In no time we were onto the traction course and as with my previous experience we would spend three out of the nine weeks travelling to Stratford. Our instructor, Clint, was an individual who we all knew and liked tremendously. He was the type of guy who his colleagues least expected would become an instructor. Long hair, shirt always unbuttoned, often late on duty or would not turn up at all, and he was always up to some sort of practical joke. The one he was most famous for was blocking the plughole on Budgie's motorcycle side car (a bath tub on wheels) and filling it with water. Budgie was a shunter at Great Yarmouth with a very vivid imagination. He wore a deerstalker hat and smoked a pipe with an extremely long stem. If you believed all of his reminiscences then he should have been about 120 years of age.

Clint would make learning fun. He would use colourful language and paint an alternative picture using comic phrases and stories that would generally have a racy tone to them. Furthermore, while Friday meant an early day most of the time, when we were in London it meant a cultural trip out to visit pubs in the London area. I would often arrive home later on a Friday than I did when I was travelling to Ilford on my first course.

One particular afternoon we indulged in maybe a few beers too many and eventually managed to find our way back to Liverpool Street. Once on the train, and with the evenings drawing in, we settled down with the heating on and tried to sleep off the effects of the beer before we got back to Norwich. Clint was soon snoring and leaning against the window when one individual decided to make a massive paper hat out of a copy of The Times. With a bit of amateur origami, he made a nice pointy hat for him.

In an attempt to try and sober up some of us had gone to the buffet and bought some cans of fizzy drinks. Once consumed we decided to tie them to Clint's shoe laces which actually worked quite well. After a while and feeling a little bored, one of us (not me I hasten to add) decided it would be a good idea to set light to Clint's paper hat..... as the flames slowly began to build up Clint must have become aware of the smell of smoke and awoke from his alcohol induced slumber. He was soon cursing us and patting the paper trying to extinguish the flames. Clint was never one to hold back and not only did he question our collective parentage, but used a whole repertoire of expletives to express his anger and embarrassment.

Once he calmed down he decided to go to take a pee. He got up to walk to the nearest toilet only to be accompanied by two Coke cans on each shoe. There followed a further tirade of cursing and the line, "I suppose you twats think that's bloody funny!" which of course ... we did, even the more so after having had far too much beer.

I have many very happy memories of Clint and was shocked beyond belief when I received a phone call one day in 2004 to be advised that he had collapsed and died in the back of a taxi. He was in his early forties and had lived life to the full. I know it's a common saying, but they definitely broke the mould when they made Clint Adams, one of the best. Clint was the man who introduced me to 'Strangers in the Night' by heavy rock band UFO, one of the best live rock albums ever recorded. Rock in peace Clint.

In what seemed like a very short time I was at the end of the nine weeks traction course and we were approaching Christmas. I was advised of the date of my second attempt at rules and traction which to the best of my memory was 18th December 1987. I was paired with fellow Norwich secondman Richard Long so I was very confident that I would have a competent and diligent partner in both exams. Again I was to travel to March training school for the rules exam which filled me with dread. The good news was that we were to be questioned by an inspector from York, Tim Weir, who again I had no knowledge of.

When we arrived we were asked by the 'secretary' as she described herself (I think she was the caretaker/cleaner) if we would like tea and then followed the offer up with, "I'm afraid he's in a bad mood, his work's Christmas dinner has just been cancelled...he has to hold an inquiry due to a serious incident over the weekend." My heart sank and Richard who was understandably on edge was now at a heightened state of edginess!

We waited a while and eventually were called through. Mr. Weir explained that there had been a serious incident where two trains had ended up on the same single line during engineering work at the weekend so he would have to lead the inquiry thus missing his Christmas 'do'. He asked us if this was our first attempt and both explained our position. I had the words of my Ilford instructors ringing in my ears about how much harder it was second time around.

Mr. Weir made us at ease with his soft northern accent and his gentle probing. Richard and I breezed through the questions and after what seemed like only a couple of hours we were done. I actually felt much better about my answers and perversely was beginning to enjoy the experience.

Mr. Weir gave us the good news that we had both passed, he shook hands with both of us while we tried to contain our elation, me for actually getting through and Richard for nailing it first time. I recall walking over to the station, which is not the best place to be in high summer let alone mid winter, and waited for the Birmingham to Norwich service that would take us home. Richard was over the moon and we relived certain parts of the exam as we travelled home on the train. I was just relieved but my thoughts immediately turned to the next day's examination.

The following day it was again back to Stratford for day two of two for me with Allan Waites. I had again prepared to be tested on all elements of the Class 47 but as it turned out poor old Richard got the lion's share of the questions. Allan was only interested in those elements of the exam I failed some six months previously which was in one way a relief but also a bit frustrating given the work I had put in. I had taken certain elements such as the air systems to such a level that I knew them inside out and had actually memorised the complete procedure to the point that I would draw it on the blackboard. When we broke for lunch Allan had indicated that I was pretty much done so I proceeded to draw the main air system on the board. Richard found a fault with it....thanks Richard!!

Despite that minor setback we both passed and I was now to be designated 'driver'. Only days before I had received a letter stating that I had been successfully allocated to a driving vacancy at Norwich on the December vacancy list, which is reproduced below. At the time of the letter being written I was labelled 'driver in training' which I could shed due to my success.

NAME	GRADE	SEN.DATE	PRESENT DEPOT	DEPOT OF FIRST PREFERENCE (WHERE APPLICABLE)
	DRIVERS' VACANCIES - EASTERN REGION continued			
LEEDS (D) - 24				
D. Whitehead	Relief Driver	8. 7.74	Tinsley	Tinsley 8(b)
C.D. Haddon	"	16.10.78	York	York 8(b)
D. Sherwood	"	12. 2.79	York	Exeter 8(b)
P.A. Blow	"	12. 2.79	York	York 8(b)
A.G. Priestman	"	16. 7.79	York	York 8(b)
J. Dickson	"	15.12.80	Carstairs	Motherwell 8(b)
19 vacancies cancelled				
NEWCASTLE (D) - 3				
B. Earle	Relief Driver	25. 6.79	Newcastle	-
2 vacancies filled by Clause 8(b) registrations				
NORWICH (MT) - 7				
D. Bellchamber	Relief Driver	18. 6.79	Norwich	-
P. Palgrave	Drivers Assistant	18. 6.79	Norwich	-
S. Green	Relief Driver	16. 6.80	Norwich	-
A. Taylor	"	16. 6.80	Norwich	-
G. Holmes	Drivers Assistant	16. 6.80	Norwich	-
D. Tyson	"	16. 6.80	Norwich	-
S. McLean	Relief Driver	16. 6.80	Norwich	-
SHOEBURYNESS (E) - 2				
M. Howlett	Drivers Assistant	7. 7.80	Parkeston	Parkeston 8(b)
A.J. Argent	"	3. 6.85	Stratford	Gidea Park 8(b)
SUNDERLAND (D) - 1				
J.C. Williams	Drivers Assistant	1.10.84	Darlington	Newcastle 8(b)
TYNE YARD (D) - 2				
M. Dodds	Relief Driver	14. 5.79	Tyne Yard	-
M. McGuire	"	25. 6.79	Tyne Yard	-
		Exhausted Vacancies		
BLYTH CAMBOIS (D) - 9				
N. Geeson	Drivers Assistant	22. 4.85	Exeter	Exeter 8(b)
D. Rushby	Driver	13. 4.70	Eastleigh	-
HUDDERSFIELD (D)-1				
A. Tordoff	Drivers Assistant	25. 3.85	Doncaster	Doncaster 8(b)

continued

Training did not end there. Truth is training and learning never ends but I would soon embark on a period of learning and signing for all the routes Norwich drivers worked and there was a whole host of various types of traction to learn as a conversion from the basic Class 47. It would still be several months before I would actually be fully qualified, but the pressure was off.

As for it being harder second time around.... was it balls!

Chapter 23 - Training Never Stops

CHRISTMAS 1987 WAS a time for celebration. I had finally cleared a hurdle that I expected to be the last major challenge in my railway career. The past twelve months had been spent either in the classroom or out and about learning the finer details of the job. However that was not the end of the training, far from it. I had passed the rules, basic traction and practical driving examinations so technically I could drive a train. In reality the only train I could drive was one hauled by a Class 47 locomotive. I still couldn't drive anywhere because I had not signed to say I was competent to drive over any of the numerous routes covered by Norwich drivers.

Over the next few months I would either be engaged in extensive route learning or training on all the various forms of traction that Norwich men drove: Class 08 pilots, 31, 37 and 86 locos, and Class 101 diesel multiple units (DMUs). Most of these courses were known as conversions with the exception of the DMUs which involved a three week course including brake handling.

Route learning was also time consuming as the Norwich route card was extensive and included lines from Norwich to London via Ipswich as well as Cambridge, the East

A Class 101 diesel multiple unit at Kyson Point near Woodbridge on the East Suffolk line from Ipswich to Lowestoft on 30 March 1991. (Alistair Barham)

A Class 08 pilot locomotive—08661—at London Road engineer's depot, Ipswich, on 24 August 1978. (Alistair Barham)

Suffolk line from Ipswich to Lowestoft, Manningtree to Harwich and Ely to Peterborough. There were also the local, or as some called them the bucket and spade lines which included Norwich to Lowestoft, Great Yarmouth and Sheringham. There was also the freight only line from Wymondham to North Elmham via Dereham. Not to forget any diversionary routes such as via Southbury in the London area. We were also expected to sign for all the depots and sidings such the Goods and Passenger Yards and Crown Point maintenance depot.

Most secondmen knew many of these lines almost as well as any experienced driver. We had spent the last six or seven years working over the routes and on many occasions the driver would put us in the chair. My father would let me drive when on the odd occasion we were rostered to work with each other. There were many times when my father and I would actually be on opposite shifts so we rarely saw each other. This caused my poor mother a great deal of hassle and she often complained about having two men on different shifts which meant having to prepare meals twice a day. When I look back on those days I feel a deal of guilt in that both my Dad and I should have done more to help her by preparing our own food as we were perfectly capable.

Some time before I passed out, I was rostered to work with my Dad for a full week. The daily list showed Driver; Tyson.... secondman; Tyson. We were subject to a deal of ribbing from our colleagues especially if we were taking a tea break and I would say, "Dad... do you want a cup of tea?" This would be followed by several colleagues saying, "Dad ... I fink I've got it wrong again!" which was reference to a couple of characters on the Dick Emery TV Show, the 'Father' played by Roy Kinnear and the 'Son' by Dick Emery who would generally mess up some scam they were executing, followed with the punchline ..... "Dad ... I fink I've got it wrong again!" Both of us took this ribbing in the spirit that it was meant but a few drivers questioned whether we should have actually been rostered together, although not out of malice. They seemed to be more concerned that if there was a serious accident and both of us were killed then things would have been doubly tough on my mother.

We had been rostered on an early morning trip to Great Yarmouth to pick up some coaching stock, work it to Norwich, then use the locomotive to back onto a London train which we would take to Ipswich where we would be relieved. Once at Ipswich we would work a parcels train to Harwich. With no trains to work back to Norwich we were booked to return 'on the cushions' (travelling as passengers). He put me in the chair so that we shared the driving. There were times when we would not speak too much as we had pretty much exhausted our conversations as the week went by so we often would speculate as to what we would be getting for tea that evening!

At Harwich Parkeston Quay there was a depot and it was also the main station where the international crossings were made on the ferries to the Hook of Holland. Every day, after dumping the train in the yard, we would make our way up to the station and wait for our train to Manningtree and then a connection on to Norwich. As it was mid winter we would pop into the station staff messroom to make tea and keep warm.

One lunchtime we were in the messroom making a brew when in walked Violet. Violet was not the smartest dresser and looked an absolute picture with her baggy BR uniform, beret hat, 'Dame Edna' glasses and a fag dangling from her mouth which was bereft of her false teeth. I had never seen her before but was aware of her reputation having spoken to other colleagues. True to form she took one look at my father, who was always immaculately dressed, walked up to him and greeted him with, "Ello darlin'... less 'ave a feel or yer balls?" and then tweaked my father in the area of 'his balls.' This was clearly a source of great amusement to Violet as she walked away cackling. To my Dad it was a source of acute embarrassment, not only that he'd been tweaked by Violet but it was in front of his son! I assured my father that his secret was safe with me and I would not tell Mum!

In between the various conversion courses I would fit in my route learning. All I had to do was advise the roster clerk as to which routes I would be learning so that he could roster me accordingly. Each route had an agreed timescale as to how long we were expected to spend on it which I stuck to rigidly. I had signed for the various yards as well as the Great Yarmouth lines and Lowestoft. Once I felt happy to sign a route I would pop into the foreman's office and sign the route card. The cards were a standard format with each route listed. You would have your name and depot written at the top and would sign and date to confirm competency for each line.

I was in a position to begin the process of filling in the route card so I popped into the office. Barry Ketteridge was the acting foreman (he was a driver but could be asked to cover the foreman's job as and when required). We discussed the various routes I was willing to sign for and he filled in all the details. I signed for the yards at Norwich, and the line from Norwich to Great Yarmouth via both Acle and Reedham. Accidentally Barry had filled in a guard's route card which was considerably different to that of a driver's. Rather than rip it up Barry put it to one side and with his usual, "Haw, haw" proceeded to fill in the correct route card.

A few weeks went by and I signed off the Lowestoft and Sheringham lines, then moved on to learn some other routes. Several days later I walked into the signing on area when 'Jakie' the roster clerk came out of his lair and shouted to the foreman, "Here he is," pointing at me. With that the foreman came out of his office with a route card in his hand. "David, have you signed for Sheringham yet?" he asked. "Yes," I replied. "You fucking liar, you fucking lying little bastard," was his reply. I was somewhat taken aback by this response but I stood my ground.

"I can assure you I have signed for Sheringham, I did so a couple of weeks back," I retorted. By this time the foreman was red in the face and pointing at the route card. "You're a fucking liar, look at this, you haven't signed for Sheringham at all!" he bawled at me. Looking back I am pretty sure he was going to use this as evidence to report me. Although I was pretty shocked by his outburst and not used to being spoken to in such an aggressive manner, I kept my cool as I knew that I had right on my side. "Can I look at the route card?" I asked. The card was thrust in my direction and, as I suspected, in bold capital letters at the top of the card it stated 'GUARD AND CONDUCTOR'S ROUTE CARD'. I turned to the foreman and the roster clerk, both of whom seemed to be relishing in what they clearly thought was my discomfort. I advised them of their error. "If you take a look at the route card it states... 'Guard and Conductor's route card'."

I then went on to explain that it should have been destroyed after it had been completed in error and the correct card should be on file. It was clear that they didn't believe me but went to the filing cabinet and started rummaging around until the correct card was located which clearly was not what they were expecting. Their faces were a picture: like a couple of naughty school boys they now had to eat copious amounts of humble pie. The foreman could not apologise enough and kept ducking his head as if he was trying to bow his way back into his office. I accepted the apology but left both of them in no doubt that if I was spoken to again in the manner, then there would be consequences for the pair of them. I resented beyond belief being called a liar as I had always been brought up to tell the truth.

I breezed through the various routes but did have particular trouble learning the North Elmham and Dereham branch line. The problem being that there was only one train a day and the service was often cancelled if there were no wagons to be taken in or out. By the time I did get to sign the route it was announced that the line was to be closed to traffic so I never worked over there as a driver.

In spring of 1988 I was placed on a railcar course with Michael, Danny, Basher and a chap who we named Butch (after Butch in the Tom and Jerry cartoons) who was from King's Lynn and would be generally met with, "That's ma boy," which was the cartoon character's catch phrase. Rod Fowkes was our instructor for the three week course. The reason for its length was that it was not a conversion from the diesel locomotives as DMUs were a different animal with a mechanical engine rather than a diesel electric. It also involved an element of practical driving.

Rod was highly regarded by all the drivers he came into contact with. He was renowned for his love of the railways and his knowledge which he freely shared with the hundreds of pupils who he took under his wing. He loved a game of cards and if there was any spare time that would allow Rod to utter, "Deal 'em out mate," and the cut and thrust of a hand along with his passion would ensue.

Each day we would pitch up wherever there was a spare unit that we could play with and from time to time we would take a trip across some unfamiliar territory, generally over the line through Bury St Edmunds and across to either Ely or Cambridge. As with most courses it was vital from our point of view that we knew when we were going to get away and we would offer to work through our lunch breaks to get done early.

We were taking it in turns to drive across the Bury branch and had made several cans of tea to take with us as we went. I was sitting in the compartment drinking tea with Michael, Danny and Butch when I decided it was time to get rid of the dregs of the can. I picked it up, removed the lid and proceeded to throw the bags out of the window while they were still in the can. On many DMUs the coach window had a small glass air vent that could be slid open in hot weather to allow for ventilation. I aimed the can at the tiny window and with some considerable force threw the tea through the window. There was a loud CRACK and the tea and bags slid down the inside. For some mad reason I had made the assumption that the ventilation windows were open when actually they were not. There then appeared a large crack in the window. What an absolute idiot I thought to myself as I slunk to the driving cab to report my error to Rod. He must have thought the same himself but didn't seem too fazed about it.

After the three weeks were up it was time to sit the exam or 'pass out' as it was known. This was to be done over a couple of days with all of us going out on a DMU to do our practical driving test, after which we would be split into a couple of groups to be tested on theory. We all piled onto a DMU along with our inspector Allan Waites and first up in the 'hot seat' was Michael.

All went well as he changed through the gears with no problem and, with being on the main line, the DMU was getting towards its maximum speed of 75mph. This was unusual as they were becoming very tired after the best part of 30 years service. Soon we were approaching Needham Market, a station we had stopped at in training but very rarely used in the course of our normal working of trains.

We were all sitting behind Michael and Allan and could watch what was going on as the DMUs had a cab that had a glass partition that was open to the view of passengers. We were all starting to become a little uneasy as Michael gave the vacuum brake a 'oncer' (in other words as much brake as possible). The unit seemed to just keep going as the platform got closer and closer. The way things were looking Michael was going to overshoot the station and I could see from the look of the back of his neck and ears, which were going red, along with Allan's body language, that things were not looking too good.

The train must have hit the platform at something in excess of 35mph which may not sound much, but it was a very short one compared to the one that is there today. By some miracle the brakes bit and Michael was able to ease them off and come to a stand with the vacuum pressure rising, a text book stop. I saw Allan's head turn as he said something to Michael but obviously we could not tell what it was.

Soon it was somebody else's turn to drive and when Michael came back we all ribbed him about how close he had come to over-shooting. We also wanted to know what Allan said to him to which Michael replied with a smirk, "Good stop," though I think it a bit of a toe curler myself.

It was not long after being passed out on DMUs that I had my first driving turn, my maiden voyage as a driver. It turned out to be nothing particularly stunning in that it was a Sunday night shift at Crown Point depot ferrying units around and then just as I was thinking it would be time to go home, I was booked to travel passenger to Great Yarmouth to pick up a DMU and work the first train to Norwich. Not the most glamorous start to my driving career but nonetheless a start. I imagine most drivers remember their very first driving turn in the same way people have those 'Kennedy Moments.' I can still remember to this day what I was doing when I found out Elvis had died, and the attacks on 9/11 stand clear in my mind. I can recall exactly what I was doing when I heard about each tragedy. Obviously Dave Tyson carrying out his first driving turn was not an international event, but to me it was a big issue and remains pretty clear in my mind some thirty three years later.

Looking back it was not the shed and ferry aspect of the night's work that caused me any anxiety at all. I had pretty much been carrying out this type of work for years under the guidance and trust of fellow drivers as we would be expected to share such work with our mate. What was bugging me on that night was the fact that for some reason the signalling equipment had failed between Great Yarmouth and Acle. In reality this was not a huge deal. Pilotman working was to be installed so that no errors were made in letting the wrong train into the single line section of track. For some strange reason this was constantly nagging away in the back of my mind all night. There was potential for an error, the need to make sure all was done correctly, and for me not to make a balls of it on my first trip.

As with many of these things that played in the back of the mind, when it came to the reality of the matter there were no problems and my first trip from Great Yarmouth on a beautiful sunny morning passed without a hitch. The pilotman was waiting in good time. We did all we needed to do prior to departure and spent the ten minute journey chatting about this and that. I dropped him at Acle and off we went stopping at all the right places thus completing my first shift as a driver and feeling ten feet tall, apart from being totally knackered after being up all the previous day and night.

Communications have always played a huge part in the safe running of the rail industry. The quicker messages and information could be shared in a clear and concise manner the better, as it would lead to a more efficient and punctual system, or that is the theory. Pretty much gone are the days of poor communications. Every driver and conductor has a mobile phone and most signals are equipped with phones. In addition the driving cabs are brimming with technology which includes the G-SMR (Global Satellite Mobile Rail) network which allows drivers to contact signallers with varying levels of urgency. In the event of an emergency they can stop all trains in the immediate area affected. They can also use the same system to make calls to other groups within the rail network such as the company operational controllers.

In the late 1980s we were still using a mixture of colour light and semaphore signalling and many of these signals were not equipped with adequate communications. The much hailed NRN or National Rail Network radio system was the British Railways Board's answer to tackling poor communications. It was to be installed in every cab of every traction unit and would revolutionise the industry.

Once again it was a trip to Ilford training school for a one day course on the NRN ship to shore radio system. This was a very easy day made long by the fact that it was another trip to London for the course at my old haunt. As I walked into the school the memories of not so many months previous came back and I was even shown to my old classroom for the day's course.

There were a couple of other drivers there whom I did not know and I can't recall the name of our instructor. Sitting in the centre of the room was some new NRN cab equipment which compared with today's tech was massive. There was a phone handset sitting above a consul which included a small screen, some coloured buttons and a conventional keypad with the usual numbers that you would expect. This all sat above a grey plastic pillar and was about three feet high. I wasn't sure if it contained batteries along with support equipment, or what… it just looked a bit bulky. 'That will never fit in a DMU cab,' I thought to myself.

Each of us were expected to make a call. It was emphasised that when we wanted the recipient of our call to know we had finished our part of the message we should state, "Over" and then wait for them to reply, when the protocol would be reciprocated.

The plan had been for another instructor to take our call as we were supposed to use role play to work through some scenarios. Unfortunately this could not be done on this particular day so we were asked to phone a number we knew and work though a test call. Several drivers phoned their depots and all went off well without incident. When it came to my turn I decided to do a similar thing: I would call the joint signing on point at Norwich. This was when we still had timekeepers who checked people in and reported to the foreman if someone had failed to sign on. One of the timekeepers was Barry, an odd character, always telling jokes and larking about. (He hung a note on the foreman's shoe when he had them up on the desk during a 'power nap' which stated, 'Sod off can't you see I'm busy.') He had a peculiar habit of cutting up raw garlic then adding it to his sandwiches.

I punched the number of the JSOP into the key pad of the phone, pressed the 'send' button and with the handset to my ear, waited for the phone to ring. Soon enough the system crackled into life and the staccato sound of the JSOP phone kicked in and rang and rang and then it was picked up: "Hello ... loco!" answered the voice which I recognised as Barry. I held down the button on the handset to transmit my message."Hello Norwich loco... this is driver Dave Tyson making a NRN test call from Ilford training school, could you respond that you are receiving my message.... over!" There was a pause and then Barry replied, "Fuck off" and the line went dead. For a few seconds we all sat looking at each other and then burst out laughing. It was clearly time to call it a day.

By this time my Dad was entering the last year of his career after 48 years and so it was considered a waste of resources to train him on any new technology or traction that was being introduced. Having been trained on 156 units that were being rolled out I was given a job to conduct my Dad on the new unit that had been scheduled to work a trip to Sheringham instead of the old 101 DMU that he was passed to drive.

Conducting another driver was a common practice when he signed the route but not the traction. I was designated to drive. As I walked over to the station I was looking forward to conducting my father and thought of asking if he would like to take the seat

Class 158 DMU No. 158864 departing Ely when working the 12:57 Norwich to Liverpool Lime Street on 30 October 2020. (Tom Stageman)

just as he had done with me when I was a secondman. I met Dad on platform 6 on a sunny autumn afternoon and he was surprised to see it was me who had been booked to conduct him. Shortly before we were due to depart I asked him if he would like to take 'her' (all traction was 'her'). "I will keep an eye on you," I recall telling him. But Dad had other plans. "I'll leave her in your capable hands David," and with that he picked up his bag and made his way over to the loco. It was his last trip of the day and it was far more appealing to be at home than on his way to Sheringham. Can't say I blamed him, a true locoman to the end.

In the mid 1990s the new Class 158 units were allocated to Norwich which meant additional practical training because the braking system was an anti-slip disc brake system as opposed to the more conventional tread.(Tread brakes were applied to the tyre of the wheel whereas the disc brake would be—in many cases—situated on the axle and were supposed to improve braking efficiency.) I had been trained on the Class 158 units and was booked on the training trip for the day. Every training trip had to be manned by a driver qualified to drive the relevant traction. I prepared the unit for the trip and three drivers and an instructor boarded.

We were required to make several trips between Norwich and Great Yarmouth in between the scheduled passenger services. All was going well: each driver would take his turn at the controls with the instructor and I would be sitting in the passenger compartment ready to step in if I was needed. We got to a point where all three drivers were coming to the end of their allocated hours, so myself and the instructor sat in the train with one of the trainees. The other two were in the front. They were competent with the new braking system and were familiar with the routes. To get the best out of the training sessions they were expected to get up to maximum speed and then make controlled stops at each station.

On our final round trip of the day we were approaching Brundall Gardens station. We came to a stand in the platform and then slowly the train began to move forward. Whoever was driving made a few short sharp blasts on the warning horn and the train then came to a stand for a moment. Again there were a few short sharp blasts on the horn and we drew forward. After this happened a third time I made my way to the driving cab to see what was going on. In the four foot (as the gap between the rails is referred to) of the line ahead was a Golden Labrador dog running away from the train. Actually he was plodding along as the day was warm and clearly the dog was stressed and probably getting tired. The driver who was in the driving seat stated, "I've had enough of this, I'm gonna run the little bastard over." I was horrified and told him in no uncertain terms that I was the lead driver and he was to do no such thing. I instructed him to draw up close to the dog and then stop which he reluctantly did.

As the train came to a stand I got out onto the track and ran along behind the dog. I got within a few feet of him when I heard the rails begin to rattle and whir which was the sign of a train approaching from the opposite direction. I made an extra effort to catch up with the dog and grabbed him by the collar. He went to ground where I held him until the approaching train had passed. It was obvious to me that the dog was stressed and tired as he was panting at a rapid rate. On further investigation I noticed he had an identification disc on his collar so I gave a sigh of relief. I kept hold of the collar and walked the dog back to the unit then lifted him up into the train where one of the other drivers (Ken, the trainee who had been sitting with me) got hold of him. We proceeded to Brundall station where we contacted the signalman and advised him what had taken place. He was more than happy to let the dog come up into the signal box and he promised to try and contact the owner as there was a phone number on the ID disc.

On the return from Great Yarmouth I hatched a plan with Ken to get the dog to his owners in the event of the signalman not being able to get hold of them. Fortunately Ken lived directly adjacent to Brundall Gardens station. He suggested that we stop at Brundall on the way back to see if the dog had been collected. If this was not the case then we could take him with us to Brundall Gardens where Ken would jump off with the dog and he could stay with him until they were contacted. Clearly the animal was from the area and being a dog owner himself he was familiar with their care.

That is exactly what we did. Ken eventually made contact with the owners and they gratefully picked up their pet later that day and the dog was able to get over his ordeal. No thanks to my so called colleague who was quite prepared to deliberately run over someone's pet which in my view is a complete and utter failure to take responsibility for a situation. I have never forgotten what a coldhearted act that was. Circumstances were to transpire against this individual some years later which in many respects was due to his own selfish attitude which I guess was some kind of karma!

Training is something that never stops on the railway. This is still true on today's system where drivers are subject to regular reviews. These can take the form of what is known as unobtrusive monitoring, where a driver manager can see how a driver is performing in real time from simply logging in on a laptop and monitoring his journey as he drives from point 'A' to point 'B'.

More often the driver manager would pop over to the station when a particular unit was available and download the information from the cab data recorder. It is my firm belief that there is nothing better than a driver having his manager ride with him on a journey taking account of the application of his skills in dealing with live situations. My driver manager, Martin Steele, rode with me on a round Cambridge trip where we encountered a signal revert to danger from a green aspect, then a total signal system failure, and a later that day a passenger having to be taken off the train by paramedics. I was able to not only demonstrate my practical driving skills but also how to deal with out of course situations.

One thing that many drivers from my generation were not over keen on was the simulator or SIM days which involved driving a mock up of a Class 170 unit. During the session the driver would encounter numerous scenarios that may include single line working, signalling equipment failures or having to make emergency stops. We would also be subject to sets of random questions that would count towards us retaining our track safety certificate. The biggest gripe was having to travel all the way to Stratford to do what you effectively did day in day out, and that the lines we were expected to drive over had no resemblance to any route we drove over in reality. With the rollout of new Stadler trains in 2018 a simulator was installed at Norwich. The graphics are excellent and are based on local routes. Personally I felt being put through the various scenarios was a benefit and all part of raising the standards of driving.

My first use of the SIM was quite an experience. We were expected to do two runs, the first to get familiar with the route and the second being an economy run. I was one of the last drivers in the area to be sent on the SIM and was full of anticipation about the whole experience. I did my best and received positive feed back from the instructor who then followed it up with, "Your economy run is the best one we've had so far." This was something of an achievement and later I was invited along with drivers from other depots within Greater Anglia to engage in an eco driving competition and I came a respectable third.

Kieran, the author's son, is seen here in the 'cab' of the simulator. (David Tyson)

Chapter 24 - Can You Stop Putting the Cleaner in the Bin?

THERE CAME A time when the loco messroom was no longer fit for purpose. Asbestos had been found in the ceiling, the heating was inefficient and the roof leaked when it rained. The fitters had transferred to new accommodation at Crown Point in 1982 so the facility was considered too big and expensive for the drivers and secondmen.

We were transferred to a 'new' messroom (built in 1921) on Riverside Road directly adjacent to the station and would be sharing it with the conductors as they too were evicted from their accommodation on platform 5. Although older than the previous messroom it was more compact with better facilities and it was good to be housed with our conductor colleagues. The 'loco' became the 'joint signing on point' or JSOP and was later renamed the 'traincrew signing on point'.

Once we began to settle into the new messroom so the antics of both drivers and conductors continued as well as the regular banter. I was chatting to a colleague one afternoon when a familiar smell wafted into the room which meant that Mick Kassa was approaching. The smell was the pungent eau de cologne he would splash on. (Actually, I think he bathed in the stuff.)

Several of the older drivers really did not know how to take Mick as he was unlike anyone they had really encountered over the years. He would turn up to work with immaculate hair which he would give a comb through every now and then. Often he wore a silk baseball jacket along with gold rings and a chunky gold bracelet as well

Norwich station on the left with the JSOP on the right, showing the close proximity. (David Tyson)

as driving an American car the size of an aircraft carrier. He would also smoke rather large Cuban cigars. Later Mick would purchase a Rolls Royce which he would park right outside the foreman's office! Spawny Elvin would comment that, "Kassa's got more bloody jewellery than my missus," which knowing Spawny, was probably true!

Mick breezed into the messroom this particular day, sat down with myself and Dave Shaw and we began to have a chat. We were passing the pleasantries of the day when Mick produced a cigar the size of a tree trunk. "Bloody hell Mick, that's one hell of a cigar," I exclaimed. "Well ... yeah I'm having to cut down... times are hard my son," which I am sure was not the case given he was one of the highest earners at the depot. As he puffed away on the cigar I just could not resist..... "Mick, you look like a film star with that cigar," I said. "Oh yeah Dave ... who would that be then?' he asked.......... I was trying not to laugh as I replied, "Lassie having a shit," at which point I burst out laughing and Dave Shaw chuckled. "Oh ha ha... very fackin' funny Tyson," muttered Mick.

After gaining my composure I asked how the Rolls Royce was running... "Yeah... sweet," he said. He then went on to say, "I took it out for a spin with my missus over the weekend, we drove out to Buxton, had some lunch at the mill.... used a gallon there and a gallon back." Dave had been sitting there taking it all in and then piped up, "Mick, was that gallon of petrol, or your aftershave?" Again fits of laughter at his expense.

I hadn't been a union representative long and was in our office at the JSOP when all of a sudden the fire alarms began to ring. Being the health and safety representative I shot out of the office like a flash to locate the fire and make sure those in the messroom began to evacuate the building. There were a couple of people seated and four drivers playing the fruit machine. "Come on, everyone out of the building," I shouted and made my way out of the messroom and down the stairs to the exit.

By the time I reached the stairwell smoke was billowing out of the gent's toilets but I was on my own. Nobody from upstairs had bothered to follow me. I made my way back upstairs and into the messroom where life continued as if nothing was happening. "Are you lot coming?" I asked over the noise of the still ringing fire alarms. I was regarded with blank stares. 'Right,' I thought to myself. I opened the door and kept it open until a cloud of smoke drifted into the room. I couldn't have timed things more perfectly. As soon as the smoke wafted in a fire engine pulled up. I've never seen a group of drivers move so quickly. It turned out that the pilot light had gone out in the hot water boiler in the toilet and someone had used a lit paper towel to relight it. The flaming discarded towel was then thrown in bin which in turn ignited.

Today the messroom has become quite a sterile, impersonal place. There are still some characters about but nothing like the old drivers and conductors of the past. There are no secondmen these days: most drivers work alone in their cabs and may mix with the conductors for a short while at their destination during the 'turn around' time before leaving for their return journey. Fewer people frequent messrooms as the demands of a modern railway mean their time at work is allocated more efficiently. Often when you do enter the room, if there are any other colleagues around, they will be fixated by their tablets or mobile phones and unwilling to engage in a conversation. There are some who will not even use the rooms as they find them an uncomfortable and intimidating place.

I had been a local union rep for some years and received a phone call one afternoon from Charlie, the Area Traincrew Manager. He was concerned the messroom cleaner was being subjected to some unwanted attention by a few of the drivers. I was not quite sure where the conversation was going but was guessing it was difficult for a young woman to work in a totally male dominated environment. Lisa, being under five feet tall, was subject to what would have been described years ago as playful banter and I am sure the perpetrators believed they were doing no harm. But Charlie asked me if I could have a word with some of the drivers and maybe post a notice to refrain from putting Lisa in the waste bin! I had an idea who the culprits were and did make an attempt to put a stop to the 'banter' but I drew a line at putting up a notice asking drivers to 'Stop Putting the Cleaner in the Bin'!

Chapter 25 - New Doors Open

ONCE ALL OF my training was complete I was free to concentrate on trying to help make a difference for my colleagues at the depot. The only way I could achieve this was to get elected to the Local Departmental Committee or LDC as it was known. The LDC were responsible for drawing up the shift rotas or rosters, scrutinising diagrams (these were the numerous jobs that were allocated to the depot), implementing agreements that had been reached at a higher level, monitoring and raising health and safety issues, attending disciplinary hearings as well as resolving any disputes between drivers and the management at a local or depot level.

The LDC had been dominated by Harry Phillips who was not only Chairman of the LDC but also the Secretary of the Norwich branch of the drivers' union ASLEF. Harry was a highly principled individual who took me under his wing after I began to attend monthly branch meetings. He was infamous for almost getting himself arrested on the platform at Norwich station during the 1982 flexible rostering strike when he tried to confront a Stratford driver who had broken the strike and driven a Liverpool Street to Norwich service. I remember seeing a photograph of him in the local Eastern Evening

News being manhandled by a police officer away from the locomotive that had just pulled into the station.

Not long after I had passed out and became a qualified driver, Harry decided to retire so a vacancy arose on the LDC. I attended a branch meeting and managed to get nominated to stand for the vacancy along with another driver, Kenny 'The Undertaker' Dickerson who we were later to call 'Thingy' on account of his liberal use of the term when he forgot what he was referring to in a conversation (which was often).

Unfortunately my attempt to gain power and take over the world fell at the first hurdle. I was beaten in the election, but I was not surprised. However it was not long after Kenny had been appointed that I was contacted by the LDC. They wanted to know if I would stand in at a meeting for one of the representatives who was unavailable. I had not bargained on being co-opted but was more than happy to attend on behalf of my absent colleague. I recognised it as a good opportunity to learn what went on at these meetings.

As the months went by I was co-opted on a regular basis and began to learn a great deal about the various aspects of being a representative. It also made me more determined to get myself elected when another vacancy arose. Soon enough the chance cropped up and I managed to win the election at my second attempt. I was proud to find myself one of four members of the LDC.

I soon learned that with the role of representative came further responsibility and I needed to be on top of the game when it came to having a good grasp of driver's terms and conditions of service along with all the local staffing arrangements and agreements, of which there were very many.

I was confronted by a rather angry driver who believed he had been booked on duty incorrectly and having to bullshit my way around solving his problem. Some weeks later I was phoned at home and asked to come into work a couple of hours early to which I agreed. To my surprise the same driver I had helped out then accused me of "Breaking every rule in the book," and that "If you (me) could break all the rules then I would too... so up yours," which I felt was a bit over the top given he worked every additional hour he could. I learned that I had to be whiter than white when in a position of power and responsibility.

The LDC would be expected to attend the monthly meetings of the branch of ASLEF where one of us would give a report as to what we had been up to and we would explain agreements that had been made. Other issues such as changes to rosters were outlined and members were able to question us or raise matters that they required us to discuss with our management.

One month we reported on a change to the signing on procedures which would lead to the elimination of the need for drivers to fill out a worksheet or driver's daily ticket. Two members present unleashed a torrent of criticism and vitriol like I had never experienced to the point where I was considering telling them to poke the job up their arse. I came out of the meeting feeling despondent, depressed and stressed only to be drawn to one side by one of the protagonists who had been criticising us as a group of representatives. "David," he said. "Don't you dare give up." He patted me on the shoulder and left. Those words were to be with me for many years. It was not much later that the individual was to join me on the LDC where he offered nothing but encouragement and advice for many years to come. What also struck me was that although we had been given a severe dressing down in the branch meeting, the matter was then closed and was not personalised once the meeting was over.

As with any organisation that operates on a democratic process we were all up for re-election at regular intervals (every three years), so over a period of a couple of years my three colleagues were deselected and replaced with three other drivers all of whom had been on the LDC in the past—John Pipe, Neville Weller and Derek 'Moss Evans' Bridges. All three brought their own individual skills to the table. John was extremely eloquent so became the Chairman, Derek and Neville both had a good deal of experience in diagramming and rostering and I had become the health and safety representative. I also managed to drag them into the age of the silicon chip by getting the branch to purchase a word processor.

Compiling rosters was an extremely complex and frustrating process. It could be described as a dark art balancing out the average hours, shifts and equalise the earnings of each link. Early on in my LDC days I made several attempts at producing rosters and did a pretty poor job of the railcar or old man's link as it was known, so I welcomed the help, advice and experience of both Derek and Neville.

A typical day would begin with myself, Derek and Neville turning up around nine in the morning. We'd have a brew while we discussed the work for the day. John would turn up a little later, tell a few jokes, smoke a fag, then disappear up the "Bank" or into the messroom to see who he could upset. This would leave the three of us to get on with the job in hand.

John would reminisce about his previous days as a rep, or shop steward as they are known in other industries. John was on the LDC previously with Derek and a driver who had recently retired, Lenny Sampher, who could have a bit of a short fuse. He was also terrified of dogs.

They had been all the way to York for a Sectional Council meeting which at the time involved changing trains at Ely on the way back. They jumped on a Norwich bound railcar and managed to bag a couple of seats in the first class compartment. Although it was labelled first class there were no actual first class fares and all seats were designated second class as it was known at the time, rather than standard class these days. (*Sectional Council was the next level of the bargaining procedure and made up of six representatives elected from constituencies throughout the Eastern Region. They dealt with matters on a regional basis and would oversee the LDCs at timetable change meetings, boundary discussions, regional safety matters, individual members' grievances that could not be resolved at local level and make decisions on disputes between depots.*)

John and Lenny sat opposite a rather large lady who had a bulldog with her. Lenny could be quite abrupt at times and confronted the lady by asking, "That dog doesn't bite does it?".... "Oh no," she said. "He's very docile and it's very hot today, so he'll be no trouble." According to John, it was indeed a hot day and soon after the train departed its rocking motion combined with the heat led to Lenny nodding off. After a few minutes Lenny was nipped on his leg. He awoke with a start and confronted the woman with the dog. "That bloody dog just bit me. you told me it didn't bloody bite." The lady was somewhat taken aback and assured Lenny that it was not her dog that was the culprit. Again Lenny nodded off and again he was pinched. "Bloody hell!" Lenny exclaimed. "You need to control that bloody dog, it's a flippin' menace!" Without any further ado Lenny stormed off to find a seat elsewhere. Of course, what Lenny had failed to notice was the fact that the bulldog had been asleep throughout the whole episode, the nip being administered by John!

Sometime later they were attending a meeting in London, and Lord only knows how, but Lenny was approached by a lady-of-the-night, only this was mid afternoon. She asked Lenny if he would like to partake in some "Business" to which he replied, according to John, "That's very kind of you my dear, but I've just had my dinner."

From time to time we would have to compile the bank holiday lists. These were

INTERCITY LINK 1

WEEK COMMENCING....Base Roster OCT 2012.

	NAME	St	COVER	HRS WK	SUNDAY on	SUNDAY off	SUNDAY turn	SUNDAY hrs	MONDAY on	MONDAY off	MONDAY turn	MONDAY hrs	TUESDAY on	TUESDAY off	TUESDAY turn	TUESDAY hrs
1	C LACEY			34:11	11:43	21:10	228	9:27	12:27	20:53	34	8:26	12:27	20:53	34	8:26
2	A TROREY			33:33				0:00	05:43	14:31	24	8:48	05:34	13:41	8	8:07
3	D VARGESON			33:28			*	0:00			FD	0:00			FD	0:00
4	M GIBBS			33:52				0:00	06:33	13:50	29	7:17	07:23	16:50	30	9:27
5	M COUPERTHWAITE			33:20	13:43	23:13	231	9:30	14:00	22:20	SP	8:20	14:00	22:20	SP	8:20
6	N PHILLIPS			34:53			*	0:00			FD	0:00			FD	0:00
7	D EGERTON			35:00	06:00	14:00	271	8:00	13:27	22:29	38	9:02	12:53	21:53	36	9:00
8	D SHAW			33:20				0:00	05:30	13:50	SP	8:20	05:30	13:50	SP	8:20
9	S BAUM			32:55			*	0:00			FD	0:00			FD	0:00
10	G CUTTING			38:33				0:00	07:24	15:50	31	8:26	07:24	15:50	31	8:26
11	M PENNY			34:05	14:50	23:29	233	8:39	14:32	22:32	41	8:00	15:43	00:20	45	8:37
12	M MIDDLETON			41:40			*	0:00			FD	0:00	06:00	14:20	SP	8:20
13	P WILKINSON			41:17	08:39	16:39	225	8:00	13:35	21:55	SP	8:20	13:35	21:55	SP	8:20
14	B GATES			30:24				0:00	04:43	10:43	21	6:00	04:43	10:43	21	6:00
15	B DANN			35:20			*	0:00			FD	0:00			FD	0:00
16	S CHAPMAN			33:33				0:00	05:24	13:36	7	8:12	05:24	13:36	7	8:12
17	G PEART			35:56	05:30	13:30	260	8:00	13:13	22:13	72	9:00	13:13	22:13	72	9:00
18	A MCNAUGHER			35:45			*	0:00			FD	0:00			FD	0:00
19	N MATTIN			35:56	05:39	13:39	221	8:00	11:43	20:42	33	8:59	11:43	20:42	33	8:59
20	T BROOKER			33:20				0:00	06:15	14:35	SP	8:20	06:15	14:35	SP	8:20
21	K BROWN			33:20			*	0:00			FD	0:00			FD	0:00
22	N TURNER			33:43				0:00	05:17	12:31	23	7:14	05:17	12:31	23	7:14
23	E KERRISON			34:06	16:23	00:23	210	8:00	14:27	22:53	40	8:26	14:27	22:53	40	8:26
24	M HURSEY			33:58			*	0:00			FD	0:00			FD	0:00
25	M ROWE			41:00	06:39	14:39	223	8:00	12:53	21:53	36	9:00	15:32	23:29	44	7:57
26	D TYSON			33:20				0:00	05:35	13:55	SP	8:20	05:35	13:55	SP	8:20
27	A BAILEY			35:12			*	0:00			FD	0:00			FD	0:00
28	G JOHNSON			34:48				0:00	04:54	12:35	5	7:41	04:54	12:35	5	7:41
29	K MURRELL			32:24	13:50	22:29	232	8:39	12:43	21:39	35	8:56	15:37	23:46	13	8:09
30	C FISK			41:22				0:00	07:23	16:50	30	9:27	05:43	14:31	24	8:48
31	D FRANCES			34:39			*	0:00			FD	0:00			FD	0:00
32	I PATTERSON			30:00	09:47	19:29	227	9:42	07:47	13:47	32	6:00	07:30	15:50	SP	8:20
				1118:13	OK			93:57				180:34				190:49

	NAME	WEDNESDAY on	WEDNESDAY off	WEDNESDAY turn	WEDNESDAY hrs	THURSDAY on	THURSDAY off	THURSDAY turn	THURSDAY hrs	FRIDAY on	FRIDAY off	FRIDAY turn	FRIDAY hrs	SATURDAY on	SATURDAY off	SATURDAY turn	SATURDAY hrs
1	C LACEY			FD	0:00			FD	0:00	12:43	21:39	35	8:56	13:27	21:50	135	8:23
2	A TROREY	05:43	14:31	24	8:48	05:00	12:50	6	7:50			FD	0:00			FD	0:00
3	D VARGESON	14:32	22:32	41	8:00	14:32	22:32	41	8:00	14:27	22:53	40	8:26	14:27	23:29	139	9:02
4	M GIBBS			FD	0:00			FD	0:00	05:05	13:25	SP	8:20	04:43	13:31	121	8:48
5	M COUPERTHWAITE	14:00	22:20	SP	8:20	14:00	22:20	SP	8:20			FD	0:00			FD	0:00
6	N PHILLIPS	05:24	13:36	7	8:12	07:23	16:50	30	9:27	07:24	15:50	31	8:26	06:43	15:31	127	8:48
7	D EGERTON			FD	0:00			FD	0:00	13:32	21:26	39	7:54	14:43	23:47	141	9:04
8	D SHAW	07:40	16:00	SP SUD	8:20	07:30	15:50	SP	8:20			FD	0:00			FD	0:00
9	S BAUM	12:53	21:53	36	9:00	13:32	21:26	39	7:54	14:32	22:32	41	8:00	17:32	01:33	146	8:01
10	G CUTTING	04:43	10:43	21	6:00			FD	0:00	07:20	15:40	SP	8:20	06:20	13:41	106	7:21
11	M PENNY	13:27	22:29	38	9:02	14:27	22:53	40	8:26			FD	0:00			FD	0:00
12	M MIDDLETON	06:00	14:20	SP	8:20	06:00	14:20	SP	8:20	06:00	14:20	SP	8:20	06:00	14:20	SP	8:20
13	P WILKINSON	13:35	21:55	SP	8:20			FD	0:00	13:35	21:55	SP	8:20	14:32	22:29	140	7:57
14	B GATES	06:17	15:29	28	9:12	06:17	15:29	28	9:12			FD	0:00			FD	0:00
15	B DANN	13:13	22:13	72	9:00	13:13	22:13	72	9:00	13:27	22:29	38	9:02	14:13	22:31	137	8:18
16	S CHAPMAN			FD	0:00			FD	0:00	04:55	13:15	SP	8:20	05:04	13:53	103	8:49
17	G PEART	12:43	21:39	35	8:56	12:53	21:53	36	9:00			FD	0:00			FD	0:00
18	A MCNAUGHER	07:23	16:50	30	9:27	05:43	14:31	24	8:48	06:17	15:29	28	9:12	06:13	14:31	125	8:18
19	N MATTIN			FD	0:00			FD	0:00	13:13	22:13	72	9:00	15:22	00:20	142	8:58
20	T BROOKER	06:15	14:35	SP	8:20	06:15	14:35	SP	8:20			FD	0:00			FD	0:00
21	K BROWN	14:30	22:50	SP	8:20	14:30	22:50	SP	8:20	14:30	22:50	SP	8:20	14:30	22:50	SP	8:20
22	N TURNER			FD	0:00			FD	0:00	07:23	16:50	30	9:27	09:43	19:31	131	9:48
23	E KERRISON	15:43	00:20	45	8:37	15:43	00:20	45	8:37			FD	0:00			FD	0:00
24	M HURSEY	07:30	15:50	SP SUD	8:20	07:24	15:50	31	8:26	05:30	13:50	SP	8:20	05:43	14:35	123	8:52
25	M ROWE			FD	0:00	15:30	23:50	SP	8:20	15:43	00:20	45	8:37	17:23	00:29	145	7:06
26	D TYSON	05:35	13:55	SP	8:20	05:35	13:55	SP	8:20			FD	0:00			FD	0:00
27	A BAILEY	11:43	20:42	33	8:59	11:43	20:42	33	8:59	12:27	20:53	34	8:26	12:43	21:31	134	8:48
28	G JOHNSON	04:24	11:50	1	7:26	04:43	10:43	21	6:00	04:43	10:43	21	6:00			FD	0:00
29	K MURRELL			FD	0:00			FD	0:00	15:32	23:29	44	7:57	16:45	00:07	115	7:22
30	C FISK	05:17	12:31	23	7:14	04:54	12:35	5	7:41	05:24	13:36	7	8:12			FD	0:00
31	D FRANCES	12:27	20:53	34	8:26	12:27	20:53	34	8:26	11:43	20:42	33	8:59	11:43	20:31	132	8:48
32	I PATTERSON	07:24	15:50	31	8:26	05:17	12:31	23	7:14			FD	0:00			FD	0:00
					201:25				191:20				184:54				169:11

			Sunday	Monday	Tuesday	Wednesday	Thursday	Friday	Saturday
TOTAL Spare hrs	300:00	SP		5 41:40	7 58:20	8 50:00	7 58:20	7 58:20	2 16:40
		FD		10	9	8	9	10	12
		SP SUD		0 00:00	0 00:00	2 16:40	0 00:00	0 00:00	0 00:00
TOTAL DIAGRAMS (exc sun)	98	diagrams	11	17	16	16	16	15	18
TOTAL DIAGRAM HRS	818:13	diagram hrs		138:54	132:29	134:45	133:00	126:34	152:31
% of FDs in Roster	30.21	% FDs		31.25	28.13	25.00	28.13	31.25	37.50
Ave Sundays Hours	2:56								

An example of the rota for Norwich drivers in the InterCity link. Each driver follows the roster day to day from left to right and at the end of each week drops down one line to the following line of work to commence the next week.

a list that would involve a daily sheet where drivers would be booked to jobs based on a specific criteria which differed from the normal day to day booking out procedures. The reason for the LDC's involvement was to determine jobs were allocated fairly to individual drivers as Bank Holidays came with additional payments and a day in lieu.

Our duty was to scrutinise the diagrams which showed what a driver was expected to do on a particular day. It included time on and off duty, the duration of the turn in hours and minutes and work content. Each diagram had to comply with the national conditions of service so we would spend several hours making sure that they were 'legal' which in most cases they were.

AR/22/1
Modifications to Former Anglia Driver Diagrams
SO 27th August 2022

Diagram	Activity	Train Working	Arr	Dep	WTT	StopCode	Route	Unit	DOO
STP NR 130									
DVR	MOB	Norwich	(07.25)	08.27	1K65			601	CDR
On 08.14		Ely	09.24	09.27	1K65			601	CDR
Off 17.50		Cambridge	09.44	(09.48)					
Hrs 9:36	RELD	by CA 106 at 09.44							
	REL	CA 109 at 10.19							
Days SO		Cambridge	(10.19)	10.20	1K66			610	CDR
From 27/08/2022		Ely	10.36	10.37	1K66			610	CDR
To 27/08/2022	AP	Norwich	11.39	(11+49)					
	IMM							608\620	
	PASS	Norwich		12.00	1P35			553	
		Ipswich	12.40						
	PNB								
	MOB	Ipswich	(13.01)	13.16	2D80			607	CDR
		Lowestoft	14.42	14.57	2J81			607	CDR
	IMM	Norwich	15.33	(15.45)					
	PNB								
	MOB	Norwich	(16.34)	16.40	2P28		Acle	703	CDR
		Gt Yarmth	17.12	17.17	2P29		Acle	703	CDR
	IMM	Norwich	17.49	(17+57)					

An example of a Norwich driver's diagram: the diagram shows time on/off duty and each train to be worked. The example shows a trip from Norwich to Cambridge and return, then travel as a passenger to Ipswich to work a train from Ipswich to Lowestoft and on to Norwich. Finally a trip to Great Yarmouth and return.

The LDC would also be assisted by a representative of the Area Manager who would normally be one of the foreman or as they were known by then train crew supervisors or TCS. Normally the task fell to Jim Beswick or 'Jam Butty' as he was known, yet another of the many nicknames I am clueless about. However he was unavailable so the baton had been handed to Brian who was a more junior TCS. Brian was a very self confident individual who would often like to wind people up. Generally as he walked into the LDC office he would greet us with the phrase "Morning girls," which we duly ignored.

We were in the process of scrutinising the diagrams for New Year's Day when we discovered a glaring error in a late evening duty which was clearly a breach of the diagramming principles. John summoned Brian to the office along with the roster clerk Richard Page and explained the particular problem with an illegal diagram. Brian agreed to take the matter away and discuss it with the diagramming office while we worked up some alternative schedules that would comply. Soon enough Brian returned and told us that the diagram office were not prepared to alter the job and it should stand. We offered up some alternatives which he again agreed to take away and get back to us.

Soon enough Brian returned and made it clear that the diagram office was not prepared to change the job and that we (in his own words), "Would have to suffer the consequences if we did not agree." Neville went into orbit and in a raised voice asked Brian, "What the bleedin' hell does that mean?" to which Brian just shrugged his shoulders and walked out of the office followed by Richard.

Clearly we felt that this was a threat and we were not going to take the matter lying down. John picked up the phone and contacted ASLEF head office in London where he spoke to someone in the industrial relations department. They promised to raise the matter and see what they could find out.

At the time the industry had been preparing to split into various sectors in advance of the Government's policy of privatisation. Many depots were beginning to rearrange the workloads to comply with sectorisation, which became extremely unpopular with the workforce. After an hour or so the phone rang in the LDC office. John answered it and listened intently to the voice at the other end of the line which terminated with John saying, "Very well then." We quizzed him as to what had been said but he would not let on. He once again summoned Brian to the office.

Brian returned and John told him to sit down. Before he revealed what head office had said he gave Brian the opportunity to retract the statement he made relating to 'suffering the consequences'. Brian was adamant that the statement was true and despite being given the opportunity to back down gracefully, he stuck to his story. "Well!" exclaimed John, "I phoned head office earlier today as you know Brian." Brian nodded. "I explained the threats being made by the diagramming office. So our people made phone calls to all the various shadow companies that have diagramming involvement at Norwich, Regional Railways, InterCity and the various Freight Sector companies. All have denied making such a statement. Now then...." He paused for effect just before John dealt the killer blow. "Head Office have been on to John Prescott's office who, as you know, is the Shadow Minister for Transport, and he has tabled a question for him to ask in the House of Commons in the debate on rail privatisation. It will be used as an example of how employee relations will deteriorate under a privatised railway." With that, John lit a fag. Brian turned white while Richard tried not to laugh from behind his clipboard.

I actually cannot remember if we got the diagram altered but the bombshell John had dropped on Brian sticks in my memory. Once he left, John proceeded to analyse the situation and we all agreed that Brian had tried to pull the wool over our eyes with some cock-and-bull story about ringing the diagramming office. We think there was no call, but once committed he could not lose face.

The following morning we were in the office again to complete the rosters for the Christmas break when in walked Richard. "Order, order," he announced as he walked through the door. He then went on to tell us that after John had explained what head office had done, both he and Brian had walked over to Grosvenor House where the area manager's office and personnel departments were. The second in command of personnel, Phil Chamberlain, came out of his office and asked them both to step inside. Brian being Brian, said he would make a cup of tea first to which Phil roared, "IN MY OFFICE ....NOWWW!" and proceeded to rip Brian a new arsehole. Apparently the phones in the personnel department had been red hot after the matter had been brought to the attention of the British Railways Board.

From time to time we would have to travel to what became known as town hall meetings. These were generally when there was a timetable change in the spring or autumn when new drivers' diagram or work programmes were issued and work was allocated to each depot. Each LDC from the various depots in the region would gather to discuss work allocations and if work was being lost to another depot they could make the case to retain it. All this was overseen by the next level of representatives known as sectional council: there were six members of the council all elected from various constituencies from within the region. These meetings could last several days with a staff side meeting taking place to discuss the proposals, disputes between depots were highlighted and a format agreed for discussion the following day with the management.

I was always amazed at the amount of representatives who attended and wondered if any trains were running on the days we were meeting! Generally the meetings were amicable affairs with the council letting each depot make their case and attempting to resolve any issues that arose.

At one of these particular meetings, one of the reps from Parkeston depot approached us and told us on the quiet that he was in possession of a secret document and passed over an orange A4 sized book. It was a book with all the questions and answers to the rules and regulations examinations that had just been introduced as part of the newly implemented driver bi-annual examinations. One of my colleagues thanked him for the book and said he would get it back to him as soon as he could. Some weeks passed and we were summoned to a town hall meeting at the unusually named Fan Makers' Hall just outside Liverpool Street station. The hall was an impressive building which had a display of fans dating back to the early 1700s.

Just before the staff side meeting was to commence, we were sitting in our seats drinking tea when an irate Graham Turner from Parkeston confronted us and began swearing. "Where is that bloody branch secretary of yours, I gave him that book and he still hasn't returned it to me, what the fuck do you idiots at Norwich think you're playing at?" He continued his barrage of abuse to the point where our LDC Chairman John Pipe stood up.

By this time the room had fallen silent with all eyes on Graham and us. In a loud commanding voice John addressed the Chairman of sectional council. "Excuse me Chair, I have a point of order to raise." The Chair, Howard Smith, looked at John in a questioning manner. John continued, "Chair, I'm raising a procedural point here before we begin our meeting, can you please ask the member from Parkeston to shut up or else I will seek your permission to stick one on him." John, being an ex-professional boxer meant business and Graham realised this. He apologised and slunk off back to his colleagues with the rest of the room somewhat in a state of shock.

We were later approached by the Chair of the Parkeston LDC, Andy Morrison, who apologised. We had a great relationship with Andy and he was later to become the area's district organiser. In fairness, we should have returned the book in good time but I guess there are way of going about things.

Over the years we travelled to various corners of the district and I always enjoyed the town hall meetings. It meant we got to mix with colleagues from other depots and would share snippets of information about what was going on at higher levels of the union or gossip about future proposals that were mooted as coming forward.

As time went by the Chairman of our LDC encouraged me to become more involved in making a contribution on behalf of the depot at these meetings. I would prepare the paperwork for the issues he was to highlight at the forthcoming meetings. In the early 1990s the BRB began to change its policy regarding freight traffic. Many trains would be made up of various wagons which were dropped off and picked up at locations on its route. These could include wagons with coal, minerals, gases, grain etc. In their wisdom, the BRB decided that from a pre-determined date they would concentrate on bulk traffic only, so proposals were issued to slash freight services in the UK.

Bulk traffic would be made up of trains hauling mainly coal, oil, steel, aggregates and Freightliner containers. The idea of drop off and pick up was to be abandoned and those companies relying on the railways were to make alternative arrangements which meant hundreds of thousands of additional lorry journeys were to be created. This may have been good for the road haulage industry but it was bad for the environment and rail workers who would lose their jobs as a result.

Norwich's freight services, which were not huge, were to be decimated and there would be a loss of work which had the potential to lead to redundancies. We were extremely worried about this and tried to make a case for the retention of some of the work much of which was seasonal traffic that came from the grain silos in the area. Wroxham alone, which only had a small siding, was yielding 34,000 tonnes of grain each year. There were also other silos at North Elmham and Eccles Road where what was known as a Section 8 grant from the European Union had led to the construction of a rail siding and silos.

Despite me making a strong case for the retention of the trains, the decision was made. It was a complete travesty and a false economy as it led to thousands of lorry journeys and a huge environmental impact. It did mean that reps from other depots and sectional council were beginning to get to know me.

The other three members of the LDC were not interested in taking on the role of health and safety representative so it fell to me. I knew nothing about what I had to do so I enrolled in a TUC course at Norwich City college where I encountered the affable tutor, idealist and communist, Ken Bradley. Ken was a great tutor and had a legal background. His advice and knowledge was invaluable which helped me grow into the role I had taken on. He taught us how to identify risks, how to progress such matters, and how to use the legal framework available to us to get matters listed and resolved.

I began to use my new found skills by identifying risks around the various yards within my constituency and then setting up regular meetings aside from the usual LDC meetings with management. I was of the view that LDC meetings were taken up with other matters and any safety issues were given little or no attention. By compiling a safety meeting agenda I was able to drill down into the issues in more detail and get them resolved more quickly.

One morning I was approached by one of my colleagues. He had been walking back to the station after taking a train to Crown Point and was taking the unofficial walking route. The unofficial route involved walking under Carrow Road bridge, across the running lines and into the sidings adjacent to the station platforms. As he approached the ramp to walk up platform 5 he was confronted by an individual in a suit and a bright orange high visibility vest. The individual identified himself as a manager of some kind and began to question Dave as to why he had walked across the tracks and not used the official walking route. The questioning turned into more of an interrogation to which Dave took offence and there was a harsh exchange of words after which the manager threatened to discipline him.

The official walking route had been a bone of contention for some time. Part of it ran along Lower Clarence Road, which had begun to get a reputation for being a no go area especially at night. There had been muggings, cars were stolen and vandalised and a stabbing had taken place. It was also the local red light area. I recall being approached by a young woman one evening as she sought to drum up some business to which I replied, "I'm actually at work at the moment." I relayed this to my wife who asked what I would have done if I had not been at work!

Things began to get out of hand so I decided to review the route and a week or so later I submitted a report to my manager listing various hazards that needed dealing with. Some of these related to the risks drivers faced on Lower Clarence Road, but also walking through a factory with poor underfoot conditions and no lighting. A particular hazard was an unlit underpass where there was no room for a pedestrian and a vehicle to pass safely.

Dave was still facing the possibility of disciplinary action and it was getting to the point where drivers were going to refuse to walk to Crown Point if the management insisted upon them using the official route. It was later relayed to me that our local manager had made a flippant comment that he couldn't understand why we were unhappy about being approached by a prostitute. This led me to write a letter accusing him of failing to treat the matter seriously and I recall writing, 'It may be acceptable to you to be approached by a drunk, mugger or prostitute, but it is certainly not acceptable to the drivers at Norwich.' I then posted a copy of the letter in the health and safety notices case.

I clearly touched a nerve. Within a day I received a letter from him demanding I remove the letter posted in the case and that I had caused an 'affront to his personal integrity.' The matter was urgently progressed to the Regional Safety Committee which was now based in Birmingham as we were being split into sectors in readiness for privatisation. A high ranking driver manager commented at the meeting that where he lived, in the Midlands, he could walk out of his home to the left and the street was lined with expensive houses and was an affluent area. If he walked to the right there was a red light district. He more or less accused us of making a mountain out of a molehill and decided he would walk the route late one night when he was on a visit to Norwich.

Some weeks later my manager approached me with a story that I could not believe. The regional manager did walk the route, however he insisted that Arthur, the driver manager for Norwich, accompany him. They proceeded to walk along Lower Clarence Road and after a short while they were approached by two ladies of the night. What happened next meant Arthur would be dining out on the story for years to come. The two ladies spotted Ian, the regional driver manager, and in a broad Midlands accent said, "Ooohhh, hello Ian, got your black BMW with you tonight?"

Within a matter of weeks the route was changed to avoid Lower Clarence Road, improvements were made to the lighting and underfoot conditions through the factory, speed bumps were installed and lighting provided in the underpass!

Chapter 26 - Company Council - A Step Up the Ladder

AN OPPORTUNITY AROSE that I could not turn down. The Conservative government had narrowly been returned to power with John Major as Prime Minister and an overall majority of one seat. Despite such a slim majority the ethos of privatisation instigated by Thatcher was to continue which meant that rail privatisation was firmly on the agenda. Changes had been negotiated with the unions to alter the manner in which employees were represented through what was called the machinery of negotiation. New bargaining procedures were to replace the old machinery and while local committees would remain, sectional councils were to be abolished in favour of profit centres.

Norwich was to form part of Regional Railways Central which stretched from Barmouth in the west of the UK to Great Yarmouth in the east with Birmingham being its epicentre and headquarters. I was elected to form one of four members of the profit centre council along with three other individuals, Mick Blackburn from Shrewsbury, Walter Lawson from Nottingham and Keith Morum from Birmingham.

I was firmly of the opinion that I would relinquish my role as local rep as I felt there would be a conflict between the two positions. However some reps in other profit centres chose to do both. I was entering into a completely different world to the one I had been used to under the former Eastern Region. I was now mixing with colleagues who were operating under the former Midland and West Coast Regions where things were done entirely different to the manner I was used to.

The four of us were soon to meet up and I was to find the majority of our meetings were to be in Birmingham. This meant a heck of a lot of travelling which could be extremely gruelling with a four hour journey in each direction.

Mick was elected Chairman and Keith Secretary. Walter, or Wally as we called him, was the most senior hand being in his late fifties. I was the young pup but keen to learn from my peers. Both Mick and Keith, although being based in the Midlands, had broad London accents but were two completely contrasting characters. Mick was slightly built with greying hair, gently spoken, protruding front teeth and loved a fag and a pint. On the other hand Keith towered over him, was thick set with a shock of thick black hair and was most certainly not shy in coming forward.

From the moment we met we hit things off and found that many of our goals and beliefs were shared. Our relationship soon built up and it wasn't long before Keith got the chance to take the micky out of my Norfolk accent. We had been summoned to Crewe to attend a meeting with the regional diagramming office where timetables were compiled and drivers' diagrams were developed. As we walked out of Crewe station a tractor trundled by with a trailer full of manure at its rear. "Ere Dave, there's a tractor with a load of shit on the back, bet that makes you feel at 'ome," he chortled!

We soon became embroiled in the cut and thrust of the business of the council where the Government's future plans for the industry began to manifest themselves. Birmingham New Street (a passenger depot) was among one of the largest in the country and was to be subject to a loss of work along with Saltley (a predominately freight depot). This centred around the high profile and what was considered more sexy InterCity work at the two depots. Both had elements of high speed passenger work and it was to be moved out to a new depot that would be taken ownership of by the new operator. This would lead to redundancies and drivers having to move around the company. The proposals were hugely unpopular with the workforce as InterCity work was considered to be at the top of a driver's aspirational goals with mileage payments and high speed passenger train work.

Over several months we had meeting after meeting trying to protect the work and eek out information from managers as to how many drivers would be involved and what the numbers would be at each depot. For some reason there was a reluctance from the management to reveal the number of drivers required at Birmingham New Street. As a council we were becoming increasingly frustrated at the lack of information. However an opportunity presented itself that gave us the information we required. We were attending a joint meeting at Bescot, just north of Birmingham, with the various councils who represented the depots to be affected where we continued to press for the numbers at New Street but still came up against a brick wall.

During a break in the meeting the four of us sat contemplating our next move. It was here that Keith came up with the idea of focusing on the new accommodation that would be required at New Street. He advised Mick to ask how many lockers would be needed. We agreed it would be worth a try and that we should direct the question at the head Driver Manager from New Street rather than the Chairman.

We returned to the meeting and after a while Mick did exactly as planned. The manager concerned stated that they would be supplying 250 new lockers. There was a pause and then the management side Chairman, Jan Glasscock, asked for a short adjournment. We readily agreed and the management team filed out to the room next door where, after a few seconds, Jan exploded. The walls were thin and we could hear every word, of which every other one seemed to be an expletive. Our change of tack had worked and revealed the figure we had been seeking for weeks.

After many weeks of talks the scheme was imposed without agreement and we then began a process of dealing with the numerous redundant drivers who were to be displaced. As with many redundancy rounds, there were no compulsory redundancies and drivers were moved to depots of their choice, or temporarily moved until a vacancy arose at their first choice. We also made sure that they did not incur any out of pocket expenses such as removal fees and, at that time, there was assistance with interest payments on their mortgages.

The travelling backwards and forwards to Birmingham would often take its toll on me so occasionally I would be afforded a hotel to stay in. Alternatively Keith made it clear that I was always welcome to stay with him and his wife Kathryn. They are a lovely couple and they made me more than welcome in their home. The only trouble was if I did stay with Keith I would end up feeling worse for wear the next morning after he had insisted on taking me to the pub or his local social club.

When I was not on council business there were frequently other jobs to be done. Members would often get themselves into trouble and face disciplinary action so I would be asked to represent them at hearings where we would try to mitigate any disciplinary action. Most of the hearings were relatively mundane and would last no more than thirty minutes where you would put a defence case to the manager, he would listen and then decide on the punishment. If you had done a really good job the member may be cleared, or if there was overwhelming evidence then it was a case of trying to get the lowest form of punishment possible.

Later in my career I represented a member at Shoeburyness who the reps thought was going to get the sack. They did not want to touch it with a barge pole as it had racial connotations, so they called me in. He walked out with a reprimand, just about the lowest form of punishment possible. Two of the reps met me after the meeting and were dumbfounded. “How the bloody hell did you achieve that Dave?” one of them asked. In all honesty, I don’t really know!

I recall my friend and colleague with whom I was later to be on the unions executive with, Sean Madden, telling me a tale of a member he represented. Prior to the hearing he went through the charge sheet, known as a ‘please explain’ or ‘form 1’. Sean tried to build a case around the issue and asked the member if he had any other previous disciplinary issues. The member told him he had a clean record.

At the hearing Sean built a picture of a model employee, always punctual, did a great job and that this was his first incident. It was at that point that the hearing officer brought the proceedings to a halt and asked Sean if they could have a word in private. Sean readily agreed thinking that there was going to be a deal to be had, or the member was going to be let off.... far from it. Once the member had left the room the manager stated that he did not know what he had been told about his colleague’s record and then produced from under his desk two thick files of all the misdemeanours the member had committed. In Sean’s words, “He made me look a right twat.” Sean tackled the member about his amnesia, to which he shrugged his shoulders and apologised. It meant Sean had his work cut out trying to protect his job.

Sackings are the worst thing to tackle and over the years I have had to deal with some pretty awful situations. In some cases members are the victims of their own downfall but there are others I felt desperately sorry for. If you failed to protect their employment you had a huge sense of responsibility. The pressure often weighed heavily on me in such situations.

It was only a matter of time after British Rail introduced the drugs and alcohol policy that someone in my area would fall foul of it. I had been a rep for a while but had never been involved in a case where a member was likely to get the sack. One evening I received a phone call from my district organiser at the time, Tony West. He advised me that a member at my depot had been asked to take an alcohol test when signing on, he had panicked and absented himself. Failing to take the test was in itself a sackable offence and he was to be issued with what was known as a 'clause nine' disciplinary summons. These are rarely issued and only in cases that are considered to be gross misconduct. Tony was unable to attend the disciplinary hearing and had decided, "It was about time you got your hands dirty." I felt the hairs on the back of my neck stand up.

I met with the member and went through the events on the day. In all honesty there was very little I could do to save his job. The policy was clear: if you failed to provide a sample or take the test you would be sacked. We made our way to the hearing venue. As I approached I had a feeling of huge responsibility. I liked the driver I was there to help and he was popular with his colleagues: maybe that was what made things even harder. After about thirty minutes I had exhausted all the arguments I could muster. I tried to keep the hearing officer talking, attempting to bring him around to at least finding my colleague a non-safety critical job, but I knew deep down his hands were tied by the policy. What made things even worse was that I had a great deal of respect for the manager taking the hearing as well and had worked with him when he was on the footplate.

After an adjournment he returned and delivered his verdict which we all knew was the only one he could bring forward. As he delivered it he had to wipe the tears from his eyes. It was an awful day. Sometime later I bumped into Brian, the now ex-driver. Fortunately he had got another job, but his marriage was on the rocks and things were not great for him.

Soon my time on the council was to come to an end. A vacancy had arisen as a result of Tony West becoming Assistant General Secretary. His vacancy as District Organiser was filled by Executive Committee member Denis Cadywould which left a vacancy on the EC: this was my goal.

Chapter 27 - The Executive

IN THE SEPTEMBER of 1994 I joined the Executive Committee of ASLEF as I had successfully won an overall majority of the votes cast. I received a call from the newly elected Assistant General Secretary, Tony West, who invited me to spend a day at the office meeting the staff and to get a feel of what was expected of me. Tony was very accommodating and introduced me to the head office manager who took me under her wing for the morning where I was given a few hours induction training.

Prior to me taking up my duties I received a letter from my Area Operations Manager who congratulated me on my election success and advised me that I would be granted two days per month to carry out my EC duties. The EC were generally in session one week per month without pay from their respective depots as the union paid their wages.

Clearly the letter was written by somebody at the British Railways Board headquarters and was part of a grander plan to curtail the power of the union in the run up to the privatisation of the industry. I was somewhat disappointed by the content of the letter and worried that I would not be able to fulfil my duties. Soon the EC and General Secretary intervened and I was afforded the same release arrangements as my colleagues.

Not only did my duties involve decision and policy formulation, I was also expected to travel to the various branches throughout my District and assist the District Secretary by covering for him at various meetings and representing members at inquiries or disciplinary hearings. As things turned out I was lucky if I drove a train two or three days per month.

I had just turned thirty in the August of 1994 and was one of the youngest members of the union to be elected to the EC in recent history. I was brimming with enthusiasm and full of ideas I wanted to put forward to change the direction of the union and reflect its demographic. Many of the more senior drivers were retiring and I wanted to see the younger element represented in a more even manner as I felt in the past the union had been dominated by the older members.

In mid September I made some calls to make sure I had accommodation at the office for the month's session but was advised that there was no meeting on the Monday morning. I was to report to Waterloo station on the Tuesday for a trip on a Eurostar train to Paris. I found this a strange instruction as the tunnel had not been formally opened. However it was explained that we had received an invitation to travel on the Eurostar and get a sneak preview of the operation of the service prior to opening. So my first day on the EC was spent at home, and the second day was a very enjoyable trip to Paris courtesy of Eurostar. This was not the cut and thrust of debate and political intrigue I had expected.

David Tyson (left) and Mick Blackburn (Assistant General Secretary) beside the Eurostar train at Waterloo before 'cabbing' it to Paris. A fact finding trip looking at in cab signalling -ERTMS. The UK rail industry was consulting on its implementation and we are still waiting 23 years later. (Author's collection)

The imposing No. 9 Arkwright Road, Hampstead, the home of ASLEF for over 80 years after purchasing it from the Beecham family in 1921. It was sold to a property developer in the early 2000s. (David Tyson)

I returned to London that evening after a very enjoyable day sampling the delights of Paris, mainly the beer but also the hospitality on the train. I then made my way to the Flask pub where I had agreed to meet with Tony West. It was here that I would spend many hours over the coming years.

Tony introduced me to Kevin Rose who was the District Secretary representing London Underground members. Kevin was an ex-public schoolboy, spoke the Queen's English, wore a tweed jacket, had brown wavy hair and wore round rimmed glasses. My first impression of him reminded me of a 1930s radio star. My father used to collect cigarette cards and had a collection that focused on these radio celebrities. Kevin looked very much like them to me.

I was taken aback when Kevin commented on my "Awful Norfolk accent" and he went on to say that there was no way somebody with an accent such as mine should be allowed to represent members at such a high level. I treated the comment with the contempt it deserved and over the years got to have a great relationship with Kevin, although we certainly did not hit it off on that night.

The following day I entered the imposing building of 9 Arkwright Road, Hampstead for my first EC session. ASLEF's head office was a beautiful old mansion house that had been purchased by the union in the 1920s from the Beecham family, the name infamous for the pill and powders, as well as the composer Henry Beecham. Hampstead, being the affluent area it was, and still is, the residents were somewhat upset that a trade union was seeking to set up its headquarters in the leafy London suburb. As with most things, money talks and the sale went through for something like £64,000.

The interior of the building was extremely grand with ornate mahogany carvings around the doors, a ballroom with wonderfully colourful mouldings on the ceiling and panelling on the walls. I was shown to the EC room which was situated across the main entrance hall of the building and next to the General Secretary's office. I passed through a set of double doors to enter the EC room. You would pull open an impressive mahogany door only to immediately be confronted with a second one which you pushed open. I assumed that this was some sort of fire regulation imposed on the building. I later discovered staff had complained so it was installed to muffle the shouting and bad language that would emanate from the room while the EC were is session!

The room itself was very much in keeping with the rest of the building. It was quite narrow with a high ceiling and windows that stretched from the floor right up to the top and overlooked a large garden. Along the centre of the room was a series of eight desks that were placed together to form what looked like a long table. Each EC member had his own designated desk and at the far end was the President's desk and table which formed a T shape where the General Secretary and Assistant would sit when the need arose.

I was shown to my desk which was at the complete opposite end to the President and had belonged to Denis Cadywould whose position I had taken. He had now become the District Secretary for my area. Behind the President was a bookcase and down one side of the room was a bank of filing cabinets, each of which was allocated to an EC member. At the opposite end of the room were some fake leather sofas, a table with a phone and another bookcase as well as a desktop computer and printer.

On each desk were piles of papers, books and trinkets each member had used to personalise their domain. I noticed that Stan Godwin, who sat opposite me, and was the EC member elected from London Underground, had a small lump of concrete sitting on his desk. When I asked what it was, he explained, "Well bruvver, that is a piece of the Berlin Wall." He went on to tell me that someone had given it to him a while back. I teased him saying that it was probably nicked off some building site in London!

I soon began to settle into the routine of EC sessions and initially I was surprised by the pace of things around the table. Prior to each session we would be issued with an agenda which generally would be agreed between the President and General Secretary. Files would be brought down to the EC room that related to each item, and the President, Willy O'Brien, would read the relevant documents aloud. Once Willy had concluded, the item would be discussed by the EC and a policy decision formulated which would be recorded in 'resolution form' by the minute taker, who would also be one of the EC members. The whole system was cumbersome and certainly not what I had expected. Nevertheless it worked and remains in place today.

One resolution that was passed almost within days of me joining the EC was to instruct the General Secretary to run my re-election! The vacancy I had filled was a casual one and the three year term of office was up at the end of 1994, so the process had to be re-opened. Fortunately, those who ran for the position against me had the decency to refrain from running so I had a clear run in my election with no challengers.

Towards the end of 1994, two members of the EC retired, President Willy O'Brien and Bill Russell or 'Pitman' as Stan Godwin called him, due to the fact that Bill had worked down the pits before joining the rail industry. Willy had been beaten in his election by a younger candidate from Edinburgh, Graham Wilson, and Bill was leaving the EC to become the District Secretary in the north east. Several retirement functions were arranged including one held by the TUC which the infamous Ray Buckton attended. I was in awe. This was the larger than life character that presided over the union when it had 90,000 members and was an iconic figure throughout the trade union and labour movements.

I was also invited to the EC Christmas dinner which was held in a private dining room at the Flask pub in Hampstead. It was tradition for the EC to have their own function along with the General Secretary and Assistant - no other guests were ever invited. I was sitting in the EC room one afternoon waiting for the session to begin when in walked Bill who wandered around to his seat and once the session was about to begin asked, "Who invited the ASLEF solicitor to the EC Christmas dinner?" All was quiet and then Stan piped up, "Well, er... I thou..." Bill jumped straight in. "Oh it was you, you twat, well let me tell you, you can bloody un-invite her!" Stan was a bit taken aback and nobody else said a word so he replied, "Hang loose Pitman, you're gettin' a bit flaky." With that Bill exploded and, suffice to say, the invitation made so generously by Stan was withdrawn.

Prior to his retirement, Willy told me about the day the EC went on strike. He explained that one morning a file had been brought into the EC room that Willy deemed important enough for the General Secretary to review while the matter was debated. The rules of the union stated the General Secretary was always present at EC sessions. This was interpreted so that as long as he or the Assistant was 'in the building' then he was present as not all items needed his immediate attention.

Willy deemed it necessary for the General Secretary, who was at the time Derrick Fullick, to be present but after several unanswered phone call to his office, which was next door to the EC room, Willy decided to summon him in person. He knocked on the General Secretary's office door and went in only to be told by Derrick, who had a liberal use of the 'f-word', to "Fuck off, I'm busy!"

Willy stormed into the EC room and then turned to his colleagues and red-faced stated, "EC adjourned.... right you lot follow me!" It was half past eleven in the morning and, somewhat bewildered, each EC member obediently followed Willy out of the building and through the back streets of Hampstead to the White Bear pub. He explained that he was not used to being spoken to in such away especially as President of the EC, so the EC were effectively on strike for the day.

Later that afternoon Derrick made his was to the EC room to find that it was empty. He scoured the building for all eight members but was unsuccessful in his endeavours. He had received a letter from the British Railways Board that required the urgent attention of the EC. He called Lew Adams who was his Assistant at the time, and instructed him to find them.

Sometime later Lew finally located the by now inebriated EC in the White Bear. However no further business was carried out that day and a clear message was sent to Derrick as to where the power in the union lay.

Over the coming months I was to learn a great deal about the way in which the union functioned at its highest level and I began to meet members from all over the country. I was enjoying my new role. Late one afternoon Lew entered the EC room and commented that he was on his way over to the House of Commons and invited one of us to accompany him. I jumped at the chance. I had never been there and felt it would be an opportunity I may never get again. We jumped into a taxi and made our way through the busy London traffic to the Palace of Westminster.

On arrival we passed through the security checks and then on to the central lobby where Lew advised someone we were here to see John Prescott. My jaw dropped. We had an appointment to meet the Deputy Leader of the Labour Party who would soon be Deputy Prime Minister. Not only was I in awe of the chance to meet him, but I was also struck by the cathedral like architecture of the central lobby, with its high ceiling, stone pillars and the four arches that were overseen by murals of the four patron saints of England, Scotland, Wales and Ireland.

There was a hustle and bustle about the place with MPs making their way to either the Commons or any number of meeting rooms. Eventually we were greeted by the Deputy Leader's Parliamentary Private Secretary, Alan Meale, who knew Lew well as he had worked for ASLEF before being elected as an MP. On our way to John's office we passed through wood panelled corridors with various committee rooms leading off them. Alan explained that John had been extremely busy over the past weeks and it would not be unheard of for him to work so many hours that he would just catch a few hours rest on the sofa in his office.

We were shown into an outer office and then to John's main room which had files and papers everywhere. He made us both welcome and I remember him taking an interest in me as a newly elected member of the EC. Much of the discussion centred around the forthcoming privatisation of the industry and what information he would require to mount a challenge to the Government's proposals. The meeting lasted no more than thirty minutes and passed so quickly, but I was later to meet him on many more occasions over the next few years. My political appetite had increase tenfold.

One thing that did not change was the requirement for me to represent drivers at disciplinary hearings. A case cropped up not long after I had been elected to the Executive, but it was to have tragic consequences. My district officer, Denis Cadywould, had to represent a member who, the employer discovered, had a drink problem. I had met the member involved a few weeks before he was sacked when his depot had visited ASLEF head office. I recall him because he was very positive and seemed enthralled by the office and meeting the likes of myself (God knows why).

Within a matter of weeks of the visit he was charged with being under the influence of alcohol at work. He had been found slumped over the controls of a train in an alcoholic stupor while waiting to depart from a station. A bottle of vodka was found in his bag.

It was an open and shut case but the member was unable to handle the situation and some weeks later committed suicide. It came to light that he had been so embarrassed that he could not bring himself to tell his wife of his addiction and that he had lost his job. Obviously the pressure had got to him and he decided suicide was the only way out. Poor Denis was devastated as you can imagine, as were the member's family and colleagues. It was a tragic ending for him, but as with these things, his family had to pick up the pieces of their lives after he had gone.

There are some members you just cannot help. I was asked to represent an individual who was constantly late on duty. He seemed to have a problem getting to work on the early shift so, in an attempt to assist him, the company placed him on a permanent afternoon shift, which he constantly would either fail to turn up for or would be consistently late.

It fell to me to represent him at the end of a three stage process known as 'Managing for Attendance'. Once an employee was at stage three, which he was, there was a very good chance the outcome would be dismissal. The member had been in the system for at least a couple of years and his attendance had become increasingly erratic and unpredictable. Making a case to defend what was pretty much the indefensible is no mean task especially when the employer had bent over backwards to try and make life easier for him. I tried hard but it was more than clear that the writing was on the wall and the driver was sacked. The best I could do for him was get him an ex-gratia payment equal to twelve week's wages.

I always hated having to sit there with someone who has lost their job and this was no exception. After the hearing I asked the driver what he planned on doing now he was unemployed. He responded that he was able to do some cash in hand electrical work but did not seem too phased about being dismissed. I did explore whether he would be seeking employment with other train companies and he replied that this was a possibility. I offered to see if I could get him and interview with a freight operator. The EC had a role in bargaining at Freightliner and I had a good relationship with the Employee Relations Director. I also knew they were actively seeking to recruit qualified drivers.

I made a phone call and explained the situation making it crystal clear under what circumstances the member had been sacked. While his attendance was poor, his safety record was very good. I was told if he submitted an application then they would give him an interview. The driver was very grateful.

Some weeks later I was over at Freightliner Intermodal's office at Euston for a meeting on pay and the Employee Relations Director pulled me to one side. "Just to let you know Dave..." he said, "... that bloke from Chingford who got the sack... he turned up an hour late for his interview!" There really is no helping some people.

Chapter 28 - "Yeah, about those Millwall Tickets" : The Last National Rail Strike

THE RAIL INDUSTRY was in decline. There had been a distinct lack of investment over many years and the Government of the day had embarked on a series of utility privatisations. Now it was the turn of the railways. It was a period of great uncertainty for many employees within the industry. Depots were being split into two, three or even four, as sectors were created which caused a great deal of anger amongst many members.

This was clearly demonstrated at King's Cross which had a mix of suburban and intercity work. Drivers with a low seniority would be placed in the suburban links and as they moved through the ranks they would aspire to be placed in the intercity links. The East Coast intercity links and the line were considered the flagship of the BR fleet with the Class 125 and 225 trains which were the fastest on the UK network. Drivers worked trains down to Leeds, Doncaster and Newcastle, and along with this work came a bonus known as contract mileage which boosted earnings considerably. The Government's privatisation plans split the depot so that any progression from the suburban links to the intercity work halted.

Attempts were made by the unions to smooth this process over and create a special promotional move which became known as the 'Vessy Agreement' which was named after the Human Resources Manager at BR HQ who came up with the idea. Unfortunately not a single driver benefitted from the move.

While there were concerns amongst the membership about what their future would be under a privatised railway, and despite the protestations of the unions and rail user groups, as well as the opposition in Parliament, the Government continued with its blind policy of privatisation. The cost was huge and the implications lasted for many years to come especially with the creation of Railtrack which was effectively nationalised in October 2002 after fatal accidents at Southall, Ladbroke Grove and Hatfield, which was the final nail in its coffin. The then Transport Minister Stephen Byers transferred the assets of Railtrack to the newly formed Network Rail which was pretty much under the control of the Government. Privatisation had proved to be deeply unpopular with the public and remains a bone of contention to this day.

One issue that raised its head in the run up to privatisation and caused me more hassle than anything else with individual members was the closure of the Railway Savings Bank. Employees were able to have deductions taken directly from their weekly wages and paid into an account at Williams & Glynn that was administered by the pension scheme.

I received numerous phone calls, and would be confronted by members who were concerned about this. It took me a few weeks to figure out why members were getting so animated about the account's closure until the penny suddenly dropped. Once an employee had amassed a fair sum of money in their account, they could then apply for a withdrawal through the BR internal mail. A few days later a cheque would be sent to the member's depot, again via the internal mail, where they would collect it from the Supervisor's office where there was a safe. Once they had collected their cheque many drivers would then pay an immediate visit to the booking office at their local station where they could cash it in. This would be their beer or gambling money which their partners knew nothing about! There were an awful lot of drivers who were unhappy about the changes.

In the early part of 1995 we submitted what would be our final pay claim under the umbrella of British Rail. Negotiations were protracted and continued past the April anniversary date. A delegation from ASLEF included the General Secretary Lew Adams, the President Clive Jones who had succeeded Willy after his retirement, and EC member Martin Samways who had joined the EC in early 1995. They would trip off to the BRB HQ and return grim-faced with nothing positive to report. Eventually we reached the point where the BRB's final offer of three percent was rejected and we decided to ballot the membership for a national strike.

The days of simply instructing the membership to withdraw their labour had long passed and there were various hoops we had to jump through before actually embarking on strike action. There had to be a bona fide trade dispute as well as making sure every member involved received a ballot paper. All these elements were designed to slow down or curtail the power of the unions and allow for a cooling off period. We also faced an additional challenge in that two companies had already been transferred to the private sector, Rail Express Systems and Railfreight Distribution. This meant that we had to make sure we had a trade dispute with both and then ballot the members separately from those on BR.

On 2nd July we received a mandate from the membership to embark on a series on 24 hour strikes across the whole of the rail industry after sixty percent of the members voted in favour with eighty percent of members actually responding. I never worried about industrial ballots. I felt a yes vote with a high turnout legitimised the action and union leaders could use the result to force further negotiations thus gaining an improved offer.

The ballot result was widely reported in the press with the media circus camping out in the road outside the office with radio and TV vehicles from all the various companies wanting interviews with the General Secretary. Lew made a strong case in the media stating that it was the fifth time in recent years that train drivers had received a below inflation pay increase and that BR had actually made a £400 million operating profit the previous year. It was also the first national strike since 1982.

I became involved in rallying the members in the district, visiting various branch meetings and arranged a mass meeting at Stratford railway club where I was expecting a huge turnout of the membership in the area. Both Tony West and I made our way over to the railway club one Friday afternoon the week before the strikes. We knew the meeting may be difficult but I was somewhat taken aback when I walked in the room to find no more than twenty members, all of who I considered to be activists, were assembled.

This was not quite what I was expecting and once the meeting began we were subject to a level of anger and what can only be described as abuse from one particular member of whom I saw a completely different side. It was an extremely disappointing event and I began to be a little concerned that maybe we did not have the support I

PAGE 2 DAILY MIRROR, Thursday, July 13, 1995

Workers' away day

RAIL STRIKE SIGNALS LONG WEEKEND

By KEVIN MAGUIRE, Industrial Editor

HUNDREDS of thousands of workers plan to take tomorrow off to beat the train drivers' strike.

Office and factory staff are expected to stay away in their droves and enjoy a long weekend instead as the network grinds to a halt.

And motoring organisations warn that good weather will produce bigger traffic jams in tourist spots than in city centres.

The walkout by 12,000 train drivers will halt nearly all rail services from late tonight until early Saturday morning after pay talks yesterday hit the buffers.

AA spokesman Nick Simmons said: "It will be like having a Bank Holiday in July, with motorists more likely to face jams on coastal routes than on the way to the office."

The RAC's Shelley Maxwell added: "The prospect of an extended weekend at home could prove far more attractive than a gruelling struggle to work."

Parking

No extra parking spaces will be provided in London and Transport Minister Steven Norris urged workers not to drive in to the capital unless they already had a space.

"Take my advice, don't drive unless you have somewhere to park," he said. Tomorrow's strike is the first of six 24-hour stoppages called by ASLEF. The second is next Tuesday.

In London, Tube strikes are also planned to coincide with rail stoppages from July 27.

The other strikes are scheduled for August 8 and 25, and September 12.

BR yesterday refused to improve a three per cent wage offer.

And enginemen's union ASLEF rejected the possibility of bonus payments worth up to £200 a head.

ASLEF chief Lew Adams said yesterday: "Unless the board is prepared to increase the offer we can see no settlement of the dispute.

"I regret very much the inconvenience the strike will cause the public."

BR personnel director Paul Watkinson said "untold misery" would be inflicted on its two million passengers.

Trapped

The union claimed his hands were tied by the Government's public sector pay policy.

But Mr Watkinson insisted that the no-strings, three per cent offer was one of the best around.

He admitted most of the network would grind to a halt.

International Eurostar services from London Waterloo to Paris and Brussels will not be halted

Each day's strike could cost BR £10 million and lose drivers about £65.

Industry is estimated to lose up to £40 million a day in lost output

Tomorrow's strike will also cost the giant T&G transport union £25,000.

Nearly 700 delegates will be trapped in Blackpool when its biennial conference ends and will be forced to stay another night in hotels and guest-houses.

Tomorrow's strike will signal the start of the third successive summer of discontent on the railways and follows four months of disruption last year.

How the Daily Mirror gave details of the strike.

thought we had. Later that evening I returned home somewhat disillusioned and rang Tony. He was of a similar mind and expressed a view that he did not think the strike was going to end well.

The day of the first strike came and I got in my car and travelled to as many depots as I possibly could. Some had mounted picket lines but others were totally confident that nobody would break the strike so they chose not to barricade the depots. All went well and I reported into the EC who had a strike committee at head office which could deal with any matters that were likely to arise during the course of the day.

I had a pre-arranged holiday to take in between the strikes which I had offered to cancel. I was told not to be so daft, so my wife and I travelled abroad for a well earned week in the sun. When I returned to work, it was one of the few days I was actually booked on duty to drive. The first person I bumped into was a conductor. "Oh, you're in the shit," he told me to which I responded, "Why?" He was somewhat surprised that I was not aware of what had taken place while I had been away.

It transpired that the strikes had been suspended as a result of an improved offer by the BRB and the union had decided to re-ballot the membership. The suspension of the action had gone down badly as I was later to find out when I walked into the messroom at Norwich to be asked, "What the hell do you lot think you're playing at?" Not the best return to work after a pleasant holiday and I was in a somewhat embarrassing position having to ask those who had questioned me what had taken place.

By now we were into August and the results of the second ballot were to be revealed. Once again the media circus returned to Arkwright Road to see what the outcome would be. The negotiating team, now led by the Vice President, Bill Mackenzie, as Clive was on holiday, attended a further meeting with the Head of Personnel at BR, Paul Watkinson whose first words to them were, "You lot are in the shit." Earlier there had been the threat of depot closures. Even some train operating companies threatened the removal of what was know as the check off system (union subscriptions would be deducted via the members' wages and paid directly to the unions).

Although Mr. Watkinson was unaware that the members had voted narrowly in favour of a strike he must have had a pretty good idea that the ballot result was not the resounding yes vote we had hoped for. While the team were away in discussions with BR, the other five members of the EC remained at head office awaiting their return. Late that afternoon they returned to give their report on the outcome of the talks. A revised offer had been tabled which included a pay increase and the promise of the reduction of the working week from 39 hours to 37 through restructuring of the drivers' conditions to deliver a salary with the consolidation of various bonuses. The three members of the team agreed unanimously to recommend acceptance of the offer.

The tough talking was to begin. While the General Secretary and Assistant were able and expected to attend EC sessions, they were unable to vote, so the final decision to accept or reject came down to the seven EC members present. We were discussing various elements of the deal and after a considerable time decided to take a break. I popped to the toilet and while I was in there Lew came in and, as I was washing my hands, he turned to me and said, "We need to square this one up today Dave," a clear sign that he was counting on me to vote to accept.

By the time we had taken a short adjournment I was leaning towards acceptance as I was more than well aware that this would be a fight against the Government and not BR. They would be able to see us out. The second ballot had revealed a diminished vote in favour of action, but we had not taken into account the other ballots on RES and RfD. These could have quite possibly tipped us into the majority for a no vote, the margins were that tight.

I returned to the EC but Stan was not seated at his desk. Instead he was on the phone at the far end of the room. The Vice President was waiting and as things quietened down Stan began to speak to a person on the other end of the line. "Ah, yeah, hello… I'm ringing about those tickets for the Millwall pre-season friendly game next week." Lew went into orbit. "Will you put that bloody phone down for God's sake?" to which Stan turned around, replaced the receiver and, true to form exclaimed, "Alright GS, hang loose bruvver." Given the tension in the room and the height of the stakes, Stan's call was somewhat bad timing on his part.

Eventually order was restored and the Vice President summed up where we were and made it clear he was voting to accept the offer. John Glover from the north west district was of a different mind. He felt we should carry on and fight for a better deal. He considered the offer on the table to be 'jam tomorrow'. Graham Wilson was of a similar view. Sean Madden made it clear that he felt we had nowhere else to go. By that time the vote around the table was two in favour of acceptance and two against. Stan then waded in stating that he would vote to accept: three to two in favour for settling. Martin Samways then made his contribution. He was firmly of the opinion that we should continue with the strike despite having recommended the offer to the EC.

The vote around the table was now three for acceptance and three to continue the strike and I had not made my contribution. Deep down I was kicking myself for not getting my views in earlier. I found I was in a very tricky position. The future of the strike, and the union in some respects, fell into my hands. I was in a great deal of turmoil, and not sure which way I should jump. As I began to make my contribution two members of the EC encouraged me to vote for a strike. But I had a major issue with Martin. He had been at all the negotiations, he had recommended the current deal for acceptance, yet he was voting against his own recommendation!

I took my time to think through various scenarios, both for and against, and after what seems an age, with all eyes upon me, I agreed to vote for acceptance of the deal. I could see the weight lifted from the Vice President's and General Secretary's shoulders. The EC then adjourned although Martin expressed disappointment and said that he was off to the pub.

It was late evening and I was due to attend a meeting at Shoeburyness branch. I rang the Secretary and advised him I was unable to attend,. He was keen to know what our next step would be. I must admit I bottled it and told him we were still in discussions even though Lew was outside in back garden preparing to make a media statement.

The following day we were to give all the branches, representatives and district officers instructions on how the agreement would be implemented. There were also deadlines for the implementation of the restructuring deals. This was to be a mammoth task with thirty train operating companies having to strike thirty individual deals, not forgetting the five freight companies as well. The coming months were going to be very busy.

The following week was our normal EC session so I decided to visit King's Cross branch. They met once a month on Mondays in the Engine House pub adjacent to the station. I felt it was the right thing to do, to face the members and explain why we had come to the decision to accept, but going to this particular branch was a bit like going into the lion's den. This proved to be the case.

It was a hot, sticky summer's evening compounded by being in London and no sooner had I walked into the pub than I was met by Andy Cotogno the branch Chairman. "Evening Judas," were his first words. Things did not bode well. We all trooped upstairs to a pokey little room that, had it been the messroom, would have been blacked as unsuitable. The meeting was opened and I was welcomed with a stony silence. After a while Andy decided to open the floor to allow me to make my contribution to the meeting but after just a few minutes I was heckled by Pat Quigley who was an icon of the depot and the trade union. Andy tried to shut him down to allow me to finish but Pat would have none of it. I knew I was not going to win any argument. Eventually Pat moved a resolution that, amongst other things, accused the EC of 'treachery' for settling the dispute. I returned to my accommodation, which I shared with Bill, battered and bruised, but glad I had the balls to confront some of my harshest critics.

Almost thirty years later, as I write this, I am convinced that the decision to accept the deal was the right one. While my vote around the EC table had a significant impact on the Union's direction, the deal itself was thrashed out by the negotiating team led by Lew Adams. By the August of 1996 First Great Western had set the bar with a deal that would deliver the 37 hour week and moved drivers from a basic wage of just short of £11,000 a year to a salary of £20,000 per annum. As soon as the first deal was completed, so the standard was set and despite some difficulties along the way not one company came in with a deal below £20K.

The 1995 pay agreement was to cost Lew Adams his job. Once the deals were in the main implemented, I'm firmly of the view that those members of the old school who were unhappy vented their anger against him. Lew was beaten in an election by Mick Rix of Leeds, and a new era for the Union was to begin.

I recall one member in the Midlands being approached by the union reps for his views on the restructuring deal they had stuck. It hugely increased his basic salary, increased pensionable pay, reduced his hours and delivered more time away from work. His reply was "Well that means I will be at home more, so I will have to spend more on the likes of gas and electricity." There really is no helping some people. With an attitude like that it's no wonder Lew lost.

Chapter 29 - Dick W and Harry 'The Blood Orange'

DISCUSSIONS ON THE 1995 pay deal strayed well into 1996, but meanwhile a ground breaking deal was being struck on London Underground (LUL). The negotiating team of Tony West, Kevin Rose, Stan Godwin and newly elected EC member Steve Ballard were in discussions on the possibility of a 35 hour week. The process was one with many pitfalls for the team but a clear message was sent to LUL. The Union was committed to achieving what had been an aspirational policy for many years.

Towards the middle of the year, and after Lew Adams had been summoned late one evening to a judge's home for a ruling on whether a proposed LUL strike could go ahead, a deal was indeed struck. It involved agreement on a predetermined pay rise over a five year period in exchange for a reduction in the working week from 38.5 hours to 35. This was a deal that would set the standard for rail workers not just in the UK but for the rest of the world and all credit must go to the negotiating team, in particular Stan Godwin. I know I have painted a slightly flippant picture of Stan, but a more dedicated and committed stalwart of the Union there is not, and the recent award of his 50 year membership medallion was well deserved.

Prior to privatisation, BR had embarked on a round of voluntary redundancy where it transpired that too many train drivers had been allowed to retire. This created a shortfall of man-power in the industry post privatisation, so the free market ruled with companies out-bidding each other to try and attract or poach qualified drivers. One particular company had huge retention difficulties. They were hemorrhaging drivers to higher paying competitors so they made a one off offer which their representatives put before the EC. It included a £2,000 one-off pay increase, the recruitment of an additional eighty drivers and a further two hours reduction in the working week spread over two years. The only downside was a commitment to allow members to work their rest days, if they so desired, for a further two years. However the annual conference, which is always described as 'the Parliament of the Union' had developed a policy that meant all rest day working was to cease by the end of that year. In the case of the new proposal, the policy was a bit of a poisoned chalice.

This was a dilemma for the EC. Generally it is bound by decisions of the annual conference which is made up of members from the branches throughout the UK. Items are sent from branches to be placed on the agenda and if adopted, they become Union policy. Ending rest day working was policy.

In my view we would be doing the members a disservice if we rejected an additional pay rise, eighty more drivers and a 35 hour week. I knew that if the company implemented a further reduction in hours, then all the others would have to follow suit given the competitive need to retain and recruit drivers within the industry as a whole. Surprisingly some of my colleagues felt the matter needed to go back to the annual conference which would mean recalling them to debate the matter. It would also mean sending out a referendum to the members in the company, or there was the option for the EC to reject the offer. The vote was split four in favour, four against. Thankfully, the President, who by now was Bill MacKenzie (Clive had been de-selected in an election) had the sense to use his casting vote to accept the deal. True to form, once the deal was implemented, so the other train operators followed suit. In four years, four hours had been knocked off the working week. This was a huge achievement.

From the beginning of 1997 through to the end of 1999, the president of the EC was Bill Mackenzie with whom I shared a flat in the house next door to the office. No. 7 Arkwright Road had been purchased by the Union several years before I joined the EC and was split up into flats. Each EC member was elected from their own district, of which there were eight, all based around the old regions of the railway. Many of us lived far away from London in places such as the Midlands, Doncaster, Glasgow, Liverpool, the South West and Brighton. Most members stayed all week in the flats but I was able to get home one or two nights a week which I welcomed as it kept me out of the pub. I would also do my best to attend branch meetings that were within easy reach of Hampstead and with London's excellent transport links I could often be back in one of Hampstead's numerous pubs for last orders.

Both Bill and I got on well as flat mates and I was often referred to by one EC member as 'the President's batman' although I think Bill took more time and trouble to guide me than I did him. On many evenings there would be a knock at the flat door and two or three other EC members would join us, often after an evening in the pub and debates would go on for hours well after I had retired to bed. It was also a time for those EC members to relate stories of things that had happened in years gone by. Sean Madden would often tell tales of his days on Sectional Council which would have us in stitches especially regarding the Chairman and Secretary of the Midland Council.

When Sean was first elected to the Midland Council it was ruled by two individuals, Chairman Harry 'The Blood Orange' Whitehead, and Secretary Dick Waters. Harry gained the infamous 'Blood Orange' nickname as a result of him going bright red in the face if he was about to lose his temper, which was quite often according to Sean. I never met Harry, but Dick would often be seen in the Flask pub in Hampstead and would sit with us until he was full up with whisky. Dick was a slight gentleman with light grey hair that was swept back. He always wore a suit and tie, was immaculately dressed and often wore a blue macintosh rain coat.

The way the Midland Sectional Council worked was slightly different to that of the Eastern Region. If a matter was to be discussed with the management then it would involve Harry, Dick and whichever member(s) of the council were deemed relevant, generally if it involved a depot from that particular member's constituency. Long before getting elected to the executive Sean had become newly elected to the council to represent his depot, Toton, which was a freight depot. On his first day he was advised to meet both Harry and Dick on a particular train they would be catching from London.

Sean was full of excitement at his first meeting and was looking forward to confronting the management about a particular issue that had caused some problems in his area. In those days many of the coaches had a corridor with compartments that seated no more than six people at a time and were entered via a sliding door from the corridor. Sean located Harry and Dick and they invited him to sit down with them and the following conversation took place as Harry turned to Dick. "Now then Dick, today is going to be a good day." Dick responded by rubbing his hands and saying, "Oh yes Harry, I've been looking forward to this day for quite some time." Again Harry came back with.... "Indeed Dick, they are going to get it today, they have messed us about for far too long!"

By this time Sean was becoming even more excited as he imagined both Harry and Dick venting the full force of their anger on a management who had clearly overstepped the mark. "Yes," responded Dick.... "Now then Harry, would you like to go first, and then once you have wiped the floor with them, I'll come in and stick the knife in." By now Sean was sure he had made the right decision getting himself elected, this was going to be a most interesting day.

Sean was certainly not prepared for what happened next as Harry stated, "Yes Dick, I've had enough of that bloody LDC, they are going to get their backsides kicked, and today is the day." Their comments startled Sean. The penny suddenly dropped for Sean. Harry and Dick weren't talking about the management at all, they were referring to the Union's representatives at a particular depot. Sean was mortified, his illusions had been shattered.

This would not be the last of Harry and Dick's antics: neither of them suffered fools gladly. Dick could be absolutely ruthless and this manifested itself when they were at a meeting to discuss a particular matter—however a representative from Nottingham had been advised that his depot of 100 plus drivers was facing possible closure. Prior to meeting the management, the council and LDC's had what is known as a staff side meeting to discuss the agenda in private. A Nottingham representative asked if it was possible to raise the rumoured closure with the management. Dick resisted, but after pressure from other depots he relented with the instruction, "Okay, go ahead but, be brief, do you understand? Be brief!"

Eventually the management were brought in and before the agenda was discussed Harry asked if Nottingham could ask a question. With that the rep got up but unfortunately (for him) began to give a history lesson about Nottingham depot: when it was built, the types of locomotives stabled there ... blah, blah, blah. Sean told us that in contrast to the blood orange, Dick began to go white and tremble with rage when he was about to lose his temper. In the end he exploded, "I told you to be brief you idiot, I was firing on Black Five steam engines before you came out of the end of your father's prick, now get to the bloody point or sit down!" Nottingham depot remains open.

While I was on the Pension Trustee Board I came to work with Tony Cotgrave who was a pensioner nominee and had been a high ranking manager on the London Midland Region. He told me that he had come up against both Harry and Dick when he was the management side Chairman of the Sectional Council. He confirmed they were formidable advocates for the drivers and when an issue was being discussed he knew Dick was going to stop pressing a matter when he would turn the pages of his papers over to face down. Tony knew then he could breath a sigh of relief. Neither Harry, Dick or Sean are with us anymore.

In 1999 Bill announced that he was going to retire from the industry and thus relinquish his position as EC member for the southern area and ultimately the role he had held as President. He had presided over a period of relative stability within the Union and under his guidance I had learned a great deal. His humour and statesmanlike manner would be a loss to the EC but little did I expect how greatly he would be missed in the early months of 2000.

Chapter 30 - An Almighty Fallout

BY THE END of 1999 Bill had decided to retire and Stan had been challenged and lost his election to Terry Wilkinson. The EC was very different to the one I had joined in 1994. I also had a new District Secretary to work with, Andy Cotogno. Sadly his predecessor Denis Cadywould passed away after a long battle with cancer. It was such a shame to see the life drain out of him. He would attend meetings even when he was desperately ill and refused to give up. Both Denis and I worked well together and I learned a great deal from him, RIP.

Andy was a far different character. As with all officers of the Union, he was dedicated to doing his absolute best for the members and worked hard to deliver improved benefits and protect those that got into trouble. He had a motto, "We don't do sackings". We went on to work together for several years and made a good team despite the odd hiccup along the way. Andy was extremely supportive when things went badly for me.

With Bill's imminent retirement and Stan's de-selection, it was not clear who was going to fill the role of President. I decided to put myself forward and began asking my EC colleagues if they would support me when it came to voting in the following January. The EC elected its own President and Vice at the first session of each year. Sean and Martin had indicated they would support me and I was able to contact Bill's successor Andy Reed to see if he would do so as well, which he confirmed he would. I had four votes and was looking for one more to gain a majority.

Not long before the December session I received a phone call from an EC member who was not known for phoning me on a regular basis. We chatted about one or two issues but I felt he was skirting around what he really wanted to say. Eventually he got to the point and asked me how I felt about being Vice President with one of the more junior members of the EC taking the presidency. I expressed the view that I was unhappy about being overlooked and not being given a chance to be President. With that we ended the call.

It was clear I was going to face a challenge to gain the job I desired. Fortunately I bumped into Terry at the head office Christmas party where he told me that he would be supporting me for the position. This was picked up by my challenger and he commented, "Well that's it then, you've got the job." There was however an issue brewing that would cause a problem in the New Year in relation to Andy Reed's election. His employer was embroiled in an industrial dispute with ASLEF and they were refusing to allow him release to attend EC sessions. I am not sure whether my challenger knew that I had gained support from Andy but the New Year was about to become ... interesting.

The first session of the year is when all positions within the EC were up for election, predominantly the President, Vice President, minute taker along with a whole raft of other positions and sub-committees that were voted upon. I turned up at head office for a 3pm start only to find that three members of the EC were missing. Obviously Andy Reed was not present due to the refusal of his company to release him. Two other members were not there, one citing he had failed to be released from his driving duties and the other apparently delayed travelling up to London, or so we were told.

Nevertheless the General Secretary was of the view that each member knew the time and date of the session and they had a duty to be there. The elections went ahead and I was elected President, Martin Samways as Vice. This did not go down well with three members of the EC. One of them accused me of gaining the support of a drunkard by voting for Martin to be the Vice President. He was later to describe me as 'Lord Haw Haw' (a reference to a World War Two Nazi propaganda broadcaster). From that moment the cordial relationship I had with three members of the EC turned sour.

I believe I was considered persona non grata by the three of them, and after the third day of the session a coup was attempted by one EC member in the form of a vote of no confidence in me which I refused to accept. It was abundantly clear he certainly was not going to give me a chance to make things right. One issue that really got under his skin was the application of the EC standing orders. In the past our lunch break had lasted an hour and a half. To expedite the business I asked them just to take an hour. This went down like a lead balloon. As the week went on, so things just got worse and by the Friday morning the antics around the EC table had got to the point where I told the three of them to get out of the EC room, but in a less polite manner!

I returned home on the Friday afternoon with a great deal on my mind. My election as President had alienated several members of the EC. There was a strike looming on Connex South Eastern as well as the pending privatisation of London Underground along with several other issues. I had a very uncomfortable weekend and was extremely stressed. I was also doubting whether I was the right person for the job.

Things came to a head on the Monday when I received notification that we had managed to resolve some issues relating to Connex along with Andy's release. I began to contact various EC members by phone to gauge their views. By the time I got to the member from the North West I had a good idea as to where we could go with the matter. However my last call led me to my final act as President. All I got was a tirade of shouting and bawling down the phone and I was told not to phone him any more, at which point he slammed the phone down on me.

This led me to a point of reflection. After an hour or so of weighing up the pros and cons I submitted an email to the General Secretary and Assistant tendering my resignation. I was angry and upset about the way three individuals were, in my view, failing to act in the interests of the Union and its wider membership. I believed matters would get worse if I continued.

Later I advised the Human Resources Director for Anglia, the company I drove trains for, that I would not longer require release, then I unplugged my landline phone and shut down my mobile. That night a courier delivered a letter from the General Secretary stating that they had been trying to contact me and wanted to know if I was ok. I felt as if a weight had been lifted from my shoulders, but I was extremely saddened to be in such a position having resigned from a job I had been enjoying for the past five years. Over the following days I received calls from colleagues and my District Officer, all of whom tried to convince me to withdraw my letter of resignation. As things turned out, things didn't work out how I had expected.

Within a few days the EC had convened and elected a new President, Sean Madden. I was pleased for Sean and felt he would do a great job on behalf of the union. Not long after he was elected President a resolution was passed by the EC which called for a special conference to be arranged 'due to failure of the General Secretary to answer any questions from the EC.' Martin, who was chairing the session in Sean's absence, voted against this.

A few weeks later Sean phoned me. He too was fed up with the antics of the three individuals who had caused me so much grief. He read me a letter he was about to send to the General Secretary in which he advised him that he would be resigning from the EC with immediate effect. I was gobsmacked, and I was pretty sure it was an unwelcome first in the history of the Union, to have two presidents resign within a matter of weeks of each other.

Events were to take another twist when later the Vice President, Martin Samways, decided that the situation could continue no longer. So, in consultation with the General Secretary, Mick Rix, he suspended all EC sessions until the special conference (special assembly of delegates), arranged for 18 and 19 April had determined what to do. This did not go down well with EC members Glover, Carrigan and Ballard so they took matter to the Queen's Bench Division of the High Court seeking to undo the Vice President's decision to suspend EC sessions. They also submitted that they required the special assembly of delegates to be cancelled.

The complaint was placed before Mr. Justice Rougier on the final day of his session where he described the Vice President's decisions as 'eminently sensible' a phrase Martin would quote on many occasions. He also went on to dismiss the claim commenting that it was '.... misconceived, and the claimants tried to make capital.... the application was not in the best interests of the union.' He also stated that '....the claimants had indicated they had wished to postpone the special assembly of delegates despite the fact they had voted for it.' Most damagingly to Messrs Glover, Carrigan and Ballard, he suggested the request '..... cast considerable doubt on the good faith of the claimants.'

General Secretary Mick Rix (standing) and Assistant General Secretary Tony West.

On the 18th April the special assembly of delegates convened. It was scheduled to last for two days but finished by mid afternoon of the first day and resolved to invite Sean and myself to reconsider our resignations and return to the EC. A delegate from Sheffield was extremely angry about the manner in which we had been treated. The General Secretary explained that after submitting a letter to the ASLEF monthly journal in which I had explained the reasons for my resignation, one member of the three errant EC members stated, 'We've got him, we'll have his house off him now.'

The Sheffield delegate proposed that Glover, Carrigan and Ballard had a series of charges levelled against them for 'bringing the Society into disrepute..... and behaviour unbecoming of holding office in the Society.' The charges were formally laid against the three former EC members which ultimately led to their expulsion from the union after disciplinary hearings and appeals.

Unfortunately it was not the end of the matter. The expelled three, along with two retired members and an active member, decided to take what they considered to be breaches of the rules to the Certification Officer. The Certification Officer was created to monitor the statutory functions of trade unions and has a raft of responsibilities. Individuals are entitled to make complaints if they feel unions have breached rules etc. A year after the special assembly, the Certification Officer made his determination on the numerous complaints raised by the six individuals. He found that the union had breached its rules in three of the fifteen complaints, but the vast majority were dismissed or he declined to take any action. In my view the whole exercise proved to be a waste of peoples' time and money.

Not surprisingly, the actions of the EC and former General Secretary are still bitterly disputed by two of the expelled members. 'Dishonesty.... corruption.... witch-hunt' and a lack of 'a fair hearing' are all phrases used in a thread of posts on Facebook. Even a comment was made about having '....the money .... we could have made a fortune from those who made wild allegations about us.' The wounds run deep.

In the meantime the three expelled EC members were replaced and we continued to do what we did best under the stewardship of Mick Rix as General Secretary, and Martin Samways as President. That was to improve member's conditions, pay and pensions as well as campaign on many issues. Some changes were made within the Union. Tony West retired as Mick's Assistant, and was replaced by my former Central Trains colleague, Mick Blackburn. Andy Reed moved to a newly created position of National Organiser.

Tony had been a Trustee of the Railways Pension Scheme and after his retirement I was considered to be the ideal replacement given that I served on three sub committees of the scheme. I was proud to be ASLEF's nominee and was elected unopposed to the position in 2001.

Chapter 31—The Battle of the Barbecue.... a Very Unsavoury Affair!

IN 2003, WHEN Mick's period of office was due to come to an end, he was successfully challenged by EC member Shaun Brady. This came as a shock to many people within the union and the industry who expected Mick would cruise to a further five years in office. It came as a particular blow to Martin: he and Mick had been very close over the years. For the Union it meant a new era was to begin. However nobody could have predicted what was about to follow.

Concerns began to grow as Mick's term of office was drawing to an end with rumour and speculation flying around that the new General Secretary intended to make sweeping changes which had the potential to bring him into conflict with the EC. Staff expressed worries about their future to the President who reported back to the EC. This led a resolution being passed limiting the powers of the General Secretary and affording protection to the head office staff. Shaun was later reported in the press as having stated that he 'couldn't buy a jar of coffee without the permission of the EC.' I was of the view that if the General Secretary worked within these limitations, which I acknowledge were challenging, after building up a level of trust they could have been relaxed. The instruction actually placed the onus of responsibility for expenditure firmly in the lap of the EC which afforded the General Secretary a great deal of protection.

On Shaun's first day in the office both myself (now Vice President) and the President met with him in his office where he signed his contract of employment and we agreed we would work together. We also offered any assistance he required. His most immediate problem related to the absence of some staff members who had left days before he took office. The Head Office Manager had taken a severance payment, the Editor of the ASLEF monthly publication (Locomotive Journal) was nowhere to be seen, and the Head of Finance had been suspended. There were also problems with the accommodation he should have been allocated.

As the weeks passed Shaun began to get to grips with the staffing and his accommodation and the work of the union continued. He also started to meet various employers as a way of an introduction. Unfortunately some of the feedback was rather negative and I recall a manager from the freight operator, GBRf, stating to my District Organiser that after meeting Shaun they wanted no further contact.

Towards the end of 2003 the relationship between the staff and Union hierarchy deteriorated: this led members of the GMB to vote for industrial action. Not long after Christmas a letter was issued to them in the name of the General Secretary threatening to dismiss any strikers and listed several benefits that would be withdrawn. This generated media coverage and caused me to be dismayed and embarrassed. The Union was using legislation it had passionately fought to prevent against our own staff which I felt was unthinkable. Some time later I recall reading an interview with the BBC where Shaun expressed regret at issuing the letter.

New faces began appearing at Head Office, a new Journal Editor along with a temporary Head of Finance were recruited, and a new a Head Office Manager was appointed from internal applicants. In the first quarter of 2004, a further new face would also be seen in the office. Eventually he was introduced and we discovered he was in the process of compiling an investigation into the finances of the union. The EC had not been consulted about the appointment and we were very much in the dark as to what his remit was and the costs arising. It was also in direct contravention of the EC's instructions.

Eventually a confidential draft report was placed before the EC which made several allegations relating to the poor state of the finance department and the deletion of thousands of computer files prior to the change of General Secretaries. It later emerged that this report was stolen from the President's briefcase while a visit from a branch was taking place at head office and the culprit was captured on CCTV. It happened to be the same person who was the Webmaster of the website 'trueaslef.com'. Just how he knew to target the President's briefcase remains a mystery to this day.

Over the following weekend I received a phone message from the Webmaster stating that he had the report and had handed a copy to a journalist at the Mail on Sunday newspaper. An article was to be published the following day. This rocked me to the core. At that time we were not aware the document had been stolen and it was clearly marked 'confidential'. I had no choice but to buy a copy of the newspaper. When I turned to the money supplement a two page spread greeted me. It made allegations including severance payments to the former General Secretary and Head Office Manager, the deletion of files, and a long term accommodation lease that had been granted to the Head Office Caretaker. This was the sort of publicity the union could do without.

Martin had got to a point where he was worried and extremely embarrassed about the allegations being made against the Union. Prior to an EC session arranged for 26th March 2004 he approached me with a draft resolution he wished the EC to adopt. It was the longest resolution I had seen as an EC member and had huge implications. I agreed to support it. Martin called the EC to order and in a short closed session read out the proposed resolution, which Stan Moran insisted that he propose the resolution. Personally, I thought it would have been better coming from the President and myself, but Stan insisted and Martin reluctantly gave way.

Both the General Secretary and Assistant were invited to attend the session and once Stan read the proposed resolution Shaun commented, 'Clearly you've been busy on your holiday Stan!' It systematically laid out what the EC required. A QC, Mr Matthias Kelly, was to be appointed to conduct an independent inquiry into the financial operation and affairs of the union between 1994 and 2004. It went on to insist that all staff, past and present, co-operate and provide any information required.

The proposal was strongly opposed by both Shaun and Mick and a heated debate took place which led to what I considered was a threat of violence in the form of 'men in dark coats' being levelled at the EC. We were also warned that if the resolution was adopted the Certification Officer would close the Union down. It later turned out that he actually welcomed Mr Kelly's inquiry. The veiled threat of 'men in dark coats' led Terry Wilkinson to threaten to change his vote from 'against' to 'for' resolution 319/424, a number which is etched on my mind. It was adopted by a clear majority.

As the days and weeks passed, it became clear that Mr. Kelly was being hindered by a lack of co-operation from certain individuals within the office. I was present when an IT specialist, Professor Peter Sommer, who had been appointed by Mr Kelly, introduced himself to Shaun. Shaun's main concerns were Mr. Sommer's fees to which, when asked, he replied '£125.' This seemed very reasonable until he confirmed that the fee was per hour! The relationship between the President and the General Secretary was becoming more fractious to the point where we sought third party mediation to try and resolve the differences as a result of what was becoming known as 'The Kelly Inquiry.' Alas the attempt failed.

We were well into May by now and the annual conference was just around the corner. Preparations were being made although it was being hinted by a certain individual that the EC were going to be 'sacked' by the delegates.

On 20th May I was attending pay talks at Peterborough with the freight operator GBRf. The negotiations had been dragging on for a couple of months but we were close to a deal we felt the members would accept. Halfway through the talks my mobile phone rang and I noticed it was Mick Blackburn who was calling which was unusual. I suspected something must be wrong: he advised me that he needed me at Head Office as a matter of urgency. I explained I would speak to him after I had concluded the pay talks, but some thirty minutes later he rang again insisting I meet with him immediately. Fortunately we had concluded the talks with an acceptable outcome so I caught the next train to King's Cross and agreed to meet Mick at a coffee shop in Hampstead. I was soon fending off calls from EC members asking me what was going on. One of them had been told there had been a fight which, at the time, I could not confirm.

I met Mick where he explained to me what had taken place in the garden of No. 7 Arkwright Road on the previous evening which sent shivers down my spine. During an informal barbecue a member of staff was allegedly assaulted after receiving a tirade of verbal abuse from a drunk President. This led to the President and General Secretary having a fight. He went on to say that he had told the President to go home and not to return to Head Office.

Later the Union's in-house solicitor, John Usher, joined us and we agreed that he would begin to interview witnesses to try and establish the facts. I was to join him. My first reaction was to try and put a lid on the whole situation. A bad relationship had been made much worse and the fallout had the potential to be extremely damaging to the Union. I sought to get the General Secretary to agree to resolve the matter but my approach failed so John and I began to go through a process of interviewing various witnesses. By now it was late afternoon and as we spoke to various parties it became clear that a fight or brawl had indeed taken place in the garden.

I had the weekend to reflect on what course of action I needed to take. Eventually I decided to call an emergency session of the EC for 25th May. I advised both the General Secretary and Assistant to cancel any meetings they had. In addition I asked Keith Norman, the most senior District Secretary, to await on the EC on the same day. I returned to the office on the 24th May to meet with John again and compile the evidence he had gathered over the previous few days into a report. The contents of the report were kept in my personal possession and were divulged to nobody. This did not stop the General

Daily Express Wednesday May 26 2004 5

Bovver brothers

STRIKE 1 President and general secretary of rail union in BBQ punch-up

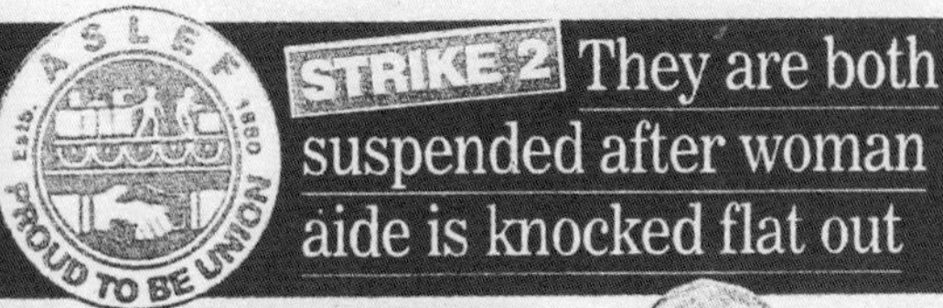

STRIKE 2 They are both suspended after woman aide is knocked flat out

DEFIANT Martin Samways at home in Doncaster yesterday

CLASH: Shaun Brady yesterday after being suspended by union

FIGHT SCENE: The garden where the brawl broke out during a barbecue

By **Jo Willey**

TWO of Britain's top union officials were suspended on full pay yesterday after a brawl at a barbecue.

The fight followed an incident in which Martin Samways, president of train drivers' union Aslef, allegedly punched a female member of staff.

Julie Atkinson was left with a split lip and sprawled on the ground as she tried to encourage Mr Samways to go off to bed when he allegedly turned up drunk.

Mr Samways is said to have begun hurling insults at his colleagues before lashing out at Ms Atkinson, who lives in a flat at the house next door to Aslef's HQ in Hampstead, north-west London.

As she lay on the ground, general secretary Shaun Brady attempted to restrain Mr Samways, but the two men, involved in a long-running feud, came to blows and ended up brawling on the lawn. Last Thursday's incident was witnessed by most of the senior figures in the 17,000-strong union. Mr Brady, 41, and Mr Samways, 57, were suspended on full pay pending an investigation. So too was assistant general secretary Michael Blackburn who said he was attempting to restrain a member of staff.

One insider claimed Mr Samways was "drunk and abusive". Ms Atkinson is said to be "traumatised" and has been off sick. "She is deeply upset because you don't expect this sort of thing to happen," the source added. "She had got up to try and encourage him to go to bed and that's when he hit her. Shaun stepped in to restrain him and there was a bit of a scuffle and a tumble in the grass. But the president's behaviour was out of order."

Mr Brady, who earns £66,000 a year, claimed Mr Samways launched an unprovoked attack.

He said: "The president, who had been drinking since 11.30am turned up at 10pm. He began verbally abusing women. He lashed out at Julie and I tried to restrain him and we fell. He came at me again. Julie was getting verbally abused. She got up and Samways hit her. It was disgraceful. It was uncalled for and it was a very upsetting." Mr Samways said the brawl was due to a "personality clash" with Mr Brady, an ally of Tony Blair.

"I'm going to go fully behind the inquiry and I don't want to muddy the waters and respond to the stupid things that Shaun has said," Mr Samways said at home in Doncaster.

"As far as 'rolling drunk' goes, I can imagine Shaun saying that but I'm not going to go into that game. I will be vindicated."

HECTOR BREEZE

"He wants to be an engine driver when he grows up"

IN THE RED CORNER

ASLEF president Martin Samways is an old-style left-winger who is locked in a power struggle with Blairite general secretary Shaun Brady.

Like most of the union board he is an ally of Mick Rix, the leader Mr Brady surprisingly defeated last year. Mr Rix, a supporter of Arthur Scargill and an opponent of the Iraq war, was close to RMT boss Bob Crow. Mr Brady's victory wrecked this alliance which promised widespread disruption across the rail network in the fight to overturn privatisation.

...AND IN THE RED CORNER

WHEN Shaun Brady became Aslef general secretary he vowed to "take the union back to the membership".

But he soon complained he was "under house arrest" by fellow board members and could not buy a jar of coffee without their say-so. Someone later left a half-full jar on his desk.

His battle with the left-wingers was intensified by his opposition to an independent inquiry into alleged misuse of union funds.

He has also been in a dispute with 25 Aslef staff over allegations of bullying. The staff belong to the GMB union, which accused him of the "worst employer behaviour" in 25 years. And he has even clashed with another union boss. As a young trade unionist, he had a punch-up with one Bob Crow.

How the Daily Express reported the incident at the barbeque.

Secretary calling me after a journalist had rung him stating that he was to be sacked the following day. I denied any involvement which was the absolute truth and dismissed it as speculation.

On the 25th May the EC convened. I reported on the events of the evening of 20th May and recommended that we suspend the General Secretary, Assistant General Secretary and President. Also that Keith Norman, the most senior District Organiser, be appointed Acting General Secretary so that the Union may continue to function. It was one of the hardest decisions I ever had to make as an EC member but I felt I had no other option with two of the most senior figures in the Union being engaged in what appeared to be an act of violence.

I then had the unenviable job of communicating the decision to both Shaun and Mick which I did separately. One individual took the news badly and accused me of conspiring to bring the suspension about (I am not clever enough for that sort of thing), the other shook my hand and asked how long the suspension would last. On being appointed Acting General Secretary, Keith suspended several members of staff who had also been present at the BBQ.

We were entering uncharted waters. The press began to have a field day as the news of the brawl and the suspensions gathered pace. Headlines such as the BBC's 'ASLEF Trio suspended over brawl', The Guardian wrote 'ASLEF Chief faces suspension after barbecue brawl' and the Telegraph focused on Martin's history of intoxication with the headline 'Chequered past of ASLEF chief in BBQ Brawl'. Clearly something had to be done and both Keith and I met with the General Secretary of the TUC, Brendan Barber, who offered any assistance we required. We resolved to appoint an independent investigation into the incident which gained evidence from various parties and later submitted a six page report which made very uncomfortable reading for all involved in the Union's affairs.

In the meantime I was Acting President and both Keith and I were engaged in meeting after meeting with financiers, the Society Trustees, various consultative groups within the union as well as assisting the on-going Kelly inquiry. We also had informal meetings with the Certification Officer.

It became clear to Keith that it would be folly to go ahead with the annual conference. The Union was in turmoil and we were short of staff as well as trying to focus on getting back onto an even keel. So the EC decided to suspend Conference. This decision went down badly with some members and through various mediums delegates were encouraged to meet at the Three Horseshoes pub in Hampstead. A view was expressed that if those delegates present were able to form a quorum then they would attempt to remove the EC. In an interview conducted by journalist Tom Baldwin with Shaun Brady which appeared in The Times newspaper on 5th June, he was quoted as stating he wanted the EC removed so that he could get back into place. Shaun later denied he had made such a statement to the journalist. However Tom Baldwin refuted Shaun's claim stating he had made detailed notes at the interview.

As it turned out a petition was signed by a few members and about thirty of them walked to the office to protest. By then we were aware this could happen so we made sure the doors and gates were locked to protect the Head Office staff. This did not stop one individual jumping over a gate and trying unsuccessfully to gain entry.

Later Keith and I made our way to the side gates to speak with some of the protestors, most of whom were peaceful and kept to the opposite side of the road. By way of compromise we made the offer to allow three of the protestors into the building so that we could explain the situation and the reasons for our decision. However they decided it was all or none... so it was none, and we left them to it. Not long after they

Suspended, three rail union chiefs in brawl at a barbecue

By **Darren Behar**
Industry Correspondent

THREE senior executives of the train drivers' union Aslef were suspended yesterday following a punch-up at a barbecue.

Three staff members were also suspended.

The union's president Martin Samways, general secretary Shaun Brady and assistant general secretary Michael Blackburn were all said to have been at the centre of the brawl.

The fight broke out last Thursday night on the terrace of a block of flats owned by Aslef, next to its headquarters in Hampstead, North London.

The union president was apparently left with bruising and a female member of staff went on sick leave afterwards.

The fight is said to have happened after 57-year-old Mr Samways returned after a night at the pub to his union flat, next to where the barbecue was taking place.

He went to complain after allegedly overhearing someone making disparaging remarks about union figures and the former general secretary Mick Rix, the Left-winger defeated by Mr Brady.

Mr Samways is alleged to have become involved in a row with Julie Atkinson, a member of the union's administration staff. Sources said she was knocked over. Mr Brady, 41, allegedly then intervened and punches were thrown. Mr Blackburn is said to have restrained one of those involved.

Legal threat: Shaun Brady

Bruised: Martin Samways

Interview: Michael Blackburn

After the row, Mr Samways returned to his home in Doncaster. Miss Atkinson went on sick leave.

She has since been suspended, along with two other members of staff.

The union is to launch a full inquiry into exactly what happened.

Aslef, which has 15,670 male and 520 female members, has always had a macho reputation.

It has also been hit by a series of internal disputes between Right and Left since Right-winger Mr Brady was elected.

Mr Brady complained earlier this year that he had lost day-to-day control of Aslef because of a bitter war with the union's Left-wing executive committee.

Mr Samways is a member of the executive and is said to have repeatedly clashed with Mr Brady over the running of the union.

Mr Brady has claimed that union funds were misused under his predecessor, Mr Rix. This led to a bitter stalemate between Mr Brady and the executive.

'Bitter stalemate'

The dispute almost led to a strike at the union's head office before the TUC intervened. A QC has now been appointed to investigate the union's finances over the past decade.

Mr Brady is furious at the suspension and is said to be threatening legal action. He said: 'I have been the democratically-elected general secretary for eight months. It has been eight months of absolute hell.

'This is not a battle between Left and Right – it is a battle between right and wrong.

'I call on the membership to get up and start fighting for the union.

'I was elected by the biggest majority ever known and I have been suspended against the wishes of my membership.'

Mr Blackburn said: 'I cannot say any more because I understand that there is to be a police inquiry and that I am to be interviewed.'

Mr Samways said: 'There was a fight and that's why I've been suspended.'

d.behar@dailymail.co.uk

The Daily Mail report on the barbeque incident.

all got bored and either went back to the pub or cleared off home.

After the publication of the TUC report, the President visited the EC to tender his resignation which we accepted. It was the end of an era. Martin had had a chequered career within the union: he had been a powerful voice from his days as a local rep and a stalwart of the annual conference through to the time he resigned as President. He had a brilliant mind, was an excellent strategist and debater, but his heavy drinking and Jekyll and Hyde character had caught up with him. Rather than face disciplinary action he chose to resign. There has been speculation in the past as to whether discussions took place with the suspended General Secretary about affording him the same facility. It was my understanding that informal discussions may have taken place and a cash offer proposed which he rejected as it fell short of anything he would consider. I was never a party to any discussions, if indeed they did take place.

The EC resolved to initiate disciplinary action against the General Secretary and the Assistant.

New staff had been recruited, and both Keith and I were working hard to get the finances of the Union back on track along with our bankers and the new Head of the Finance Department.

Later Matthias Kelly produced his report which in many respects was explosive but also gave a steer as to how the Union should operate in future. The extensive and costly report revealed that during 2003 the Finance Department had become disorganised but the long term effects on the Union were nil. There was no evidence of fraud and it also concluded that the finances were sound. It went on to state that the severance payments were authorised, legal and justified. In respect of the alleged 64,000 deleted computer files, it concluded after a detailed forensic investigation, many thousands had been deleted after the previous Head Office Manager had left the employment of ASLEF and could not have been deleted by her.

On a positive note the findings highlighted areas of weakness and made a series of recommendations ranging from Head Office management, governance, financial management (twenty one relating on finance alone), the trustees, IT, recruitment, also the running of Executive Committee.

But the report made grave reading for the suspended General Secretary in which Mr. Kelly described his lack of co-operation and his behaviour as 'childish' and that he experienced 'outright hostility' from him. He also listed the numerous attempts he tried to interview the General Secretary but found his approach 'obstructive' and '.... in direct contravention of' EC resolution 319/424. Later the EC had adopted a further resolution setting out the terms of the inquiry and stating failure to co-operate with the inquiry 'may result in appropriate action being taken.....'

Mr. Kelly's report pulled no punches and after its publication the EC levelled further charges against the General Secretary.

After several exchanges of correspondence a disciplinary hearing was held in front of the EC in mid August and was chaired by me. We had employed a stenographer to record the hearing. Much of the first part was bogged down wrangling over the method we had laid out that resulted in the suspended General Secretary's representative insisting that we withdraw the charges. This was something none of us were prepared to agree to. We did agree to defer decisions on several charges due to the non availability of two witnesses but decided to press ahead with those we could deal with.

After hearing the defence which was professional and concise (I expected nothing less from Len Worboys) the EC voted by a majority to dismiss the suspended General Secretary as we believed his actions amounted to gross misconduct. Other charges were either withdrawn or he was found not guilty. The hearing was adjourned and then

Co-operation.

The Assistant General Secretary and the EC have co-operated throughout with my Inquiry. They have made themselves available for interview and they produced what I asked them, in so far as they had access to the documents I sought. Like wise all the staff outside of the office of the General Secretary co-operated with the Inquiry.

Mr. Brady, on the other hand, refused to attend a conference with me in Chambers on 5th April 2004 after my appointment. He did so, he told me, because he would only meet with me if instructed to do so by the Executive.

I found this surprising in the light of the resolution setting up the Inquiry.

On the morning of 6th April 2004 when I went to Arkwright Road, Mr. Brady refused to come into the Executive Committee room until the Executive Committee resolved that he should. In my opinion such behaviour was childish. I found it surprising that Mr. Brady thought that this was a profitable way for anyone to spend time.

On a number of occasions throughout the conduct of this Inquiry I have encountered outright hostility from Mr Brady the current General Secretary. There has been a lack of co-operation from him. He is reported in an interview published in The Times on Saturday 5th June 2004 as saying he would not cooperate with the Inquiry. He has consistently questioned the decision of the Executive Committee to establish the Inquiry. This is despite the fact that he, himself, engaged Mr Paul Blagbrough to conduct a review of the Union's finances and administration without reference to the Executive Committee in the first instance. Mr Brady has been unwilling, on virtually every occasion I have met him, to discuss in a rationale manner the problems confronting the Union and the issues as he sees them. When I spoke to Mr. Brady at the offices of the Union on Tuesday the 6th April he made it plain to me that he would not instruct the staff to provide files and other records that I might seek. Again I found this obstructive approach surprising, being in direct contravention of the resolution of the EC (319/424). Apart from anything else it meant that my work took much longer and was more difficult since we had to track down documents ourselves. It is strange behaviour for a General Secretary who claims that he wants the facts established.

I have had to write to Mr Brady on a number of occasions. On the 28th April 2004 I wrote to him to make plain that I did not want substantial changes made to the Union's IT structure until a forensic IT consultant whom I had commissioned had had an opportunity to "image" the system and inspect the same. Mr. Brady was, until I wrote to him, determined to carry on regardless. Had he done so the IT forensic exercise would have been pointless.

On the 11th May 2004 my junior Mr Rohan Pirani wrote formally to Mr Brady seeking details of the Union's investment advisers and portfolio managers, a complete list of the current investments of ASLEF, reports relating to investments and their disposal and minutes of meetings with investment and portfolio advisers. Mr. Brady failed to respond to that letter. We still have not been given that material.

Although Penny Bygrave provisionally booked Tuesday 25 May in Mr. Brady's diary, that date was cancelled on Friday 21 May due to the unavailability of Mr. Brady's solicitor, Ivan Walker from Thompsons. On Monday 24 May Rohan Pirani explained to Penny Bygrave that I would meet Mr. Brady at any time within a 48-hour period on Tuesday 25 May or Wednesday 26 May. No response was received to that invitation.

I wrote to Mr. Brady on 24th May asking to meet him. I told him, in that letter, that he could bring a solicitor along, as he had said he wished to be accompanied by one.

Extract of the Kelly Report summary.

reconvened towards the end of August where the EC found the charge of fighting was proven and the decision to dismiss the suspended General Secretary was again carried by a majority.

September was upon us and the delayed annual conference was due to begin. As I drove up to Scarborough I was accompanied by friend and colleague Steve Wright, who was the Company Council Secretary for Greater Anglia at Norwich. We discussed the possibilities that could unfold on the first day of the conference and I remember telling him I could be on my way home soon after. Steve was firmly of the view that the EC would win through and I was encouraged by his enthusiasm. I had been working on my conference address which was traditionally first business and was hoping it would set the scene for a successful few days.

At conference the EC are generally represented by the President (myself), Vice President, plus one other. However several other EC members had requested to attend so that they could offer their support to me, but also witness how events would turn out. Both Keith and I agreed to their requests. Our pre-conference meeting was designed to scrutinise the agenda and formulate a strategy as to which items we would either support or oppose. That year was no different, but our thoughts were dominated by the rumour and speculation of attempts to unseat the EC and reinstate the General Secretary and Assistant on the morning of the first day.

On the evening of the eve of conference Keith and I decided to take ourselves to a pub in a quieter part of Scarborough away from the delegates who were turning up and frequenting the pubs in the close proximity of the hotel. Not long after settling down with a pint we were aware that three of the security detail who had been hired for the conference were sitting close by. They had been instructed to shadow us and keep us safe. I found this to be a bit over the top but nevertheless I welcomed the concern for mine and Keith's safety. We were also joined by three EC members, our Press Officer, Legal Officer John Usher as well as Nick Whitehead who was the District Secretary for the area.

After a few beers we decided to make our way back to the hotel. As we were passing an Indian restaurant I noticed Bob Crow, RMT General Secretary, sitting on his own having a meal. I knew Keith had invited Bob to address conference in a gesture of unity, but I was surprised and embarrassed to think he was on his own, so we all piled in to join him for a beer.

While we were chatting my mobile phone rang. It was the suspended General Secretary. I was intrigued. It turned out that he was calling me to discuss the possibility of some form of reconciliation. I was utterly gobsmacked. Then the battery on my phone died. I managed to borrow a phone and we had a conversation in which he explained why he felt it would be beneficial to all parties to make a statement that we would all work together. I was thinking to myself that it was a bit late in the day for such a proposal when I had suggested something similar way back on 21 May. I explained to him that I was in no position to agree to anything, the EC were no longer in session, it was the eve of the annual conference and the EC would not be in power until conference ended. The call was terminated.

I tried to analyse the reason for the call. Why would he make such a request on the eve of a conference where there was a chance the EC were going to be sacked? Maybe he would be allowed to address the delegates and even achieve his desired re-instatement? We were aware some delegates were going to try and get a motion on the floor of conference to at least allow him to address them. I came to the conclusion that he was obviously in Scarborough and had been seeking delegates' views which may not have produced the reaction he was expecting. That was, and remains, pure speculation on my part.

Eventually we were kicked out of the curry house and made our way back to the hotel. As I approached the main entrance a delegate stopped me. "President, what should I do at tomorrow's conference?" he asked. "Support your EC and Acting General Secretary," I replied. He nodded and said, "Will do President," and with that we parted ways.

At this point nobody had seen my opening address but our Press Officer asked if he could have sight of it just to check it over. I was happy to oblige so along with him and our Legal Officer we made our way up to my room. After reading it he nodded and said, "Spot on." They left and I then had a sleepless night working through all the various scenarios that could manifest themselves the following day.

Morning soon arrived with a tap, tap, tapping on the large window of my room. I opened the curtains to be faced with a huge gull standing on the window ledge staring back at me. I nearly jumped out of my skin. Some may have said it was an omen. Whether it was, I couldn't say! A busy stressful day lay ahead. I was of the view that if we got through to the lunch break without being sacked, then we would be home and dry.

I was surprised to see the level of interest the conference had generated with a great many visitors at the rear of the conference room including the suspended General Secretary, a former President with whom I had shared a flat, a former District Secretary, the 'trueaslef' Webmaster and the suspended Assistant General Secretary. The media were also gathered outside with the BBC reporter Laura Trevelyan seeking to interview me and delegates but I asked her not to. However true to journalistic form, she ignored my request. There was also the BBC's Industrial Relations Correspondent who wanted to record the morning's proceedings which I refused. The only people eligible to attend were either delegates, ASLEF members or staff.

Keith, Terry (the acting Vice President) and I took to the top table that was situated at the front of the conference hall on a stage. As the delegates filed in, one member made his way past our table, pointed at Keith's name card and commented, "That'll be gone soon," which I guess was a reference to a rumoured motion to sack the EC and Acting General Secretary. It was a bit unnerving but time would soon tell if the prediction was right. We wouldn't have to wait long to find out.

Once the delegates were seated it was tradition for the President to make his opening address. It was now or never as I rose to me feet and made my way to the lectern. I was nervous, my mouth was dry and my heart racing as I welcomed the delegates to the delayed annual conference. I made it clear to all present that the turmoil the union had found itself in was to end, that we had acted on the recommendations of Matthias Kelly and I ended by stating that I wanted to see "..... a strong and vibrant ASLEF...known for its equality, honesty, respect and integrity. Those who seek to divide us must fail. Those who seek to destroy us must fail." I also encouraged the delegates to ".... move forward in unity for the future prosperity of ASLEF, the membership, (and) their families..." I actually received a round of applause.

After my speech the conference Chairman and Vice Chairman had to be elected from the delegates. Two delegates were nominated for the position of Chairman and I knew, depending on which way the election went, it could well determine how the next few minutes would unfold. One nominee would be sympathetic towards the EC, the other in all probability would not. Fortunately Roy Luxford from Three Bridges branch was elected. The same process applied to the Vice Chairman and the same thing happened again. The Newport delegate was defeated and I was damn sure he would have been unsympathetic towards the EC. I had seen him in Arkwright Road in June, protesting against the suspension of the General Secretary. Finn Brennan from East Finchley and Golders Green branch took the Vice Chairman's position.

The Chairman took his seat alongside myself and the Acting General Secretary. As soon as the Acting General Secretary had made various housekeeping announcements the delegate from Newport placed a motion before conference. The exact details of this are not recorded in the minutes as the Chairman rejected it on the grounds that it would interfere with the disciplinary process that was already underway – I recall it was seeking to allow the suspended General Secretary to address the conference. The Chairman's decision was challenged. 'Here we go,' I was thinking to myself as Finn took the chair. I knew he would be supportive of the Chair's ruling but was not sure if the delegates would be. A counter motion was placed before the Vice Chairman which stated, "The ruling of the Chair be upheld." It went through 49 votes to 19 with 4 abstentions. We just had to get through the session and into the afternoon, as there was technically a way back for the delegates to resurrect the issue once the afternoon session began. If they failed then we would truly be home and dry.

After Bob Crow had made a passionate speech it was the turn of Matthias Kelly and his experts to give a detailed presentation to the conference on his findings and the recommendations of his inquiry. This took up the rest of the morning session. As I left the room for lunch I walked past Mick Blackburn who complimented me on my speech. That was indeed praise in itself, as despite the situation I still had a great deal of respect for him. We returned from lunch to find many of the visitors had left and the mooted technical challenge failed to materialize. We were now past the worst. Matthias Kelly continued his presentation for the rest of the day while answering questions from the delegates. By the evening we were seeing media reports of the day's events and the suspended General Secretary was described by one reporter as 'having his chance for re-instatement come off the rails'.

The following day conference debated the Kelly report and after instructing the EC to adopt a raft of recommendations (which we had already acted upon) we were instructed to report back to a recalled conference the following year on the progress we were instructed to make.

Deep down, I took no joy in the position we found ourselves in. We had won through but there were still many hurdles to jump. The disciplinary process was yet to be concluded and there would no doubt be legal challenges if the process fell in favour of the union. I had also sacrificed friendships, alienated people and colleagues for the greater good of the union and was more than well aware of the consequences for those who had been dismissed. But I had taken what I thought was the right and proper action.

Over the coming days I began to enjoy the cut and thrust of the conference. Some weeks earlier I had decided to indicate to the EC and Keith that I intended to leave at the end of the year. I had held the position as EC member for ten years (on and off) and was spending far too much time away from home. I was to embark, with my wife, on a new chapter of our life and I wanted to give the utmost dedication to her and my son. Keith would often have nicknames for people and in his world I was 'Pressie'. After the previous months of turmoil we had been through he was firmly of the opinion that I should stay and, after a particularly enjoyable evening with Brendan Barber the TUC General Secretary, he kept saying, "Stay Pressie… Brendan, tell him, he should stay." We had all had quite a few beers in a pub known as The Hole in the Wall just around the corner from the hotel. Brendan just smiled. However I was not to be persuaded.

By November, at the request of the suspended General Secretary, an appeal hearing had been arranged however. In the meantime further charges had been levelled against him. In the run up to the appeal I made meticulous preparations as it would be myself and Keith who would be representing the union. The disciplinary process against the Assistant General Secretary had been curtailed when he decided to reach a compromise arrangement with the union, as had the other members of staff who were present at the now infamous barbecue incident of 20th May.

The suspended General Secretary's appeal was to be held in front of the ASLEF Appeals Committee which was formed of eight elected representatives from each of the districts in the country. It was an intimidating experience for all parties, but we were all afforded as much time as possible. Again we employed the services of a stenographer to record what was said at the hearing which stretched to 161 pages of text.

After each side had made their representations we were able to leave. Keith and I retired to the EC room and awaited the outcome of the Committee's deliberations. They had a great deal to get through and it had been dark for some time when Andy Morrison, the Chair of the Committee, knocked on the door and delivered the decisions. I took no joy at the process or outcome but was relieved when Andy advised us the Committee had upheld the charges levelled against the suspended General Secretary but it was a sad day for everyone concerned. Now a light appeared at the end of the tunnel. At last we could begin to move on.

The Appeals Committee hearing signalled the finish of the internal process but it was never going to end there. Shaun's representative had made that crystal clear from the outset of the process which he argued was flawed. A claim of unfair dismissal was lodged with an employment tribunal. It was not until late 2005 that the tribunal convened.

The barbecue incident and the troubles of 2000 were a stain on the good name of the Union and all those involved and I include myself in that. When I look back I

Dave Tyson (seated) at an Executive Committee meeting, with (left to right) Terry Wilkinson, Hugh Bradley, Tosh McDonald, Andy Reed (National Organiser), Steve Usher, Alan Donnelly and the late Graham Walker.

think how things may have been done differently. Running for President in 2000 was not my best decision and the fallout was regrettable, but we were all big and ugly enough to make our own choices and we all had to face the consequences.

I made it clear to Keith and the EC that it was I who should give evidence at the forthcoming tribunal on behalf of the Union. I had reported to the EC and made recommendations to suspend the General Secretary and the Assistant so it was my initial findings that were adopted and acted upon by the EC. Furthermore, with me taking any criticism, it would take the heat away from the EC and the General Secretary at that time. It was agreed that I would do so.

The tribunal was an unpleasant affair for all involved but I did my very best in answering the questions that were put to me. However I was described by the tribunal Chair as being an 'unreliable witness' which did not help matters. It went on to rubbish my actions and those of the EC, from failing to assist the new General Secretary on the day he took office to heaping charges upon him once suspended. In the eyes of the tribunal we had done just about everything we could to get rid of him via a mismanaged and vindictive process. We also breached our own disciplinary procedures. Consequently Shaun Brady won his claim against ASLEF and demanded to be reinstated, something we could not agree to and so began a period of protracted legal arguments over compensation.

It was a messy and unfortunate saga but there was for me one overriding factor. Two of the most senior figures of the union had engaged in an act of physical aggression which was, in itself, an act of gross misconduct and could not go unpunished.

Thankfully, under the leadership of Keith Norman and now Mick Whelan, both ably assisted by Simon Weller, ASLEF eventually put the troubles of the past behind it and has moved on.

It is important to stress that I have not intended to set the record straight or gone into this most unsavoury affair in great detail, but merely painted a picture of what took place over a very difficult period of time for the union from my perspective. To go into meticulous detail would be of little or no interest to anyone.

Chapter 32 - A Client?...How much do they pay these people!

WHILE SERVING ON the Executive the President at the time, Clive Jones, was beaten in an election. Towards the end of his tenure he very sensibly discussed with us his exit and what positions would become vacant as a result of his departure. One of his roles was to represent members on one of the various pension committees that had been created as a result of the fragmentation of the rail industry. Prior to privatisation there had been a management committee that had overseen the Railway Pension Scheme as a whole, however the Government's policy of rail privatisation had led to the creation of over one hundred sections many of which had committees. This was an unintended consequence of privatisation and the scheme incurred huge additional costs as a result.

It was agreed that I would take over from Clive on the 1994 Pensioner's Section of the Railway Pension Scheme. The section had been created to provide assets for all of the former employees who had retired or were deferred prior to privatisation. It was intended the newly created active sections would have small liabilities (pensions) from day one. The 1994 section had been given a Crown guarantee by the Government meaning whatever assets the section held, the Government would stand by it even if the money in the fund ran out.

I was honoured to think that Clive had confidence in me to carry on such an important role and that the executive agreed, although in all honesty I think nobody else wanted the job. Helpfully, Clive took me along to his last meeting where I was introduced to the Chairman, Frank Robertson and the members of the committee. I became friendly with Frank over the years and built a good working relationship with him until his untimely death sometime later.

I knew nothing about pensions and felt quite daunted about the prospect of dealing with billions of pounds of assets: the responsibility was huge. The support staff who worked for the scheme and the Trustees were largely based a Darlington. However the investment staff worked in offices at Broad Street, just a stone's throw from Liverpool Street station. I embarked on various training sessions and over the coming months became immersed in the world of pensions. To many people, the prospect of becoming involved may seem quite dull, but there are so many moving parts to such a large scheme like the RPS that I found much of the work engaging, stimulating and challenging.

Soon I was ready for my first meeting. A week or so before I was sent the agenda, a document of maybe 100 pages plus that was full of actuary speak, investment jargon and other matters such as medical reports and meeting minutes. I threw myself into the papers but soon began to struggle with the long investment and actuarial reports with all the figures, graphs and much more. I would read some reports and fail to grasp the meaning of the paper, so I would read it again but repeatedly

Time out from two days of Trustee board meetings in Scotland: David Tyson on top of the Forth Bridge. (Author's collection)

failed to understand what was being stated. I would become frustrated and try and refer to various training material I had been given but the exercise became futile.

I attended my first meeting with a sense of apprehension. However Frank soon put my fears at rest and as the meeting progressed I came to learn that the various reports would be introduced by either the Scheme Actuary, an Investment Manager, the Committee Secretary or the various support staff. It was still hard to follow at times but their professionalism and approachable attitude made life easier.

I had been reading a particular report that had many figures contained within it and there was one figure of £165,000 which was written as £165, that did not make sense to me. As we went through the paper I still could not reconcile the figure, so with some anxiety I raised my hand to attract Frank's attention. "You have a question Dave?" he asked. I cleared my throat as I felt my mouth go dry. "Yes Chairman, I'm looking at this figure of £165,000 and it does not add up to me," I commented. I was met with silence and sideways looks from the other members of the committee. "What page of the report are you on Dave?" he asked. I advised him of the page number, there was some shuffling of pages as everybody turned to the part of the report I had referred to and a wry smile appeared on Frank's face. "No Dave, that's not £165,000.... that's £165 million, the section is that large we only deal in multiples of millions, I hope that helps." I confirmed that it did help and that I would shut up for now.

After the meeting Frank pulled me to one side. He told me not to worry and that I should never be afraid to ask what appeared to be daft questions. Sometimes the most simple ones were actually the most important. He also reassured me that getting to grips with the complexities of the scheme would take a good deal of time and effort.

In time I became involved in several other committees. The British Railways section and sometime later the company I worked for, Anglia, decided to seek nominations for three staff members to join the committee. I was fortunate enough to be elected and sometime later became Chairman. It was during my time on the Anglia committee that the company took the decision to close the section to new entrants. What riled me was the fact that they had taken the decision without consulting either the committee or the unions. The implications were quite large as it meant that over time the section would become overwhelmed by pensioners with no new money coming in from active members. Anglia were the only train operating company to do this and to my eternal regret I think I should have been more demonstrative in pressing the issue harder to get it reversed. It was only some years later that the new owner turned things around to allow new employees to join.

Towards the end of 2000 the Assistant General Secretary, Tony West, expressed his desire to retire. He had suffered a massive heart attack some years earlier but, with the constitution of a ox, returned to work after a period of recuperation. Tony had been a Trustee Director of the pension scheme for some years and expressed the view that given my involvement with the various sections of the scheme I should be the natural successor: the Executive again agreed. This was a big step up from the various committees I had been involved in as I would be a Trustee of a board of sixteen directors with ultimately overall responsibility for all the billions in assets of the scheme and its 350,000 members, one of the biggest in the UK. I decided that to continue in the roles on the other committees could cause a conflict so I resigned from all three and concentrated on the board which is a decision I certainly did not regret given the workload involved.

The board was chaired by a formidable character, James Jerram, who I came to have a great deal of respect for and with whom I had an excellent working relationship. He would not suffer fools gladly and in truth I think there were many members of the team who were somewhat overwhelmed by him. Not long after becoming elected to the board I attended a meeting which James was chairing. There had been a slump in the markets and equity values had dropped quite dramatically. From time to time the board would receive briefings from our various investment managers at what was deemed an investment review meeting.

A team of investment managers from Schroders awaited upon the board and began to give their presentation. They had several billion pounds of our money and the individual giving the presentation explained that the drop in value was down to market conditions. I was watching James and at one point I thought I saw steam coming out of his ears. After about five minutes he held his hand up to stop the presenter. “You have lost us 25% of the value of our fund,” he said to the presenter and gave him the thousand yard stare. Anyone who knew James would have taken it on the chin and agreed with him. Sadly the presenter failed to grasp his rising anger and was not aware of his reputation. “No, it’s down to the market conditions,” he stated and there followed a short conversation between the two of them. I sat there thinking, ‘This is not going to end well,’ and my expectations were confirmed when James turned to the individual and stated, “Your figures are all wrong and YOU have lost the value in the fund, now GET OUT and don’t come back until your figures are correct.” I expected tumbleweed to blow through the meeting room as the atmosphere turned decidedly frosty. The Schroders team collected their papers and left the room with their tails between their legs. My respect for James increased ten fold.

A few days later I was travelling up to London for a meeting when the train ran into Stowmarket station. As it came to a stand in the platform I glanced up from my newspaper and looked straight at a chap waiting to board the train. ‘He looks familiar,’ I thought to myself. He boarded and took the seat directly opposite me. It was the presenter James had kicked out of our meeting only the week before. ‘Bloody hell,’ I thought to myself, would he recognise me and start questioning me, what should I do? I did what any self respecting wimp would do, I buried my face in my newspaper until the train arrived at Liverpool Street station until he had left. What a sap I was! It was not so long after James’ rant that we parted company with Schroders.

The Trustee board is made up of a total of sixteen directors. Eight are nominated by the employer organisations and eight from employee groups including trade unions and pensioner representative groups. With so many trustees, which was considered unusual, there was diverse range of characters albeit at the time not a single woman, ethnic minority or anyone under fifty years of age. Apart from me— I was 36 years of age.

Three characters were on the employee side, Maurice Whittle, Ken Ball and John Mayfield. All were former high ranking BRB Directors and all three were complete gentlemen. Maurice was expert in the area of investments and would always quiz investment managers, probing them for snippets of information that may uncover some issue or another. Much depended on the character of the person who headed up a particular investment house. Their personality, competence and reputation were all key at that time, as well as, more importantly, delivering good returns for the scheme. It tickled me that Maurice would turn up for a meeting in a suit, a newspaper under his arm but due to he fact he ‘suffered with his feet’ he would wear training shoes. It was only after he passed away did we learn he had been a Spitfire pilot during the Battle of Britain.

I learned so much from these three men. Each had their own quirks and would often offer advice which I soaked up. From time to time John would call me and begin the call with, “Mayfield here...” which I loved. He was a real gentleman and a very dapper dresser. I recall him turning up for a meeting with a red rose in the lapel of his jacket.

When asked why he was wearing a red rose he exclaimed, "Saint George's day old boy!"

I would always wait to hear what John had to say when we were in a debate about some major issue. He was a man of vast experience and wisdom but he also took a calm and measured approach to the subject being discussed. Some time just before he retired we had to meet with representatives of The Pensions Regulator (TPR). We had not met before and as each of us gave a very brief description of our CV it was clear that the TPR representatives were rather inexperienced. When John came to giving a brief run down of his CV I could see their faces drop. He had more damn experience than the lot of them put together.

As the years passed so the personnel on the board would change. Trustees would come and go as would staff. Challenges would also come and go but the biggest ones were when markets fell or recession hit. We were taught that the markets were cyclical and equities would always suffer. That was why we had such a diverse range of investments from equities in the UK and abroad to government bonds, property and cash, to name but a few. However the banking crisis of 2008 was to cause the Trustees huge worries as we witnessed a perfect storm with the banking system in the UK close to collapse and billions were wiped off the value of the fund.

Some years later I was to attend an investment conference in Edinburgh where the Chancellor at the time of the banking crisis, Alistair Darling, gave a speech on the Government's reaction to it. He was abroad when he received an urgent phone call from the chief of one of the big banks in the UK who advised him that it was only a matter of time before the banks collapsed. "How long can you last?" asked Mr Darling "About two hours" was the reply!

David Tyson giving his pension report to the ASLEF conference in May 2017. (Photo courtesy of ASLEF)

Training plays a huge part of the role as a trustee. Pensions legislation and the requirements to keep up to speed are essential so that effective decision making can be undertaken. I would attend courses run by various organisations such as our actuary Willis Towers Watson, or the National Association of Pension Funds later to rebrand themselves as the Pension and Lifetime Saving Association (PLSA), a name I could never get to grips with for some reason.

After I had been on the board about three or four years, Phil White, the British Transport Police Federation Trustee, retired and was succeeded by Gary Towse. I had never met Gary but soon got know him well and came to realise that he was extremely well connected and had that policeman's instinct for sniffing out information and getting to the root of problems. He was also not frightened to speak his mind. It wasn't long before he was calling me 'Tyse' and giving me stick about all sorts of things. He also introduced me to the annual investment conference in Edinburgh run by the PLSA.

I had never deemed it really necessary to attend the investment conference but he insisted I come along to see what it was all about. It was indeed an eye opener with well over a thousand trustees attending and speakers from all over the world. It was a great way of looking into the world of investment and finding out what the big issues of the day were and what was on the horizon. At my first conference I was in awe of the keynote speaker Al Gore, former Vice President of the USA. His speech was inspiring and urged trustees to act on climate change, a call I responded to and hope I had influenced the trustees over the following years. Other speakers over the years included Norman Lamont, Alistair Darling and journalists such as Dan Snow, Katia Adler and Robert Peston. One journalist that made me sit up and take note was a guy called Misha Glenney. As a result of his presentation I immediately read two of his books which are among the most fascinating I have ever seen, 'McMafia' and 'Dark Market.' I shit a brick after reading them!!

As a side to the conference there would be a trade area where various investment banks, managers and other organisations seeking investment would have their trade stands. They would entice you to speak to them with offers of competitions with prizes, 'freebies' such as books, pens, trinkets and nibbles and drinks. I got talking to Peter on one particular trade stand. He worked for JP Morgan, a huge investment bank and not the sort of place the likes of Dave Tyson would put his money. To be a client you had to have vast assets. It turned out he happened to be the relationship manager between the bank and the Railway Pension Scheme. We struck up quite a conversation and soon established that on occasion I would drive the train he caught into work. He would catch the 05:32 out of Stowmarket each morning. This began as the 05:00 from Norwich which I would work occasionally. I advised him that I would keep an eye out for him next time I worked the train and would give him a wave if I spotted him.

Many months passed until one summer's morning I was working the 05:00 to London and sure enough, as I ran into Stowmarket there was Peter standing on the platform waiting to board. I gave the horn a short toot and waved to which he responded. Many months passed until I was up in Edinburgh at the investment conference the following year. I had been doing a tour of the trade stands, trying to suss out the ones that were handing out the best freebies and those that were serving beverages (I must admit to doing a tour of the beverages late on Thursday afternoons), as well as looking for any that may actually have something interesting to say.

Soon enough I bumped into Peter who quickly beckoned me over. "Dave, I've been dying to see you, and I'm so glad you made it this year." I was intrigued as to what he had to say. It turned out that on the day I had given Peter a wave he had been standing next to a friend who knew he worked for an investment bank. As I sailed past and waved at Peter his friend turned to him and asked, “Did that train driver just wave at you?” He responded that I had and the follow up question was, “Peter, how do you know a train driver?”

“Well, he’s a client,” Peter replied. His friend was dumfounded. “A client, you have a train driver for a client.... how much to they bloody pay these people?” I have dined out on that story for many years.

Conferences also had a social side where we would catch up with colleagues from other schemes and investment houses who we had not seen for some time. It was also good to be with colleagues in a more relaxed environment. Gary would often invite me along to various bashes he had managed to blag his way into and we would often overdo the social side of things. If I awoke the following day with a hangover I knew I had been well and truly ‘Towserized’. One particular evening we were invited to a meal at a Chinese restaurant and after a very enjoyable session we started on the sake. I had never had any before but I quaffed it like it was going out of fashion. My word, I had an awful night and the following morning I made my way to the conference hall where I decided to get a coffee and sit down for a while. I was close to the top of the escalators and as I was sitting contemplating whether to go into the conference or go back to bed, John Mayfield came gliding up the escalator and glanced across at me. He came over, looked me in the eye and said, “My God Dave... you look like shit!” It was the only time I ever heard him swear.

There was one particular incident that occurred that could be described as being ‘hoisted by my own petard’ as the saying goes, or being blown up by my own bomb as the translation is. Towards the end of my driving career there had been issues with me gaining release from my employer to attend pension meetings. This was as a result of a shortage of drivers and trains had to be covered before releasing me for a meeting, a position I accepted but it would be frustrating to prepare for a lengthy meeting only to find I could not attend. I was scheduled to attend a particular meeting, so the day before it, I looked at the daily supplementary list that is posted at noon the previous day. I scanned the list and located my name at the bottom where it stated my name and the comment ‘pensions meeting’ in the comments column. This pleased me and I made my way home happy in the thought I would be able to attend.

The following day I made my way up to London and attended the meeting of what was known as the Benefits and Funding Committee. These meetings were renowned for taking up the full day and this particular meeting was no exception. However it finished around 3pm and I made my way down to the station to catch my train home. I walked onto the station concourse and checked the display screens to see which platform my train was to leave from only to discover it had been cancelled. Just what I needed at the end of the day!

There was no use complaining. I was travelling for free and there was absolutely nothing I could do about it so I popped up to Hamilton Hall, the pub above the station, had a pint and then made my way back down to catch the next train home. As I was sitting there on the journey home I was reflecting on the day and the cancelled train when a thought crossed my mind. That thought kept niggling at me for the rest of the journey until the train arrived back at Norwich.

Before making my way home I popped into the signing on point to check the supplementary list for the following day to check what duty I was on. However my niggling head worm made me look at the current day’s list. My release was there at the bottom of the list but as I then scanned up to the job I would have been on I noticed that my name was also allocated to that job as well. The roster clerk had double booked me. He had shown me as being on a driving job and at a pensions meeting on the same day.

When I had scanned the list the day before I had located my name at the bottom but failed to notice the error! My train home had been cancelled as a result of me not turning up for work around lunchtime.... bugger! If I had paid better attention to the daily list I may well have noticed the error and prevented the cancellation.

I spent over twenty years representing members at various committees and in September 2021 I decided it was time to make way for someone else. I had enjoyed my time on the board, met and worked with some fantastic people and gained a great deal of knowledge for which I am extremely grateful. I also made some great friendships which continue to this day.

Chapter 33 - Well and Truly Stitched Up

FROM TIME TO time colleagues would either wind up each other or play practical jokes. There are many instances that spring to mind. The classic stories of telling the new boy to go to the stores to get a left handed screwdriver or a bucket of blue steam were the myths of many a work place and the railway was no exception.

There were certain characters who were very adept at this. Not long after I had joined the railway a story was relayed to me about Mike who worked on the platform. He was soon to be married and had brought some wedding invitations in to work. He also brought a wedding present booklet which his future wife had compiled. In it were presents on various pages that had been taken out of an Argos magazine with a photo and an order number. A guest could pull out a page once they had selected a suitable gift to buy the happy couple.

Steve was an invitee to the wedding and Mike gave him an invitation along with the present list booklet. Steve took the booklet home and tore out a page but also made some additions on the blank pages at the back of the book. These were taken from adverts in a porno magazine for various sex toys and lingerie. He returned the booklet to Mike a few days later. A week later a rather unhappy Mike confronted Steve about the additions that had come to light after Mike had passed the booklet on to his relatives!

Unfortunately for Mike that was not the end of saga. On the day he was handing out the invitations at work he had inadvertently left some blanks on the table in the office. Steve got hold of them and filled them in. A while later a couple of the more obnoxious characters that worked on the platform thanked Mike for the invitations and Eric, who should never have been unleashed on the travelling public, asked if it was, "ok if I could bring my missus to the wedding?" Mike became far less happy once this came to light.

Speaking of Eric, he was quite a short chap, always immaculately dressed with slicked back grey hair, thick lensed glasses and he always wore a waistcoat with a pocket watch on a chain. He also walked with a pronounced limp. His command of the English language was not the greatest and I recall him talking about a poor chap who had committed suicide. Eric stated the he believed the chap's act was "Pre-medicated". It is also said that a passenger approached him on the platform one afternoon and asked, "Excuse me mate, can you tell me where the train to London is?" Eric responded as only Eric could, "Platform 4, and I'm not your bloody mate!"

I was subjected to a wind up, that if the truth be known backfired on the perpetrator to an extent. Some particular turns of duty were quite unique to our roster. They were known as being 'as ordered' and that was pretty much what was required of the driver. One was an early morning turn where we would sign on duty at the unearthly time of 04:40 and there was also a more respectable late shift at 14:00.

These duties were created to fill any gaps that were left at the last minute. Drivers, like anybody else, were liable to sleep in or fail to turn up at the right time as is the nature of such early turns, or they may phone in sick at the last minute. It has also been known for the roster clerk to make a balls up and book the wrong person on a particular turn of duty. The as ordered man would be there to provide cover in the event of such occurrences.

The 04:40 job was a nine hour shift that could seem like twenty hours if you had nothing to do which was often the case, and there were many occasions when I would return home having only left the messroom to stretch my legs to buy a coffee from the station. If the right supervisor was on duty, I would nip into the city to do some shopping or get a haircut (the days of visiting the barber have long gone). Drivers being drivers were always looking to get away as soon as possible if they had not been allocated any work either when signing on duty or in the first few hours of the shift. Sometimes there would be additional spare drivers turning up later in the day thus freeing up the 'as ordered' man. If the right supervisor was on duty then it was not unknown for me to be home before my wife had got out of bed!!

When the turn was first created I spent my first time on the early morning shift constantly on the go and did not stop all day. I was sent to the depot to prepare and bring in some stock to the station, then sent out there with a failed train, later a trip to Yarmouth because of a delay and then just as I was thinking about going home I had to take a unit to Parkeston Quay at Harwich. I remember saying to the supervisor, "Don't you have anybody else to cover some of this work?" and was told that he did but the supervisors had a bet on to see how much work could be allocated in one shift to the 04:40 as ordered driver. I think he won the bet much to my annoyance, although being busy always made the time pass more quickly.

There were critical points during the shift that meant that there were certain trains you did not have to work as the round trip would take you over your allocated hours. Of course there was always the offer of overtime which some of my colleagues would gladly take. I was not in that camp. I did not work my free days, nor overtime as I felt the days were long enough and I have always treasured my free time away from the job.

The threshold most drivers judged things by was the 10:40 Norwich to Cambridge and return which was scheduled to arrive back in Norwich at 13:27. This meant you could do that trip just within you daily allocated hours. Generally if the driver booked to work the 10:40 Cambridge had returned to the depot on time from his trip to London and back you were considered safe. Odd trips to Yarmouth or Lowestoft may crop up, but the omen for a finish no later than noon would be good. Many of the supervisors would use the 10:40 driver as a guide. If he was at Norwich in good time then the 04:40 driver would be getting a call to, "Stop making the place look untidy," or "It's about time you weren't here."

There were certain drivers you would look out for on early London/Cambridge job who would, if they were running late, try and drag out their late arrival so as not to have a long enough break before going to Cambridge thus stiffing the 04:40 driver into covering the second part of his job. This increased the London/Cambridge driver's chances of an early day. Very unprofessional and inconsiderate but not unusual. In fact I knew one driver who became notorious for making unusual requests of the supervisor to get away early because he had 'Made arrangements for some radiators to be delivered,' in the full knowledge that he would be at work, or on another occasion he "Had to get home because his wife's hairdresser was going to give him a hair cut!"

Of course there were a few supervisors who would insist that you stayed right up to your booking off time which never really bothered me. You were paid for nine hours so that is what you should do. Alternatively there were always a few who felt it was their divine right to clear off after a period that they thought was acceptable and the allocated hours for the day were just 'advisory'! Generally, if a driver got right away early, the supervisor knew that he would get the favour back sometime in the future if he needed it. It was good man management although some may see it as what was known as a Spanish practice.

I had been allocated to the 04:40 morning as ordered shift which meant climbing out of bed at just after 03:30, a most anti-social time and was described by a colleague as being a time of day that was occupied by 'rats and twats!'

When signing on, I would study the supplementary daily list to see if there were any spare drivers signing on later in the morning thus increasing the chances of an early day. This particular day I was in luck. A driver was on duty around 07:00 so things were starting to look up already. There was also a newly promoted depot driver coming on at around the same time so he may prove to be keen to get some experience in if a local turn cropped up.

I checked who the driver was on the London/Cambridge job which was the threshold 10:40. It turned out to be a reliable colleague Lee, who was also one of the local ASLEF reps. So far so good. Next thing to do was to check out who the supervisor was on the morning shift. Not such good news there: it was one who was not known for letting drivers get away. I would just have to see how the day panned out and maybe work some magic on him over the course of the shift, engage him in chit chat at quiet times, ask about his wider knowledge of golf and how to improve my game, always good to get advice from a good player, all that sort of stuff.

I made my way upstairs to the mess and locker rooms to see who was about and to have a coffee to start off the day. To a newcomer it may be quite a surprise as to how busy the messroom could be at such an unearthly time of the day. There were generally plenty of drivers and conductors preparing to begin their shift. This would often be a time to catch up on the latest gossip or scandal, evaluate the day's possible events, or analyse any incidents that may have cropped up since the previous day's shift.

I was always full of good intentions and would often have a book in my locker. When I was a Pension Trustee or on the ASLEF executive, I would have reams of papers to read and the as ordered turns were in theory a good time to catch up. In reality, as you picked up a book or papers someone would want to ask your advice or engage in conversation about something or other. I was always happy to do so as I found I have always enjoyed the company of my railway colleagues.

Around 06:00 one of my closest friends, Michael, came into the messroom and on seeing me greeted me with the usual hello, "Morning Sword!" He was on the early shift at Crown Point depot which was not the most desirable of turns of duty but not too onerous. It was clear from his demeanour that he was not keen on going out there and complained that he had a slight headache. Once he finished his coffee he made his way out to the depot with a "See ya later old fruit".

The 07:00 spare driver signed on and appeared in the messroom and by around 08:00 it was quite lively in there with plenty of chit chat and banter.

The supervisors, who were situated in an office downstairs, would generally ring the messroom (there was a phone on the messroom wall) and ask for a particular driver or conductor and then give them the good or bad news depending on the task required of them. If the phone rang what generally would happen is everyone would look at each other as if to say, 'Well whose going to answer that then?' Depending who was up there it could ring for ages.

However there was a depot driver who was relatively new and very keen. He answered the phone and then called out the 07:00 spare driver's name. Robin drew himself slowly out of his seat. I breathed a sigh of relief as he sauntered over to the phone to get his instructions. The exclamations "Really!" and "You're joking!" were used. He replaced the phone and looked at me. "I've only got to go out to Crown Point to help Michael with the workload out there, he's got a headache coming on and wants some help!" I replied sarcastically, "Poor Michael, it's such a tough job out there, you better take him some aspirin and tell him to have a lie down, they will be so busy." Robin laughed as he collected his things together and made his way out to the depot.

Time passed and my mind began to wander as to the all important 10:40 Cambridge train threshold and whether Lee was on time on his journey back from London.

Around 09:30 the messroom phone rang again and the same depot driver answered it and ended the call by saying, "Yes I'll tell him." He looked across at me, then he uttered those dreaded words "Dave ... 10:40 Cambridge." There was a collective sucking in of cheeks and 'Ooos'. My heart sank. I had dared to think that it would soon be time to 'roll the wicket' with the supervisor as to a possible early finish. I resigned myself to a trip to Cambridge and back, which in the grand scheme of things was not too bad as it was my last shift and I had a long weekend to look forward to.

About five minutes before I was due to make my way over to the station Lee walked in, the driver who should have been on the 10:40 but was clearly late. "I've got to do your 10:40 Cambridge, Lee," I said. He looked at me in surprise and said, "Oh... thanks very much Dave... that's great!" I didn't think too much about his reaction. If he was running late he may well have expected to get 'cut out' .

I gathered my gear from my locker and returned to the messroom to fill my mug with a brew and made my way downstairs. As I passed the supervisor's office I bid Ken a "See you later." He looked up from his desk with a blank expression on his face, and bid me a "Yeah.... see you Dave." As I walked over to the station I remember thinking that Ken seemed as though he had forgotten he had given me the trip but I shrugged the thought off immediately.

Eventually I relieved the incoming driver of the Cambridge train. Just as I was setting up the cab for my trip, my mobile phone buzzed... a text. The sender was Michael with the message '10:40 Cambridge!'...... 'Cheeky bastard,' I thought. I didn't have time to call him as it was too close to departure time and using your mobile while on the move is a sackable offence so I resolved to call him on arrival at Cambridge. I thought Michael was having a laugh at the fact that I had been 'stiffed' with a trip right at the end of my shift, though I was still trying to work out how he would have found out as he was stuck out at the depot.

I always enjoyed the journey across to Ely and then Cambridge. It was one of the few that were, at that time, still controlled by semaphore signals with the traditional signal boxes all along the route. There were also the sights through Thetford Forest, Stamford battle area where the army would often practice manoeuvres with soldiers in combat gear dropping out of helicopters or the occasional tank trundling around. Fighter jets passed overhead on their approach to Lakenheath as well as the massive air re-fuelling and transport planes that would use Mildenhall. I found it a pleasure observing the ever changing seasonal colours of the forest and then the unique beauty of the Breckland.

On arrival, I shut the driving desk down and switched on my mobile phone. As soon as it was able to receive a signal it rang.... the caller was Michael, our conversation went like this.

Class 170 DMU No. 170201 in platform 6 at Cambridge on 11 March 2017.
(Alastair Holmes)

"Hello Michael."

"Dave, where are you?"

"Well, I'm at Cambridge, you ought to know you sent me a text stating 10:40 Cambridge!"

"Er, well er.... um... er ... you know that phone call you got in the messroom this morning?"

"Yeah."

"Er, well ....er um..... er .. that was actually me, not the supervisor. I just thought I would wind you up, I never thought you would actually go," he said sheepishly. Clearly my sarcastic comment about his headache had been fed back to him by Robin.

I could only respond in one way.

"You f......., hang on a minute Michael!"

I was about to let loose a tirade of abuse at one of my best mates but I found myself standing by the open cab door with passengers still disembarking from the train. I clearly needed to exercise some discretion.

"Just wait a minute, Michael."

I got out of the train and made my way to a quiet corner at the end of platform 6 and then let him have it. Well I tried to let him have it both barrels but I found I was laughing too much. Everything was starting to fall into place beginning with the new boy answering the phone and not realising it was not the supervisor speaking. The odd

Michael Lloyd—the perpetrator of the stitch up—beside DEMU No. 755405 at Cromer.

look Ken gave me when I left the signing on point and of course Lee's gratitude when I told him I was doing his Cambridge trip.

However I could not let Michael get away with this.

"You bastard, what a dirty trick, let me tell you something Michael." By this time I could not keep a straight face. Although I was the victim of the prank I found it so funny. "I have got a few years left on this job and let me promise you I will get you back for this."

Michael was very apologetic, and they say that you can't hurt your mates. I believe that, it was harmless and I saw the funny side. No sooner had we terminated the call than my phone rang again. This time it was Lee.

"Dave?"

"Yes, Lee. You'll never guess what Michael has done to me?"

Lee knew all about what had happened. It turned out that he had not been late into Norwich from London. He had been dealing with some ASLEF matters in the local rep's office downstairs at the signing on point and had only come up to the messroom to fill his flask prior to his trip to Cambridge. He had been surprised when I offered to cover for him.

For some reason Lee had not cleared off home which was fortunate.

"Dave, Michael is in a panic, the supervisor is looking for you, he wants you to work a train to Great Yarmouth!'

"Well that's going to be a bit difficult bearing in mind I'm in bloody Cambridge!" I replied.

Lee had advised Ken that he would pass the message on to me but in reality Lee worked the train. As far as Ken was concerned the train was being worked by me.

It was time to pick up my return trip to Norwich. Thankfully the conductor had bought me a coffee so I quickly set the cab up and we were off home. During the return journey I kept thinking of the day's antics and kept laughing to myself. The conductor joined me in the cab for a short while and I relayed the story to him which we both laughed about. I was a victim of a prank that got a bit out of hand, the only downside being I had a longer day than expected.

I relayed this story to many of my work mates over the years, much to their amusement. Not long before I retired, I was travelling back from a pensions board meeting in London. Ken, who had been the supervisor on that fateful day, was travelling back to Norwich and sat with me. He had taken a promotion and was no longer a supervisor. I told him the story and he was somewhat was taken aback, but as with everyone else saw the funny side. I think he was surprised such antics had transpired right under his nose without him knowing at all. It was with some good fortune that Lee had decided to hang around for a while on that day. If the Yarmouth train had been cancelled we would have had to spill the beans so to speak which could have led to some rather tricky questions and consequences.

Well, did I manage to get my revenge on Michael......?

Chapter 34 - Revenge

THE TRUTH IS.....no. I retired from the industry somewhat earlier than I anticipated so any plans or opportunities I had to capitalise upon did not come to fruition. The best I can do is tell a tale about my great friend Michael Lloyd.

I think it is fair to say that most employees who work in the operations of the railway will at some point in their career make a mistake which, if they were lucky enough, they could get away with. These days the technology and more intense scrutiny means this is unlikely. As I often stated when representing members at incident reviews and disciplinary hearings as a result of operational mistakes, the 'culprit' does not have a delete button. Once the error or breach has been committed it is there to see for all who care to look.

When we first moved into the joint signing on point we were able to park our cars at a space behind it. (It's gone now after the station was redeveloped and a new multi-storey car park built on the site of the old goods yard.) We were issued with permits that we were expected to display in the window of our cars. Woe betide any individual who forgot to display their permit as there was one particular station manager who seemed to take great pleasure in clamping any offender's car. A terse message would be left on the windscreen informing them of their misdemeanour and the fine. He would be out there with his wheel clamp and a look of smug satisfaction on his face as the offender's wheels were clamped.

Unfortunately one day he picked on an individual who was not prepared to put up with such a petty action. Joe made his way over to said manager's office and invited him to remove the clamp with the comment, "I'm working the 13:00 to London in a little while. The train will stay in the platform until the clamp is removed." Consequently the clamp came off.

Michael (my Cambridge prankster) was spare one particular morning and had little to do during the course of the day. Half way through his shift he was contacted by the Train Crew Supervisor and given a job along with another driver, Tim, which involved them walking out to the maintenance depot at Crown Point and taking two units which were coupled together. One was to go to Cambridge and detach with the second travelling on to Peterborough where Tim was to work an empty unit back to Crown Point. They were advised by the supervisor that once they were back in the depot they were free to go home. This was music to Michael's ears and given that the depot was a good twenty minute walk from the signing on point, he decided to drive his car out to Crown Point and once they returned he would drive straight home.

They arrived at Cambridge, where Michael decided to travel to Peterborough with Tim and then back to Crown Point. However on arrival at Peterborough it transpired that there was no empty unit to work back so they had to jump on a service train. Later they arrived at Norwich station.

Michael returned to the signing on point and went through the usual routine we all generally go through, putting his bag in his locker along with all those other bits and pieces he carried about. He closed the locker door and made his way to the car park. He had recently purchased a sky blue Mark III Ford Escort that was his pride and joy, yet when he went into the car park to get it there was just an empty space. He got that sinking feeling and then looked around just to make sure he had not parked the car in a different place to the one he thought he had left it in. No, there were no sky blue Escorts in the car park so Michael came to the grim conclusion that the car had been stolen. After his initial panic had passed he pulled himself together and rang the Norfolk Police to report the theft. He then had to go through the process of describing the car with all the details such as registration number, colour, where it had been left and his personal details.

Michael lived only a few miles from the station so gloomily walked home to relay the bad news to his wife. I can imagine that he was feeling quite glum at the time having lost the next biggest investment second only to his home. There was the insurance company to advise and the prospect of not ever seeing his beloved car again or maybe worse, it could end up being located as a burnt out shell. There was also the prospect of having to arrange alternative transport.

Some five hours after the car had been reported as stolen Michael sat down to his evening meal with his wife. It was as they were sitting there talking about the events of the day that Michael had what can only be described as a moment of clarity. His blood must have turned cold when he suddenly realised that the car had not actually been stolen but was sitting where he left it, at Crown Point. His elation at having remembered that his car had not in fact been stolen but was sitting patiently waiting for its owner to return can only have been short lived once he realised that he would have to inform the local constabulary and the insurance company of his glaring omission. I would love to have been a fly on the wall when Michael made those calls and listened to the reaction of the police.

Michael got his beloved car back and, some would say foolishly, told his mates about his oversight.

Chapter 35 - Humble Pie

I WAS SCHEDULED to work the 07:40 fast service from Norwich to London one morning so, as is the usual practice, I conferred with the conductor about the stops we were booked to make on the journey. For some reason when I said Diss, Ipswich and London he retorted that I was not correct. I took what he said a face value and then ignored it and walked off to the front of the train with my cup of tea and set the cab up ready for departure.

Departure time came and the signal remained at red. I began to think that something was wrong, maybe a points failure or a fault on the swing bridge at Trowse. I powered up my mobile phone. As soon as it got a signal it rang—it was Ken the Train Crew Supervisor. "Dave, is everything ok?" he asked. "Fine thanks Ken, I was just about to ring the signaller as we don't have the road yet," I replied. "Oh, where are you?" ….. "I'm on platform 2 with the 7:40 London!" 'Strange question,' I thought to myself. To my surprise Ken came back with, "No Dave, you're on the 08:00 London, your train is on platform 4!"

I felt the blood drain out of me. No wonder the conductor had quoted different stops to the ones I had, I was on the wrong bloody train! I quickly shut the desk down, got my bits and pieces together, jumped out of the cab onto platform 2, got back into the cab to get the cup of tea I had left behind, and then made my way on the short route to platform 4. No way was I going to do the 'walk of shame' all the way to the back of the train on platform 2 and then walk the length of the now late 07:40 London thus enduring the wrath and scowls of the passengers. I whipped around the front of my train, over the rails and onto the locomotive of the train I should have been on a few minutes earlier.

We were soon on the move albeit about twelve minutes late but given the amount of recovery time we were allowed and the efficiency of the conductor we were almost on schedule by the time we passed through Shenfield and arrived a couple of minutes late at Liverpool Street. Once we arrived at the Street I quickly disappeared into the engine room to make a 'check' on the equipment and spare myself from any further scowls or rude comments from passengers. What a wimp! On my return to Norwich I popped in to see the supervisor to apologise for my error. He advised me I had 'made the log', not just for my glaring error but also my spirited attempt to successfully make up the time I had lost!

Throughout my entire railway career I have never had to encounter any form of disciplinary action, although I have made a few errors that were brought to my attention and needed dealing with. When I first joined the footplate many incidents and errors would be covered up, but as the years passed and technology has improved that option has slowly been eroded and in my view that is for the better. Drivers may have twenty years of incident free driving but then underlying issues, such as health or personal problems, may lead to a lack of concentration which can lead to mistakes being made.

Once a driver has had a safety of the line incident it will be investigated and an action plan agreed with him and his manager to try and learn lessons from what took place and to reduce the risk of the error reoccurring. In most cases this does the trick,

(Above) The view ahead: looking through the fly encrusted windscreen of a DVT at Liverpool Street prior to departure. (David Tyson)

(Left) Class 90 at Norwich about to haul the 18:00 departure to London on Christmas Eve 2017: this train then formed the 20:30 from London to Norwich, the last Down train to Norwich before the two day shutdown for Christmas. (David Tyson)

but from time to time further errors occur so more intensive action may have to be taken such as increased monitoring and additional training. Ultimately it can lead to the driver being removed from the grade and deployed elsewhere.

The vast majority of drivers will go through their career and at some point will make mistakes. Those that say they have never made an error are either liars or very lucky. It could be speeding, failing to stop at signals, or maybe the most common error, failing to call at a station. The potentially most dangerous of these mistakes are known as signals passed at danger or SPADs and are treated with the utmost seriousness. A SPAD has the potential to lead to collisions and fatalities, so as soon as a driver is involved in one he will generally be removed from driving until the matter is fully investigated and a plan agreed to get him back driving, or not, as the case may be.

I have failed to call at various stations over the years, one being Harling Road on the Norwich to Cambridge line. It is a rural station and at the time the only working that stopped there was an evening train to allow commuters to alight. I had stopped at the previous station, Eccles Road, and then once on the move I powered up to 75mph. On the approach to Harling Road there is a line speed increase to 90mph so I opened the power controller to full and once at maximum speed and about 100 meters from the platform, I realised I was scheduled to stop there. By the time I had realised my error it was too late, so I continued on to Thetford where a group of disgruntled passengers alighted and were advised to make their way over to the opposite platform where a Norwich bound train would pick them up and make a special stop. About two years later I did exactly the same thing on a Saturday morning: I missed Harling Road in the opposite direction. Fortunately there were no passengers on the train or the platform but I still called in the error.

My most memorable fail to call was at Stratford in East London. I was working the 20:30 train from London to Norwich and was booked to stop at Stratford to pick up only. At this time the line between Chelmsford and Norwich was being upgraded by the use of a train known as a high output ballast cleaner. The train was the longest in the UK and was formed of a mixture of empty wagons at one end, some ballast clearing/ laying machinery in the centre, and wagons loaded with ballast in the rear. It was an amazing collection of machinery and once on site it would clear out all the old ballast stones that held the track in place, then replace them with new ones. The track would then be 'tamped' by an on track machine and once completed the track would be fit for trains to run over at maximum line speed. The work would be carried out overnight and about 500 meters would be completed each session. If this work had been carried out in the more conventional way it would have taken several nights or weekends with a 20mph speed restriction slapped upon it for the duration.

The train I was working from London that night was to be the final through train of the day as the high output ballast cleaner would be going on site at around 21:30 somewhere between Colchester and Chelmsford. Passengers catching a later service would have to endure a train as far as Chelmsford, then the dreaded bus replacement service to Colchester, and then back on a train to any one of the stations to Norwich.

I left London bang on time and powered up to 70mph. I was also trialing a tablet based App that was supposed to advise the driver of his route and alert him to the next stop as well as measure the train's progress. If the train was running early it was supposed to suggest a suitable speed below that of the route to assist in energy saving and keep the train in its booked path. The App was hopeless and despite being told not to interfere with it while on the move, I attempted to get it to work..... and failed in the process! I shut off power to coast through the neutral section at Bow Junction and then normally I would coast to a point where I would apply the brakes to stop at Stratford. Unfortunately, my frustration with the App had boiled over and I was not applying myself to the standard I usually set and instead of applying the brake I applied power.

It was only when I hit Stratford platform at 70 mph and noticed it was packed with passengers did I realise that I was supposed to be stopping there. By that time it was far too late and even if I had stopped I would not have been allowed to set the train back into the platform. I buzzed the conductor but he was already through the cab door wanting to know if I was ok and why we had not stopped. There was nothing I could do but inform Anglia Control of my error. Not much later I passed the high output ballast cleaner entering the worksite.

I had to face the music with my manager the following day and was issued with an action plan to mitigate any further risk. I was also informed that the company's Twitter account went into meltdown on that evening with angry passengers baying for me to be sacked. I can quite understand their frustration, but as I stated earlier, drivers do not have a delete button, our errors are there for all to see.

Chapter 36 - Slip Slidin' Away

AUTUMN IS KNOWN as the leaf fall season, a period that has caused so many issues as a result of a chain of events and circumstances which forty years ago would not have been so much of a problem. I do not recall too many major incidents apart from railcars developing 'flats' on their wheels. Flats occur when the driver applies the brakes and the wheels lock up. The metal tyre on the metal rail causes the tyre to become flat which results in a 'lump... lump... lump'. As the train moves along the lumps increases in frequency as the train gains speed. Prior to the 1990s, rolling stock had what were known as tread brakes where a brake block would apply to the tyre to slow the train down. This in turn kept the tyre clean so the chance of wheel slip was reduced.

Years ago railway embankments in many areas were devoid of foliage. These days trees have been allowed to grow on the line side. Also, the profile of the wheels on modern trains is much narrower, and the phasing out of the old tread brakes in favour of the more efficient discs leads to a build up of rail contamination. This combination has led to an increase in low rail adhesion which has become a major issue on the rail network.

Gradually, railcars, which were over thirty years old, were replaced with a new fleet and it was around 1990 that the Class 158 units were introduced at Norwich. 158s brought with them disc brakes rather than the more traditional tread brake. This meant that the training conversion course was a couple of days longer than normal as each driver was expected to master the new system.

Not long after the introduction of the Class 158 units autumn arrived. I had been elected a Union representative and was in the office when a driver came in, clearly in a state of shock. I asked Tony what the problem was. He explained that as he was making his final approach to Norwich and had applied the brakes on the 158 at which point the anti-slip (ABS to you car drivers) system kicked in but failed to overcome the wheel slip and he got to a point where he was not in control of the train.

As part of the training on the 158s we had been tutored on the anti-slip system but had not experienced it in action as the majority of it had been carried out during the summer. I promised Tony that I would look into the matter and raise it as I was the health and safety representative. I was also aware that there had been trouble in the past in the London area. The Class 315 units had been fitted with a similar braking system which had led to drivers being disciplined for incidents that were out of their control. In turn this had led to the Union threatening to black the units if the disciplinary action went ahead.

Some weeks later I was approached by another driver who had experienced a worrying problem relating to the 158 braking system. As Andy approached Brandon station, he applied the brakes as normal, but the anti-slip was kicking in to such an extent that he thought he was going to overshoot the platform. He applied the brake controller to step three which was a full service application. The braking instructions were to apply the brake to either step two or three and leave the anti-slip system to 'do the work'. Andy had, by accident, applied the brake controller past step three and into emergency. As soon as he realised his mistake his natural reaction was to bring the brake controller back to step three.

I should explain that the brake systems we had been brought up with were solely based on an air pressure, so if the driver made an emergency application he could bring the brake handle back to release and the brake pressure would eventually rise thus releasing the brakes. On the new Westinghouse three step anti-slip system this was not the case. It was an electrical system that sent a message to the brake distributer which would allow air pressure to the brake cylinders. Once emergency was selected by the driver the brakes would only release once the on board computer had recognised that the train had come to a stand even if the brake handle was moved away from emergency accidentally.

Andy advised me that after he placed the brake controller back to step three the brakes released back to the step three brake pressure and he was able to use the system normally. This most definitely should not have happened as the system was 'fail safe' yet here he was, in a situation where the computer controlling the braking system had been fooled into thinking the train had come to a stand.

Between the two of us we came to the conclusion that all the axles on the train had locked up at the same time thus fooling the system into believing the train had come to a stand. This was a most serious situation. I asked Andy to submit a report which he did and I banged off a letter to my Area Traincrew Manager. I also involved ASLEF Head Office and the District Organiser Tony West.

Over the coming weeks I raised the matter in various other forums. Each time I was given the same answer: 'It's impossible for all the axles to lock up on a 158 or any other unit fitted with the anti-slip system'. I simply did not accept this explanation. Tony was extremely supportive of the stance I had taken and the matter was pushed up to the Regional Health and Safety Committee where he would again raise our concerns with the directors of our region. Again we were knocked back.

In the meantime I was working a train between Ely and Norwich and scheduled to stop at Thetford. Prior to stopping I had to bring the train down from 90mph to 60mph. I applied the brakes and watched the anti-slip kick in. I was over a mile from Thetford, but the train stopped at the far end of the station with just the rear coach in the platform! The passengers alighted via the crew door and I made my way rather gingerly back to Norwich. I now had first hand experience of what could happen in a wheel slip situation, which I duly reported.

Some weeks later I received a call from the Area Driver Manager at Norwich, asking me if I would go on a wheel slip weekend on the Bedford to St. Pancras line the following Saturday and Sunday. I jumped at the chance. It was an opportunity to get my point across to the people who may be able to make a difference. On arrival at

158799 working the 13:51 Liverpool Lime Street to Norwich service passes the disused signalbox at Thetford as it arrives into the station on 31 August 2021. (Greg Kiteos)

Bedford, I met Graham Morris, another ASLEF representative who later became the Regional Organiser for the Southern Region.

A test train had been kitted out with a massive amount of technical equipment. A complete coach had its seating stripped out to accommodate all the tech. Graham did not hang about and began making the point that drivers were being disciplined for station overruns, signals passed at danger and other operational incidents. All due to inadequate training and a failure to acknowledge that drivers were no longer in control once the anti-slip system took over.

We were then dealt a bombshell. The technicians had wired up every single bogie, axle and wheel on the unit which had four coaches (two more than a Class 158) and they confirmed that the train could indeed get into a situation where there was a total slide. This confirmed my fears and certainly vindicated what we had been telling the management for some time. As a result of these findings I think it is fair to say that over the years the level of training for drivers has been adapted to cater for wheel slip conditions as well as alterations to instructions.

Millions of pounds has been invested in braking technology and training. Each year Network Rail operates rail head cleaning trains on an hour by hour basis so as to try and prevent low adhesion problems. I would like to think that my actions and those of some of my colleagues at Norwich who took the time to report the problems played some small part in improving things.

As the years progressed the industry gained more experience, information and data about low adhesion. The train operators, in collaboration with Network Rail, were able to assess when best to pinpoint the leaf fall season and what actions to take. Each year just prior to and during the season, drivers would be briefed on the dangers of low adhesion with the mantra 'THINK EARLY - BRAKE EARLY' being drummed into all of us. The season would be designated as beginning on a certain date and running for a period of several weeks. Each day during this period would be assessed and colour coded with black being the day of the most severe form of low adhesion. Every depot would post notices as to what the next day's adhesion conditions were expected to be.

In addition to railhead treatment, sand boxes on the Class 90 fleet would be topped up every time they arrived at Norwich (many trains were fitted with sanders to help combat wheel slip). Some train sets would complete four trips to London and back each day. In addition the electric rheostatic brakes would be isolated on the locomotive so that the tread brakes would be used to keep the wheels clean. (The 'rheo' brake uses the electrical power on the locomotive to reverse the traction motors to slow the train down which is a much more efficient form of braking than the old tread brakes.)

I was driving the 13:30 from Norwich up to London one Saturday afternoon two days before the official leaf fall season was designated to begin. All was going well until I passed through Bentley automatic barriers on the way to Manningtree station. The approach required you to bring the train down from 100mph to 75mph, then to 60mph through the point work of Manningtree junction, along with an overhead power neutral section and a road crossing before entering the platform. (*Overhead power neutral sections are just a few yards long and keep wires fed from different sources electrically separate from each other.)*

I applied the brakes to step one, which on the Class 90 is designated as the brake you use to hold the train in platform. I then went to step two and immediately the speedo fluctuated and dropped to zero. As soon as this happened I felt the anti- slip brakes on the coaches kick in which led to the train snatching backwards and forwards. I knew I was going to have a battle on my hands to bring the train to a stop in the platform. I applied the engine brakes to clean the wheels and applied the train brakes and let the system do its job. Thankfully I had left myself a good distance and soon the train began to perform as it should in such a situation. The speedo rose from zero to show me that the wheels were gripping and after a few more slips and slides the train came to a stand in the platform.

Stopping at Manningtree in such a manner caused me some concern as I had never experienced low adhesion to such a degree on an approach from the Norwich direction. I knew from experience that leaving the station was going to be a challenge as it was a long steady incline up the bank and through a cutting with a vast amount of overhanging trees.

Station duties were completed quickly and I soon received two buzzes on the bell buzzer, my signal to depart. Experience had taught me that if I could get the train up to 15mph I should achieve enough momentum to climb the embankment through to Ardleigh. I took power and the train slowly drew forward. Even with minimal power being applied the wheels were beginning to slip. The wheel profile that had contact with the rails was no more than two centimeters and I had a highly powerful Class 90 locomotive with ten coaches which amounted to about 400 tonnes.

The Class 90s are fitted with sanders to assist with rail adhesion, which used air pressure to blow the sand onto the rail head. No sooner had the locomotive begun to slip than I commenced use of the sander button, but for some strange reason the sanders made no impact whatsoever and the locomotive continued slipping. I was feeding as little power into the traction motors as possible but just enough to gain momentum and slowly we crawled up the bank toward Ardleigh with my finger constantly on the sand button.

The longer I kept trying to apply sand, so the air pressure in the main reservoir began to drop from 140psi. By now the pressure was down to about 100psi and falling. I was beginning to worry that if the pressure got much lower the low main air protection system would kick in. This would lead to an automatic application of the brakes and a stranded train. I was also conscious that it was a Saturday and the Thunderbird rescue locomotive was only manned Monday to Friday. All I could do was too persevere and hope I could get the train to the top of the bank. By this time Kate my conductor was trying to contact me to see what the problem was. The driver/guard communication system was not the best and all I could hear was a load of static when I pressed the 'speak' button. *(The 'Thunderbird' rescue locomotive was on standby to rescue any train that had problems, and was manned from Monday to Fridays only. The location at which it was based varied over the years, but it was usually at Colchester, this being around half way between Norwich and London.)*

After twenty minutes of constant wheel slip with only brief moments of traction adhesion we reached the top of the bank. Slowly the train gathered speed and we arrived into Colchester after thirty minutes: the journey would normal take just ten. I coasted into the platform with a red signal at the end. I contacted the signalman who wanted to know if all was well and I advised him of the problems I had experienced but confirmed the train was ok to continue. He also told me that the railhead cleaning train was not scheduled to begin operations until Monday morning which was of absolutely no use to me at all!

A few days later I was contacted by Sarah, one of the Driver Managers at Norwich. She wanted to know what had taken place and asked for a report which I was happy to supply. She also told me that it appeared the sanders were empty and probably were before I departed from Norwich. The data recorder also revealed that the train had actually come to a standstill at some point while climbing the bank.

I had similar problems some days later when I was approaching Colchester station in the up direction. This time I was brought to a stand at the inlet signal to the station where I had difficulty stopping but again applied the policy of 'Think early, brake early' so all was well until the signal cleared to a single yellow. The inlet signal is located in a dip and as I began to apply power the wheels were slipping all the time. It took me over five minutes to get into the station and again there was a stop signal at the end of the platform.

I contacted the signalman who advised me that the Norwich service in front of me had come to a stand just past Chitts Hill crossing and needed to be pushed through. There comes a time when the driver has to use his knowledge and experience to make a decision which is contrary to what is being requested and this was one of those times. I advised the signalman that I had enough trouble getting the ten coaches I had into the platform, so getting to Chitts Hill was more than likely to cause more problems with two trains being stuck rather than just the one. I suggested that they get the driver of the stranded train to change ends and drive back to Colchester to clear the line.

A few moments later I was advised that my train had been cancelled and we would be shunted into the up direction passing loop. We were to wait there so that we could pick up our return working from Colchester just over two hours later. A few moments passed and the train that had been stuck at Chitts Hill passed into the station (the line in that area is what is known as bi-directional which means trains can be signalled in either direction on the same line). Normal working was resumed except that all Norwich trains travelling to London were given a not to stop order for Colchester so that they could get through Chitts Hill without any issue.

Another example of the power the driver wields. I had been driving over thirty years before I received a not to stop order and I consider them to be extremely rare. Generally additional stop orders were more common: these would be issued if preceding trains were cancelled.

Chapter 37 - Annus Horibilis

I HAD BEEN driving for over twenty years when I had what can only be described as my 'annus horibilis'.

I was working a service to London one bright sunny morning, the 07:40 express train which used to be named 'The East Anglian'. It even had a name board that a fitter would attach to the front of the locomotive prior to departure.

I had passed through Colchester at 90mph and was then heading up towards Marks Tey. Everything was fine, the Class 90 locomotive was performing well, we had green lights all the way and were also bang on time. Every few moments I would check the speed which was sitting nicely on 100mph. All was well with the air pressure gauges and fault lights. It was after doing this cursory quick check I looked up to see that the next signal was displaying a red aspect.

My first reaction was to slam the brake into emergency and I thought, 'Did I miss two sets of yellow signals?' I immediately questioned my own competency so glanced up at the automatic warning system (AWS) indicator. It was displaying black which meant that the previous signal was green (if it had been either a yellow or red signal the indicator would have been black and yellow) so my conscience was clear. By this time the speed of the train was down to about 70mph and we passed the signal at danger. Marks Tey station was looming and I could see that the next signal was green. I assumed there had been a problem with the previous signal. I shot past the green signal and came to a halt in a lump.

This was before cab secure radios were installed in the Class 90s so I walked along the platform as the fans on the locomotive were screaming to cool things down. There was dust emitting from the brakes along with a burning smell which I guessed was also from the brakes. For some reason the signal I had passed at green was situated halfway along the platform at Marks Tey rather than at the far end. As I walked along there were several passengers awaiting the next train behind me, all of whom were giving me rather odd looks wondering why I had come to a grinding halt. I bade them "Good morning," and contacted the signalman. It turned out he was unaware that signal had returned to red. He also asked me if I was okay to continue after reassuring me that there were no other trains in front of me, and it was safe to proceed.

I climbed back on the locomotive, contacted the conductor, and we made the necessary arrangements to proceed. It was only then did I realise that my hands were shaking and I considered the endless possibilities of what may have befallen me. There could have been a serious track defect or another train fouling the line. I also noticed that everything on the locomotive sounded much louder. I later learned, when on a human behaviour course, that post incident the human senses go into a heightened state for a while. It is generally at times like that that your confidence in the system can take a bit of a knock.

Only a matter of a few days later I was driving across to Cambridge between Ely and Waterbeach when the signal in front of me turned from green to red. I brought the train to a stand and contacted the signalman who advised me that there must be a fault

Class 90 locomotive No. 90012 leading a London bound service at Brantham, between Ipswich and Manningtree. (Alistair Barham)

with the system. Fortunately the signals on this particular stretch of line are situated well apart and given it's on the edge of The Fenland and very flat there are points where you can see as many as four signals in advance of you. I was beginning to wonder if I was jinxed! I thought little of the situation and the rest of the journey continued without incident.

A few weeks passed and I was working an early afternoon train from London to Norwich. Again it was a bright sunny day and the train was bang on time as I approached Witham at 100mph. The approach to Witham from both directions is dead straight and if both the up and the down direction Norwich/London trains are on time they usually pass each other at Witham. This was the case on this particular day. I must have been something like a quarter of a mile from the station as the up direction train hit the platform. I remember seeing what appeared to be a cloud of dust suddenly billow up from around the locomotive very similar to what happens if new ballast stones have been laid and a train travels over it at speed in dry weather. My first thought was 'There hasn't been any ballast laid there over the past few days.' With both trains travelling at a combined speed of 200mph we were soon at the point of almost passing each other when the stark realisation of what had occurred struck me.

Across the yellow front of the up direction train was a large streak of blood. By now both trains had passed each other. I had the brakes on and entered the down platform where I saw a torso and a leg laying in the four foot of the up line. (*The four foot is the space between the running rails of the track).* I felt sick to the core and it hit me that the plume of dust was either the impact of the body or the brake pipe air pressure being vented to atmosphere or more likely a combination of the two. By now I had decided there was little to be gained by stopping. For some reason I had not made an emergency brake application. There was no doubt in my mind that my colleague would have come to a stand by now and would be reporting the matter. I called the Colchester signaller on the NRN radio and advised what had taken place and asked if I could be relieved at Colchester. I was shaking like a leaf and was also worried about my colleague. I operated the driver-to-guard communication system to attract the conductor's attention (the code is 3 buzzes and pause then 3 buzzes). Derek, my conductor for the day, soon came through and was shocked to hear what had taken place. By this time though we were almost at Colchester.

On arrival at Colchester I again advised the signalman that I was seeking relief if possible and he replied that the Thunderbird driver was going to relieve me for which I was grateful. No sooner had he arrived than he was called by Control and told to get in a taxi to Witham to relieve the driver of the train who had been involved in the fatality. I could not disagree with that. His need was far greater than mine. I agreed with Control that I would take a few moments at Colchester and then take the train to Norwich. If I felt it was not safe I would dump it at Ipswich. Fortunately on arrival at the next station, which was Manningtree, there was a driver who was travelling back to Norwich who very kindly offered to work it back for me.

Given that my message had made its way to Control, I was somewhat surprised to find on arrival at Norwich there was nobody to meet the train and check on my welfare. Still being quite shook up after witnessing such an incident I was not really looking forward to my next trip which was to Sheringham. I thought to myself that maybe I would be ok once I had taken my break.

I popped into the Driver Manager's office at Norwich and told them what had taken place. They were not aware of what I had witnessed. The first words out of the senior manager's mouth were, "You're not going anywhere else today, go home and I'll make sure your next trip is taken care of." I was very grateful for this intervention and I was impressed by his decisiveness on my behalf. I can't explain how relieved I felt, not just to get my next turn of duty covered, but on my return home to see my wife and my little boy who were at the door when I arrived. It is family that make life all the more worthwhile and to have their support is a huge comfort.

Obviously the person who had been hit on that day did not survive. I am led to believe that passengers and staff who witnessed the incident were also traumatised as was my colleague who had experienced the second fatality of his career. He did receive extensive counselling and support and is still driving as I write this.

This was not to be my only near miss that year. One Sunday morning I was travelling between Manningtree and Colchester when, in the Ardleigh area, I noticed a person standing between the rails of the line I was travelling along at 100mph. I sounded the horn but the person made no effort to move. Again I gave a longer blast. By this time I was closing down the distance at a rapid rate so there comes a point when a decision has to be made as to whether to apply the emergency brake. I decided I had reached that point so simultaneously killed the power and applied the brake to emergency and made a continuous blast on the horn. As I got closer to the individual I noticed he was standing under an overlying bridge and had a mobile phone to his ear which he then he held above his head.

I must have got within 200 yards from him when he casually walked off the track and up the embankment beside the bridge. By this time I had passed through and as I looked to my right I saw him ascend the embankment steps that were there for track workers to use: standing close by was also another individual. In my mind, once again, I had thought I was going to hit the person and would have struck him at about 50mph. The train came to a grinding halt and I called the signalman to explain the situation.

Later I began to analyse what had taken place. I came to the conclusion that it was a hoax and the phone call may well have been to somebody attempting to coerce them into doing something. I think the individual was holding the phone up to give the person on the other end the line the impression that he was going to be hit by the approaching train, given I was making a continuous sound on the horn - and believe me the horns on the Class 90s are very loud.

All these incidents occurred within six weeks of each other, so it was an eventful time. There was one final act that was 'The Straw that Broke the Camel's Back' as the old saying goes. I was working a late evening train from London: the clocks had gone back so it was dark as I approached Ipswich. I had timed the train to perfection as it came to a stand in the platform. Unusually the signal at the end of Ipswich down direction platform was displaying red so I assumed there was a problem.

We waited a few moments and then, from the holding sidings next to the station, a Network Rail test train began to emerge and crossed out in front of my train and along the mainline in the direction we were supposed to be travelling. I was livid! I could not understand for the life of me why the signalman had delayed a schedule passenger service for a test train which could have easily tucked in behind me. Both the conductor and I shared our views on such a stupid decision which was to cause us an unnecessary delay.

Eventually the signal cleared to a single yellow, station duties were completed and I was given two on the buzzer to depart. We slowly made our way along until passing through Claydon where the signals ahead changed from a yellow (caution) to green (clear). I was able to open up the power controller to maximum and the Class 90's power kicked in. Soon we were up to 90mph and increasing as we passed an up direction Norwich to London train.

The approach to Needham Market is around a quite sharp left hand bend where the next signal was situated. It should have been displaying a green or yellow signal but it was red! Not for the first time in the past few weeks I gave the brakes an emergency application. However this time it was dark. I had been following a slower running test train and my immediate thoughts were, 'Any second I'm going to see the tail lights of that train I am following.' I was seriously worried and in no time we passed the red signal and then came to a grinding halt: I had passed the red signal by six coach lengths. I tried to call the signalman via the NRN radio but we were in an area of poor signal quality so I walked back to the signal where I intended to get hold of him via the signal post telephone. It was not working. That was something I had never experienced.

My only other option was to contact the signalman via my mobile phone. I fired it up and waited. Soon enough he answered and I advised him of my train code and told him that the signal was showing red. His reply sent me into orbit. "Sorry to put the signal back against you driver, but the driver of the up direction London reported sparks coming from under a train, I couldn't remember if it was your train I needed to stop or the one in front of you.... are you okay?" I can only say that it is the only time in thirty eight years on the footplate that I lost my cool and acted in a most unprofessional manner. "NO I'M NOT BLOODY ALRIGHT!!! And after hearing what you've just told me you need to get a grip, the train in front of me, which you should know, is a test train that omits a strobe light underneath the test coach. So no, I am decidedly un-alright and will take the train to Stowmarket where I will decide if we go any further."

Frankly, at that moment I could not believe the incompetence. However on reflection I guess he had to make a quick decision as we all do in such circumstances. Having said that the test train's presence had been advertised in the weekly operating notice with the warning that when operating it would admit a bright strobe light. After having so many incidents in the past few weeks my confidence in the system was beginning to seriously wane.

I made my way to Stowmarket where I took five minutes, still shaking, more with anger than anything else and then set out for Norwich. I am pleased to say I was met by the supervisor Peter Francis who told me to go home.

Chapter 38 - Failures, Near Misses and Incidents

FOR THE MAJORITY of train drivers a day at work is relatively mundane: sign on duty and check the daily notices, travel to various destinations over routes they have driven on too many times to recall and then go home without any incident. Somebody commented to me once that working over all these routes must be great. However after doing the job day in day out over many years occasionally it feels a bit like watching the same TV programme with different adverts in between.

Generally any variety means that things have gone wrong which is never for the best. There are periods when things just don't seem to work out, or it feels that the odds are stacked against you and whatever you do seems to go wrong. There may be days when you try to keep to time or make up any delay, yet events thwart any advances you make. There was one conductor whom I would work with: I knew if we got delayed, no matter how hard I tried to make up time his glacial dispatch at stations would lose any gains I had made every effort to claw back.

I can remember several drivers having unfortunate incidents that were not within their control and yet they must have thought, 'What am I doing wrong here?' There was a time when my first mate, Felix, became derailed three times in one week on the night shift while working trains to and from the loco sheds and the station. None of which were attributed to him, it was just a weakness in the track that gave out as he travelled over it.

Or there was the extremely unfortunate Albert Brown who worked a lunchtime London service from Norwich. As he passed through Brentwood station a person jumped in front of his train and was killed. This is one of the most distressing things to happen to any driver and it is not unusual for some to have been involved in multiple fatalities throughout their careers. I believe the unenviable record is held by a driver from Nottingham who had been involved in nine and I am aware of a Colchester driver who had been involved in six. These days there is a great deal of support for drivers as they get paid time away from duty, counselling and a staged return to work. However I have also known of colleagues whose mainline career has been curtailed as a result of one or more fatalities.

Albert had his fatality at a time when it was considered to be just one of those things or an occupational hazard. He returned to work the following day on the same turn of duty he had been on the previous day. As he approached Brentwood he noticed somebody standing in a rather precarious position on the platform and as his train entered the station at 70mph the person stepped out in front of it. For the second day on the trot Albert was involved in a fatality. The odds against that happening two days on the bounce must have been millions to one and at the same station too. Well it was off the scale. At that time there was a psychiatric hospital just up the road from Brentwood station so it was quite a common occurrence for patients to wander down the road and end their lives in this way.

What drives someone to take their own life in such a manner is difficult to comprehend. In many cases it comes to light that their actions are those of a highly disturbed individual and they may have made unsuccessful attempts in the past. Standing in front of several hundred tonnes of train travelling at speeds up to 125mph is final. Mental health issues, debt, drug addiction and family breakdowns are common causes of such terrible incidents and the victims are the families, friends, the emergency services and traincrew who have to deal with the individual's actions. Many say they are the actions of a selfish person. I think that displays a terrible misunderstanding of the individual's circumstances and their mental state at the time they decided to take such action. I thank my lucky stars that I have never had such a terrible experience.

As the old railcars were replaced so we were unfortunately introduced to the single coach Class 153s unit which were given the uncomplimentary name of 'Scuds' after the missiles developed by Saddam Hussein's regime and used to very little effect in the first Gulf War. The nickname was given because when they left the station they rarely hit their intended target. Failure rates were very high and the 'space saver' cab was a complete nightmare. The driving position made you feel your nose was almost pressed against the windscreen. Along with the addition of various radio equipment and all the other switches and our personal equipment there was very little room for the driver.

Class 153 No. 153 335 at Norwich on 6 August 2013. (Alastair Holmes)

I was on the Norwich to Lowestoft run again on this particular day and had the pleasure of driving the 153 from the space saver cab. I approached Haddiscoe station which is situated at the end of a long sweeping right hand bend. There is a set of user worked crossing gates prior to the station. User worked gates have been the source of many incidents and accidents over the years mainly because the people using them do not follow the very simple instructions which are posted on clear notices right next to the gates: 'STOP...... Always telephone before crossing with vehicles or animals to find out if there is time to cross.' Additionally the instruction also states 'Open the far gate before crossing with vehicles or animals.' Simple instructions but so many people ignore them.

I noticed a red estate car sitting in the middle of the track. I sounded the horn but the car failed to move. Instinctively I applied the brake to the emergency position and blew the horn continuously. By now I could see that the driver of the car had driven onto the crossing, the passenger had closed the gates to its rear and was wandering across to open the gates for their exit. They should have opened both sets of gates before driving onto the crossing!

I was facing a potentially fatal accident and given that I was in the space saver cab I considered I had the potential to be the one who came off worse. I was extremely relieved when the driver of the car (an old Eastern Bloc built Lada) moved closer to the exit gates and was able to pull off the track altogether as I whizzed by and came to an unceremonious halt with the brakes fully on. Once the emergency brakes are applied they should not release until the train comes to a stand, even if the brake controller is pulled away from emergency to the release position while the train is moving.

I was livid with the idiot driver and his passenger for committing such an act which put themselves along with my passengers and me in danger. I jumped out of the

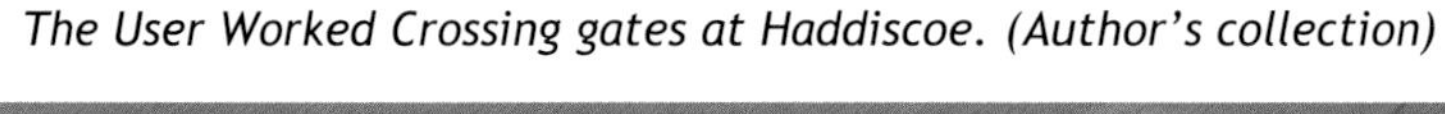

The User Worked Crossing gates at Haddiscoe. (Author's collection)

cab and ran back along the track to have a pop at the pair of them, but by the time I had got to the crossing the car had moved off. Fortunately there was only an Anglian Water Authority depot and a house on the other side of the gates which were adjacent to a river. I also counted my lucky stars that the car was a crappy old Lada which were renowned for being poorly built. The owners were at far more risk than my passengers and I!

I immediately called the signalman from the telephone at the crossing and asked if anyone had phoned for permission to use the crossing. He confirmed that he had not. 'No surprise there' I thought to myself. I advised him of what had taken place and that I could see the car parked at the house next to the Anglian Water Authority depot. I would investigate and report back. I took a walk though the yard and managed to get the registration of the car which I then relayed to the signalman on my return to it.

On my return journey to Norwich I was met by Conductor Manager Paul Reeve at Brundall station. He had been sent out to meet me to see if I was ok. I had again received a bit of a shock but by the time I had got back to Norwich I had calmed down. I was still smarting at the idiocy of the car driver and was more than happy to not just fill in a driver's report but also make a statement to the British Transport Police. Apart from relaying the story to some of my colleagues over the next few days I forgot about the whole saga.

Many months later, my wife told me a story that had been relayed to her on the bus by a lady she was friendly with who happened to work in the courts at Norwich. It transpired that my statement was read out in court and formed part of the prosecution's case against the driver of the Lada. She told my wife that he was an old boy and when asked if he had anything to say he replied that he had "....done nothing wrong," and he went on to explain in his defence that he had been crossing the line in that manner for the past twenty years ... talk about putting your arse where it can be kicked! After that he was found guilty and fined! Frankly, bloody good job too, my only regret is that I was not asked to give evidence against the silly old twat!

When I first passed out as a driver in December 1987 I had to learn all routes Norwich drivers were expected to drive. These routes included the Norwich to London line. Unfortunately my opportunities to drive over that route were curtailed due to my low seniority which meant I was placed in a roster that did not have any London work contained within it. After a while my knowledge became out-dated and I was not afforded any refresher training which led to me crossing off the route from my card. I was disappointed about this because it was considered to be premium work which brought with it the chance to earn extra money through the mileage bonus system. The majority of my work was spent either going to Peterborough and back or on the local services. Nonetheless I was happy to be driving at the tender age of 22.

It was some years before I would actually return to mainline driving due to the manner in which the link structure was altered as the industry was privatised in the mid 1990s.

Eventually my seniority took my into the InterCity Link No.2 where I re-trained on the Class 86 locomotive and the DBSOs. *(A Driving Brake Second Open [DBSO] is a type of railway carriage converted to operate as a control car. Fourteen vehicles were converted from standard class coaches. Modifications included adding a driving cab and TDM [Time Division Multiplex] equipment to allow a locomotive to be driven remotely. Using a system known as push-pull, the driver in the DBSO can drive the locomotive, even though it is at the opposite end of the train.)* These had a poor reliability reputation and could be a bit of a handful to drive. My first week out on the mainline turned into a baptism of fire as was described to me by my Operations Manager Phil Barrett when he bumped into me a few days after the following events occurred.

The country was in the middle of a hot spell of weather and as with all climate extremes I have come to learn that it means trouble at work, be it wind, heavy rain, snow and ice or heat. This Friday was no exception. I was half way into my maiden voyage to London when I left Colchester bound for London. We were on time but the heat in the cab was unbearable as none of the locomotives had any form of air conditioning. That would come with the introduction of the Class 90s. Lowering the drop light side window would create a draught but once the train reached speeds of 60mph and above it became impossible to keep the window open as the pressure and noise would be too much: also dust would start flying around the cab. I soon learned not to open the air vent that had been retro fitted as a so called modification on the driver's desk as the first time I used it I got covered in dead flies!

As the train was approaching full speed the power suddenly cut out and a fault light appeared. I tried to regain power but to no avail so pressed the 'pan up/re-set' button which was supposed to cure most problems. This did not yield any results so I was left to scratch my head as to what the fault could be. I decided that I would let the train coast as far as possible. If I was lucky I would have been able to get to Witham where following trains could be diverted around me, whilst if I stopped on the mainline then trains would just stack up behind.

Good fortune was smiling on me this particular day and all the signals ahead were showing green. In the meantime I contacted the signalman via the NRN and advised him the train had lost power and I was attempting to coast to Witham where I would investigate. I also was paying attention to the overhead wires. They were stable so this indicated that the pantograph was intact. If there was any sign of them bouncing about then I would have had to bring the train to an immediate stand so as to minimise any damage to the cables and pantograph.

I rolled into Witham up direction platform and began my investigation. I checked the driving desk for any obvious faults of which there were none. I moved into the transformer compartment where everything was normal with no fault flags showing and the oil in the transformer was full. I returned to the cab but still could not gain power. By this time that I was worrying that I had missed something simple and was causing an unnecessary delay.

My mobile phone kicked into life. Anglia Control advised me that the Technical Riding Inspector (TRI) was on his way and would be with me shortly at which I breathed a sigh of relief. *(Technical Riding Inspectors—known as TRIs—were based at Norwich and Ipswich, and also at Liverpool Street in the evening peak. They could give technical advice over the phone in the case of faults, and could also be sent to the location where a failure occurred.)* Maybe he would get to the bottom of the problem. Soon enough he turned up and began his investigations. He came back and told me the transformer oil had overheated which would have explained why the cooling fans were constantly running. The only thing that could be done was to let them do their job until the oil reached a safe temperature at which point I could go on my merry way. The bad news was that he estimated it would be a good hour before they cooled enough to allow power to be regained.

As my TRI, Neil, and I were standing on the up main platform a Norwich to London train passed on the adjacent line. Driving it was a good mate of mine, Terry. As he passed he gave me a 'Harvey Smith - V sign' with his fingers. "Bloody charming!" I exclaimed to Neil who agreed. I rang Anglia Control and advised them of the situation and they instructed me to wait and then make my way back to Norwich under reduced power. Neil was going

(Above) A London to Norwich service arrives at Colchester with the DBSO leading on 30 June 1991.
(Below) The author pictured in the DVT of a late evening service from London to Norwich: the photographer commented that he took the photo as "it was such a rare occurrence to see you actually driving I thought I'd capture it for posterity!"
(Both photos by Alistair Barham)

to remain with the train to make sure all was well but soon received a call advising him to get up to Chelmsford. Terry had failed and couldn't rectify the problem..... I think they call that karma, or it appeared the powers that be worked very quickly that day!

Soon enough things cooled down and I was shunted across the mainline into the down passing loop where I sat for another hour or so. By this time it was the evening peak with trains passing every few minutes so I had to wait until things had quietened down before moving off back to Norwich.

The following day was equally hot and I was on a return journey from London so driving from the DBSO when I lost power and the brakes applied. I immediately knew it was the TDM system which allows the driver to control the locomotive from the DBSO. I went through the required procedure to try and re-awaken the TDM which involved what can only be described as a re-boot. This involved walking back to the locomotive, dropping the pantograph and knocking out the batteries. Then waiting a few moments until I could reinstate them and raise the pantograph. If all that failed then, in the words of my instructor, "You're screwed" .... and we were. The only thing left was to detach the locomotive from the rear, run it around to the leading end, attach it to the DBSO and drive as a conventional train. This all took some considerable time but we got on the move with me questioning whether this was normal for the InterCity Link. I was glad to see the back of my first week in the new role.

I had to reboot a class 90 and DVT after the old class 86/DBSO fleet had been replaced with cascaded stock from the West Coast Main Line. The train had passed through the neutral section at Bow Junction between Bethnal Green and Stratford and de-configured. My attempts to reconfigure from the DVT had proved fruitless so I made my way back to the 90 to carry out my duties.

Again it was a boiling hot day as I trudged along the ballast. As I approached the last three carriages which were the first class accommodation, a gentleman poked his head out of the coach door window. He looked down at me and said, "I say old chap, can you do something about the air conditioning in this coach, its frightfully warm in here?" My immediate thought was, 'Bugger me, as if I haven't got enough to worry about.' I diplomatically responded by saying, "Well it's like this Sir, I can come up there and poke about for a few minutes and maybe get it going, or I can get on the locomotive and try to get this train on the move, which would you prefer?" He came back with "Right you are old chap," and with that poked his head back into the train. Ten minutes later we were on the move.

The introduction of the 'new' Class 90 fleet with the Mark 3 coaching stock along with driving van trailers (DVT) was not the best experience. *(A DVT [Driving Van Trailer] is a purpose-built control vehicle that allows the driver to operate with a locomotive in push-pull formation from the opposite end of the train.)* The locomotives were constantly de-configuring through certain neutral sections and each day became a gamble as to whether you would actually get to London or not. I for one was really pleased to see the replacement stock. It was technically streets ahead of the old fleet and should have been more reliable, but the initial few months were trying times for the drivers, fitters and more importantly the poor old long suffering passengers.

Some weeks later I had been signalled into platform 8 at Liverpool Street. I applied power and got up to about 10mph when there was a lump as the power dropped off. I was coasting along but I knew if I did not regain traction power then there was no way the whole train would make it into the platform. There were no fault lights visible but I still pressed the reset button and prayed to regain power. I had no such luck and soon enough the train came to a standstill with five coaches in the platform and five out. To make matters worse it was the evening peak. I advised the signalman and conductor of the problem and began to investigate. As much as I checked, double checked and even triple checked, I could find no fault at all. I advised the signalman the train was a failure and he thanked me for "Fucking up the evening peak service," to which I replied, "It's my pleasure!"

We detrained the passengers which included one Ian Hislop, editor of the satirical magazine Private Eye and regular team member on the popular TV show 'Have I Got News For You.' I don't think we made the magazine or TV show thankfully. I was also joined by a driver from the Thunderbird rescue locomotive, Bernie Earles, who had been deployed to assist a failed train on the next platform. He asked me if I had tried this and tried that, to which I replied, "Yes Bernie," each time. He then asked, "Have you tried sticking your thumb in your ear and pressing the reset button?" I thought he had gone nuts but realised we were at the point of desperation. "Worth a try Bernie old boy," I replied and of course it didn't work!

I rang Alistair Barham at Anglia Control who was an excellent person to have onboard in a crisis. I advised him of the situation and that we appeared to be a failure to which his comment was, "No problem Dave, I'll get Bernie on the Thunderbird engine to untie from the train on platform 9 and push you in." It was a great plan to which I replied, "That's all well and good Alistair, but my train is so far out of platform 8 it's blocking him in." His reaction was one that has become a mantra of all those who have reached the end of their tether. "Oh Fucking Hell!" he cried and that's from a chap who hardly ever swears!

True to form Alistair came up with a plan that involved an up Norwich driver and locomotive dumping its train at Stratford and then travelling light (locomotive only) to Liverpool Street to push my train into the platform so that Network Rail could get the trains moving again. I was pleased to see Terry arrive (no Harvey Smith V sign today). We tied up and gently pushed my train clear.

The good thing about most of these incidents and about the railway in general is first and foremost, there is generally somebody around who is willing to help out and does not want to see a colleague struggle. Secondly you can have the most horrendous day at work, everything can be total chaos but, when you return for your shift the next day, it's back to normal and all the stresses and worries from the previous day have gone.

Chapter 39 - Last Thoughts

AFTER FORTY ONE years on the railway, I attended my final meeting of the Trustee Board of Directors of the Railway Pension Scheme in September 2021. My career had come to an end.

I had never seen the railway as a stepping stone to greater things. I was happy to join the footplate and make my way up to driver and would have seen my days out doing just that. But as I came to learn, the railway industry is huge and with it comes many opportunities. Those that presented themselves to me I grabbed with both hands and did my best in each role. In that time I have come across a wide range of characters some of whom I have written about in this book. I soon came to learn that it is the railmen and women that make the industry what it is.

I have always been a great believer in passing on knowledge and encouraging others to try and better themselves and on most occasions, when asked, I would let colleagues drive if they were route learning for example. However there was one incident where I let a colleague drive as he was on the final day of route learning the London line. We left Liverpool Street with Jim driving and as we passed through Bethnal Green he opened the power controller to full power and we were soon up to 70mph. Shortly after, we encountered a preliminary caution (double yellow). He acknowledged the AWS warning but kept the power controller open. We were soon bearing down on a single yellow so I called out for him to dump the brakes into emergency. It was as if he had been in limbo for a few moments. He came to his senses and dumped the brakes. By now we were fast approaching a red signal. It was more than clear we were going to fail to stop and as the red signal loomed ever closer I could imagine myself filling in the report forms and facing a disciplinary investigation. With that the red immediately changed to a single yellow, then a double yellow and finally green. I breathed a massive sigh of relief. This incident put me off allowing colleagues to drive for a while.

Sometime later a colleague of mine was in a similar position. Julie was route learning London and was on her final day before being assessed. She asked if it was ok

The author of this book, David Tyson, being greeted by Driver Manager Martin Steele on arrival at Norwich after working his last train before retirement.

to drive which I duly agreed to. Her run up to London was perfect and as we began to crawl into Liverpool Street I reminded her she needed to draw up quite close to the buffer stops at the end of the platform so the rear of the train would not be foul. She coasted in beautifully then touched the brakes just a moment too early. We stopped about twenty feet short of the buffer stops which was not ideal but I just hoped we were clear at the rear. As she began to shut the driving desk down a passenger walked by and took a long look at the gap she had left between the locomotive and the stops. "What's he looking at?" she exclaimed. I could not help but reply, "I think he's going to seek a refund on his ticket after having to walk half the journey." Fortunately she saw the funny side.

I have enjoyed my time on the railways although there have been lows where I have struggled and on occasion the stresses have been huge, but I believe they have made me the person I am today. I was most surprised when, at the 2019 ASLEF conference after giving my pensions speech I was presented with an honorary membership medallion by General Secretary Mick Whelan. This is something that is only given to a handful of members and I was close to tears when he said the kind words in his presentation to me. ASLEF has a special place in my heart and I have always done my best, although some would not necessarily agree. However that's their problem, not mine.

In this book I have tried to portray some of the more humorous things that took place over the years although there have been some more serious and tragic elements at times. I wish to stress that day in day out the industry runs safely and professionally despite the ridicule in the media when things go wrong. A generally well run and efficient railway does not make headlines. But the people who clean the trains, work on the

David Tyson being awarded honorary membership of ASLEF. From left to right are Dave Calfe (President), Mick Whelan (General Secretary), Dave Tyson, Howard Kaye EC member District 5 and Nigel Gibson District Organiser District 5.

the stations or in maintenance depots, the track workers, signallers, planners, train staff and many more, all do their job professionally and for the good of the travelling public.

It takes the best part of a year for a driver to become fully qualified and then they are subject to vast amounts of monitoring. Some may think drivers are overpaid. In fact a finance director at a freight company told me that once, a comment I disputed of course. But, to the person who has never driven a train with 2000 tonnes of cargo, or the best part of a thousand passengers on board, then maybe they should think of this. Imagine getting in a car and driving at 100mph in thick fog, snow or in a thunderstorm either during the day or at night. It is a strange sensation just seeing your reflection in the windscreen then having to pick out various points on the journey such as speed limits and restrictions, bridges, junctions, signals (that more often than not would display cautions in bad weather) and then applying the brake at the correct point to stop in a station. It takes skill, nerves and an excellent knowledge of the route. Ultimately the safety of the public and your colleagues depends on everyone doing their job properly. Also we must not forget the millions of pounds worth of machinery you are in charge of. It is not for the faint hearted and driving at such speeds in such conditions for up to twelve hours is mentally draining.

There are many who criticise, generally politicians and the media, or disgruntled members of the public when there are times of industrial strife, but I bet many of these armchair experts wouldn't even get past the entrance exam!

David Tyson (July 2024)

Deltic D9000 at Liverpool Street after working up from Norwich on Bank Holiday Monday, 26 August 1998 service from Yarmouth (Alistair Barham)

References

Much of this book has been written from memory and in places names have been changed so as to protect their identity.

Chapter 17

- Pages 91/92 Re; British Rail (Dispute); Hansard Volume 27 5th July 1982.

Chapter 28

- Re: Train Drivers pay claim, various newspaper articles including 'The Independent' article by Barry Clement 3 July 1995. Daily Mirror Article July 13th 1995.

Chapter 30

- My resignation, letter to ASLEF Journal February 2000. EC Resolution 105/407 26 January 2000.
- Special AAD EC resolution 147/407 7 March 2000.
- Comments made by General Secretary, Mick Rix, Special Assembly of Delegates 18 April 2000.
- Complaint by three EC members to Queens Bench of the High Court Case No. HQ0002017 7 April 2000 (also referred to in decisions of Certification Office - 2 March 2001).
- Decision of Certification Officer 2 March 2001.
- Comments on Stan Godwins's Facebook thread on 11 August 2022 from John Glover and Steve Ballard.

Chapter 31

- EC resolution 668/422 restricting General Secretary's powers.
- 'Couldn't buy a jar of coffee' quote, various newspapers including Times online 25th May 2004, Independent online 25th May 2004, Daily Express 26th May 2004 and Daily Telegraph 26th May 2004.
- Threat to sack GMB members at ASLEF Head Office letter 29th December 2003 signed by Shaun Brady. Also article by journalist Kevin Maguire Guardian online 26th May 2004.
- Interview with Shaun Brady by Tom Baldwin of Times Newspaper calling on members to take back the union, 5 June 2004.
- TUC Report into fight chaired by Professor Aileen McColgan June 2004.
- Appointment of Matthias Kelly QC EC resolution 319/424.
- Report of Matthias Kelly QC September 2004.
- David Tyson quotations of his speech to delayed 2004 conference, ASLEF AAD 2004 minute book 27 September to 1 October 2004.
- Challenge of the Chair of AAD, ASLEF 2004 AAD minute book 27 September to 1 October 2004.
- David Tyson 'unreliable witness' comments by chair of tribunal Val Cook, EAT decision 4th November 2005.

Acknowledgements

THERE ARE MANY who have helped bring the book to finally see the light of day, first and foremost Rob Boyce who made contact with me once I announced my intention to publish. I am indebted to him for his help, assistance and advice, not to mention his hard work, editing skills and patience. Rob was ably assisted by the 'grammar-miester' Geoff Hutton who corrected my grammar and then passed it back to poor old Rob for yet further editing.

I was urged to write about my experience by Rachel Casey: a short comment sent me on a long and enjoyable journey.

I would also like to thank Chris Pearson for his assistance in clarifying many things where the passage of time has clouded my memory in certain areas, in particular when referring to the Fakenham branch line. Also Michael Lloyd for his help with chapters 33 and 34. And Phil Briggs, who enlightened me on issues relating to our driver training at Ilford. Also all those railway colleagues who contributed to the comments relating to the chapter about serial prankster Gary Strange. Donald 'Don' Murdie is thanked for providing useful extracts from his archives. And not forgetting the many colleagues who provided information or photographs that we simply did not have space for.

There are also those who contributed the numerous photographs that have been used and I thank Alistair Barham, Stephen Dey, Chris Harkins, David Lacey, Derek Pears, Martin Steele, Alastair Holmes, Tom Stageman, Greg Kiteos, G. D. King and Dom Shaw for their generous contributions.

From time to time I have passed drafts of random chapters to friends and family for comment which has been invaluable, especially to see what people with a non-railway background think. So I am indebted to my late father-in-law Gerald Kemp who read the whole manuscript (and he was a person who never read books) and my mother-in-law Valerie Kemp. Also Mike Craston, Frank Johnson, Andrew Nobbs, Simon Thompson and Dean Ward, all of whom offered constructive criticism and have been supportive of my efforts. Not forgetting my son, Kieran, who has offered words of encouragement.

I cannot forget the assistance and encouragement I have received from friends and colleagues within ASLEF including Mick Whelan, Keith Richmond (who gave me a crash course in grammar over a couple of pints) and Howard Kaye.

I would like to pay tribute to my agent Guy Rose of Futerman Rose Associates who recognised a good story when he spotted one. Also Peter Cox who runs the 'Litopia Popup Submission' YouTube channel where drafts are reviewed weekly: his criticism and advice were invaluable.

Behind every man is a good woman. My wife Yvonne was thrust into the life of a train driver's when we married in July 1990. Over all those years she has put up with the onerous shift patterns and the no-shows when I have been delayed, also having to spend weekends alone due to the nature of the job. Once I became a member of the ASLEF Executive my hours became longer and I would spend days away from home which sometimes stretched into weeks only for me to return at the weekend. There are times when I should have been at home and was not. She has been my rock and I would not be without her.

There is a group of people who are far to numerous to name, the railmen and women with whom I have worked over the years and who have been a source of the tales I have been able to recount. Without them there would have been no book.

Finally, although not related to the book, I cannot thank enough the people in the Norwich Area NHS, in particular those in the urology and oncology departments at the Norfolk and Norwich Hospital who have looked after me through my battle with cancer since 2016, and continue to do so. If it were not for them, then I most probably would not have lived to tell my story.